WITHDRAWN

D1626543

Prison Violence

Prison Violence
The Dynamics of Conflict, Fear and Power

**Kimmett Edgar, Ian O'Donnell
and Carol Martin**

WILLAN
PUBLISHING

Published by

Willan Publishing
Culmcott House
Mill Street, Uffculme
Cullompton, Devon
EX15 3AT, UK
Tel: +44(0)1884 840337
Fax: +44(0)1884 840251
e-mail: info@willanpublishing.co.uk
Website: www.willanpublishing.co.uk

Published simultaneously in the USA and Canada by

Willan Publishing
c/o ISBS, 5824 N.E. Hassalo St,
Portland, Oregon 97213-3644, USA
Tel: +001(0)503 287 3093
Fax: +001(0)503 280 8832
e-mail: info@isbs.com
Website: www.isbs.com

First published 2003

ISBN 1-903240-98-0

British Library Cataloguing-in-Publication Data

A catalogue record for this book is available from the British Library

Typeset by TW Typesetting, Plymouth, Devon
Project management by Deer Park Productions, Tavistock, Devon
Printed and bound by TJ International Ltd, Trecerus Industrial Estate, Padstow,
Cornwall, PL28 8RW

Contents

List of figures and tables

Figures

Tables

About the authors

Kimmett Edgar is Research Manager, Prison Reform Trust and formerly Senior Research Officer at the University of Oxford Centre for Criminological Research.

Ian O'Donnell is Research Fellow at the Institute of Criminology, Faculty of Law, University College Dublin, and an Associate of the University of Oxford Centre for Criminological Research.

Carol Martin was formerly Research Officer at the University of Oxford Centre for Criminological Research.

Acknowledgements

We are grateful to the prisoners whose views and experiences form the heart of this book. We hope that we have properly reflected their concerns about prison safety. We are obliged also to the governors and staff who made us welcome and facilitated our tasks. In each establishment we visited, we were received with courtesy and enthusiasm. Our work was supported at every stage by Prison Service Headquarters.

The first of the two projects that form the core of this book was funded by the Home Office Research and Statistics Directorate and the second by the Economic and Social Research Council under its Violence Research Programme. We acknowledge these sponsors with thanks and are pleased to have been supported by them while we carried out our work. Chapters 3–5 are based on the study commissioned by the Home Office. The views expressed are those of the authors and not necessarily the Home Office (nor do they reflect government policy).

The University of Oxford Centre for Criminological Research, where we all worked at various stages over the past decade, provided the necessary administrative support as well as a congenial and stimulating work environment. A special word of thanks is reserved for Professor Roger Hood, Director of the Centre and Fellow of All Souls College, who oversaw both research projects from conception to completion. Professor Hood was always unstinting in his support, generous with his time and constructive with his comments. The successive drafts of this book have benefited greatly from his insightful guidance and academic rigour. In addition, he ensured that Kimmett Edgar could devote sufficient time to the completion of this book.

We would also like to thank Dr Diego Gambetta, Reader in Sociology at Oxford University and Fellow of All Souls College, for his comments on the penultimate draft of our manuscript. Ian O'Donnell acknowledges the generosity of University College Dublin, which made possible his contribution to the writing of this book, through the grant of a President's Research Award.

Kimmett Edgar, Ian O'Donnell and Carol Martin
July 2002

Chapter 1

Introduction and overview

Stewkley

I'm in his cell and I'm talking to him. We were talking sensibly. Then a mate of mine comes in and grabs my arm and tries to pull me out. As the door opens, there were loads of heads there and that must have made him change his mind – he started saying, 'Get out! What you doing there, you little monkey?' and he started pushing me. He threw me out like I was a rag doll, and I thought that was humiliating, so I retaliated by punching him in the face. He picked me up and steamed me into the wall. I said to myself, 'He's big but he's slow'. He's still trying to grapple with me – I'm still hitting him to the head and face. I was upset because I didn't want to resort to that over something so trivial. I don't remember it at all but he fell down and I carried on kicking him. I heard the alarm bell and my friend pulled me out and I went into his cell and washed my face and got some of the blood off. I was hoping the officers wouldn't know who was fighting but they came for me and took me down the Block. They started to tell me it was assault but when I mentioned my solicitor, they said they would do me for fighting.

Warslow

I saw Stewkley come up the stairs and he came in my cell and pushed the door to. He starts being abusive to me. The way he was stood – side on and his hand kept going towards his pocket – I said, 'You're tooled up, are you?' I called him a kid and told him to get out. I'd avoid a confrontation if possible unless I'm being hit. I told him to get out but he had his foot against the door. I wanted him out of the cell, so I put my hands on his shoulders and moved him to the side through the door. As he went through the door, he swung his hand round and punched me in the face – he knocked my front tooth out. I put my hands back on his shoulders to push him out. He tried to hit me again but he grabbed my shirt and I tripped over. Whilst I was on the floor, he kicked me three times in the face. An officer was there and shouted and it just broke up. He knew something was going on. Stewkley went into his friend's cell and I went into my cell. Staff came in straight away and said I had been assaulted. I then made a statement and signed it but I don't know why I got charged with fighting. I was taken to Health Care and then the Block.

The harm caused by imprisonment is multifaceted. Most evident are the material deprivations of prison life, isolation from families and reduced prospects for future employment. In addition to these, the prisoner runs the risk of becoming a victim of crimes such as theft, robbery or assault; and more rarely, rape or murder. Violent incidents, such as the fight between Stewkley and Warslow,[1] seem to confirm a stereotype of prisoners as volatile and dangerous individuals. Our aim is to explain the nature and extent of *interpersonal* prison violence and victimization; that is, incidents that arise between individual prisoners, including fights and assaults, but also threats, robberies and bullying. We will not deal with the uses of force in relations between prisoners and prison officers, nor will we discuss collective violence, such as rioting or destructive demonstrations.

This book brings together evidence from two major pieces of research on prison life (both conducted in England and Wales). The first, 'the victimization study', focused primarily on the extent of different forms of harmful behaviour, ranging from assaults with weapons to social exclusion. It was funded by the Home Office Research and Statistics Directorate (as it was then). The second, 'the conflicts study', grew out of the first. It gathered detailed information about the tactics prisoners used in dealing with problems that arose between them, and the circumstances that resulted in physical violence. It was funded by the Economic and Social Research Council.

Both projects were carried out at the University of Oxford Centre for Criminological Research. This book grows out of a long assocation with the centre, where all the authors were employed at various periods between 1992 and 2002. Each project pioneered new approaches to the study of prison life and led to a number of publications (including Edgar and O'Donnell 1998; O'Donnell and Edgar 1996, 1998a, 1998b, 1999; Edgar and Martin 2000; Edgar *et al.* 2002a, 2003). What is novel about *Prison Violence* is that, for the first time, it weaves together the two studies to construct a detailed account of the forces shaping individual prisoners' experiences of conflict, fear and the struggle for power.

We aim to focus systematically on prison violence in a way that might lead to a deeper understanding of how often and why it occurs, and to develop thinking about how this problem can be minimized. Our primary sources are the prisoners' recollections of their thoughts, feelings and interpretations, especially when they found themselves in conflict. We describe the prison experience as seen through the lens of troubled relationships.

The prison subculture

The sociology of prisons has been extensively discussed, and we do not intend to review the general literature here. Indeed, rather than attempting to incorporate fleeting references to numerous studies, we have concentrated on a modest number of sources, some drawn from beyond the confines of traditional criminal justice research. By freeing up the text in this way and concentrating on prisoners' narratives, we hope to lower the barriers between the reader and the lived reality of prison violence. However, a brief sketch of how others have described the functions and meanings of violence within prison culture will set the scene for the chapters that follow.

The classic works of prison sociology describe the processes of acculturation, particularly the defining features of the inmate 'code'. Donald Clemmer initiated this research tradition with his landmark text, *The Prison Community* (1940), a work of extraordinary breadth and detail. Clemmer compiled a dictionary of prison slang, elaborated the structural dimensions of social differentiation and organization, and studied sexual and economic behaviour among prisoners. He developed the concept of prisonization, which he defined as 'the taking on in greater or less degree of the folkways, mores, customs and general culture of the penitentiary' (ibid.: 299).

Almost twenty years later, Gresham Sykes described how prisoners maintained an uneasy balance between solidarity and mutual exploitation. His book, *The Society of Captives* (1958), is short and elegantly written. The prisoners Sykes studied were united in opposition to the prison authorities, 'their captors', but were also engaged in a war of all against all. Sykes (ibid.: 77) summed up the situation facing a prisoner in New Jersey in the mid-1950s in words that still ring true today: 'While it is true that every prisoner does not live in the constant fear of being robbed or beaten, the constant companionship of thieves, rapists, murderers and aggressive homosexuals is far from reassuring.'

Like Clemmer, Sykes believed that prisoners' lifestyles reflected the particular adaptations they had to make to prison environments. This understanding came to be referred to as the 'deprivation model' of prison adjustment. Within this school of thought, violence was seen primarily as a tool prisoners used in securing for themselves as comfortable a lifestyle as was possible in the deprived environment of the prison. In the institution described by Sykes, prisoners used violent force to:

- deter others by shows of toughness
- exploit others through robbery
- maintain their image against insults
- obtain sexual gratification.

Other writers, such as John Irwin and Donald Cressey (1962), emphasized the ways the inmate code reflected values that offenders brought with them into prison from their criminal networks outside. Breaches of the code which governed their behaviour (for example, passing information to staff) were met with violence. It was largely assumed that prisoners' conduct was shaped by conformity to the code. The general thrust of this theory, which is labelled the 'importation model', was to untangle the ways that inmates' behaviour in custody was an extension of the 'criminal subculture' more generally. Hence, the importation model tends to stress the extent to which prisoners enter custody already committed to values that support the use of violence.

Martin Grapendaal (1990) and others have since advocated an 'integration theory' proposing that some of the aspects of culture in prison are imported from outside and some originate in the special conditions of confinement. Prisons are not seen as monolithic environments and prisoners differ in their perceptions of, and responses to, similar experiences. Kenneth Adams (1992) provided a useful summary of research on prisoners' culture from the deprivation, importation and integration perspectives. He charted the developmental nature of adjustments to institutional life. For example, self-mutilation, emotional disorders and rule infractions are most likely during the early phases of incarceration. Adams argued that 'maladaptive' behaviour in prison has much in common with maladaptive behaviour in the community and that programmes that result in positive changes in prisons should spill over to community settings. In other words, there

4

would be a diffusion of benefits associated with improvements in prison safety.

General descriptions of prison culture acknowledge that within prisons the potential for violence is ever present, but rarely do they explore the consequences of fights and assaults for the prison as a community. They say little about how the extent and threat of victimization structure social relations among prisoners.

Violence and social order

More recently, research has examined the structures and processes which generate and maintain 'order' within the prison community. Richard Sparks, Anthony Bottoms and Will Hay (1996: 119) defined social order partly in terms of the absence of violence. In the interpersonal context, they viewed order as a kind of reliable predictability:

> ... an orderly situation is any long-standing pattern of social relations (characterized by a minimum level of respect for persons) in which the expectations that participants have of one another are commonly met, though not necessarily without contestation. Order can also, in part, be defined negatively as the absence of violence, overt conflict or the imminent threat of the chaotic breakdown of social routines.

Their book, *Prisons and the Problem of Order* focused on 'the *perennial problem* of securing and maintaining order in prisons, rather than the *special problem* of the occasional complete or near-complete breakdown of order' (ibid.: 2, emphasis in original). Their definition viewed violence as an interruption in social order. None the less, they also recognized that prisoner culture could create competing understandings. In a later essay, Bottoms (1999) made clear that, among prisoners, violence might become routine, part of the everyday expectations that participants have of one another. Rather than being disruptive, violence can be seen as a convention. He described prison societies in these carefully balanced words (ibid.: 275): 'The evidence that we have about the prisoners' own world suggests both that it is a special kind of social context unusually weighted toward coercive power and that it nevertheless frequently contains elements of predictability and order.'

Bottoms also cited evidence that most prisoners seem to feel safe most of the time. These insights raise key questions about the influence of violence at the level of prisoner culture. How can it be that prisons exhibit high rates of assault, threats of violence and other unsettling behaviour, yet prisoners are not disabled by fear? How is it possible for institutions to function if violence – and the threat of violence – is routine, a way of life?

Violence, then, appears to have three possible roles in regard to social order:

1. When order is conceived as stable relations based on a minimal level of (mutual) respect, violence represents chaos and disorder, a break in social stability that requires resolution before orderly routine can resume (violence as disruption).

2. In other contexts, chaos might be brought to an end by violence used as a regulating device. In these situations, violence has a temporary function, to restore order, at which point the need to inflict harm comes to an end and routine is re-established (violence as regulator).

3. If human nature is viewed as naturally violent; if violence is believed to be inevitable, and interpersonal harm seen as the way things are; if we imagine a society in which violence is the expectation each party has of everyone else; then violence is part of everyday reality (violence as convention).

Clearly the first and third meanings are mutually exclusive: violence cannot be a break in the order and order itself. Bottoms's reference to the role of coercive power and predictability implies that prison culture might exhibit a perverse kind of order in which violence is the norm. Joe Sim (1994: 104) has gone further and related the ordinariness of violence to the expression of masculinity:

Violence and domination in prison can therefore be understood not as a pathological manifestation of abnormal otherness but as part of the normal routine which is sustained and legitimated by the wider culture of masculinity: that culture condemns some acts of male violence but condones the majority of others.

The extent to which violence is a disruption of social order, a regulating device or a convention is partly an empirical question. If violence could be shown to be extremely rare, it would then be difficult to support the claim that it is part of everyday prison life. If most prisoners are likely to experience or witness physical violence over the course of a period in custody, then the prevalence of violence would seem to confirm the hard image of prison as a place where each member might reasonably expect everyone else to attempt to inflict physical harm. One of our major aims is to clarify the extent to which prisons are ruled by force, to investigate whether Sykes's war of everyone against everyone reflects prison life in general.

The relationship between violence and order can be presented as a difference of perspective. Take, as an example, an assault on an informer. Prisoners for whom violence is a convention would accept this as an inevitable (and normal) part of everyday prison life. Those who subscribe to the values of inmate solidarity might judge that the beating was necessary as a regulator of inmate conduct, punishing the betrayal of the inmate code. For prison management, the private justice such a beating represents would typify violence as a break in the social order.

Kieran McEvoy (2001: 45) described how prison violence was used in a strategy of resistance pursued by paramilitary prisoners in Northern Ireland. He wrote:

> Violence against prison staff or other inmates (normally from opposing factions) is a direct challenge to the prison authorities, it is a direct appropriation of power. The state's monopoly on the use of force is challenged in a place which should be the zenith of the state's capacity for power and control . . . Violence is resistance through infliction.

McEvoy's study dealt with cohesive and organized prisoner groups, which have little in common with the shifting alliances of ordinary prisoners. Republicans for example avoided behaviour, such as assaults on sex offenders, which would offer the authorities the opportunity to portray them as ordinary prisoners. However, his study highlights the importance of setting violence among prisoners within the framework of the sometimes tense relations between the keepers and the kept.

In a related vein, Mary Bosworth (1999) analysed the way that women prisoners strove to resist the restrictions placed upon them by imprisonment. The crux of this resistance was negotiations of identity, their achievement of a sense of self. Her focus was largely on how inmates resisted the deprivations of prison, 'despite their subordination and confinement' (ibid.: 127). 'Yet,' she concluded, 'despite the restricted choices and opportunities that characterize all penal institutions, most prisoners find the ability to express their agency and to resist. Few prisons are run by coercion alone' (ibid.: 131). Resistance can take the form of refusing to eat prison food by becoming vegetarian, demanding Halal or Kosher meat; low-level verbal challenges to the authority of officers; forming lesbian relationships; the nature of one's religious observance; and self-harm and suicide. Our analysis extends this understanding by honing in on the uses of violence among women in prison.

The work of McEvoy and Bosworth implies a fourth possible connection between violence and order: violence as rebellion against an imposed order. Violence is a resource which may be deployed to redefine or renegotiate relationships. Erving Goffman (1961) described the adaptations inmates make in response to the deprivations of institutions. He distinguished between adaptations that conform to the objectives of the institution and those by which inmates resisted the power of the institution to shape their identities (Goffman terms these 'secondary adaptations'). Following the insights of McEvoy and Bosworth, the use of violence by prisoners can be defined as a secondary adaptation to prison life, that is, a way of resisting or rebelling against the prison authorities' attempts to impose their own sense of order.

The relationship between violence and social order cannot be defined for all prisons in terms of any one of these four models. The research upon which this book is based enables us to compare and contrast a range of different social settings, including populations of young males, female prisoners and adult males. We are also able to observe the influence on prison culture of short-sentence and remand facilities, and high-security regimes for long-term prisoners. Thus, in the discussions of prison violence to follow, we hope to develop ideas about how particular prison cultures shape the interactions between prisoners that result in violence.

Focusing on the mundane

Although routine, prison violence in England and Wales rarely results in life-threatening injuries. In 2000, for example, there were three homicides in an average population of 65,000. The previous year there were none (Sattar 2001: 17). Hans Toch (1997: 168) has argued that most of the time, violence in prison is mundane: 'The point about prison-violence experience that matters is its unrepresentativeness ... Prison life is not continuously suffused with imminent violence. This fact is hard to accept because it is drab and unexciting.'

A more spectacular rendering of prison violence – for example, lurid depictions of sexual assault, murder or rioting – would obscure the ordinary, day-to-day victimization which characterizes institutional life. William Davies (1982: 131) suggested that, despite its mundane character, 'everyday' violence has a profound impact on the lives of most prisoners: ' "Endemic" violence, although less newsworthy than either riots or hostage-takings, is probably more feared by inmates. Although an individual is relatively unlikely to be involved in either a riot or a hostage-taking, there is the constant threat of assault from another inmate.' A fascination for the rare violent incident that results in serious physical injury can lead to a distorted perception of prisons, according to which every assault is potentially lethal and the principal risks to the inmate are of murder and rape. In contrast, we will show that the routine victimization represented by endemic, low-level violence creates a social order in which each member of prison society has good reason to suspect that the others are plotting an assault or some other form of predation, potentially leading to a perverse cycle in which the individual prisoner perceives a need to use force for self-protection. When the individual uses force in this way, the consequences for the community are that it becomes less safe. In this context, it is important to recognize that violence is never a totally isolated act. It needs to be seen as a process, with a history and a future. Thus, a theme running through the following chapters will be the consequences for inmates of exposure to a regular threat of minor harm.

Interpersonal dynamics

Thus far, we have painted the context against which violence arises in social terms. But much of our argument will be based on a more detailed look at the way individuals interact with other individuals. The motivations that guide an individual actor are the stuff of psychology. The structures that shape behaviour within particular social groups are the subject of sociological study. Our emphasis – particularly in Chapters 6 and 7 – is at the level of paired interactions ('dyads'). At this level, decision-making, and even recognizing that there is a dispute, is strongly influenced by the reciprocity between the two people involved. We propose to explain interpersonal violence in part by exploring how the prisoners directly involved interpreted the course of events and how each person's actions influenced the reactions of the other party. We will provide a more comprehensive explanation of this approach when we deal with methods and key concepts in the next chapter.

Bottoms (1999: 212) wrote that 'Researchers ... have rarely addressed the minutiae of the average prison day, or considered in detail how violence can arise within the social order'. We attempt to rise to this challenge by presenting uniquely detailed accounts of specific occasions of violence and conflict.

Fundamentally, the concept of violence involves harm to people. But violence is also a form of communication. It has important symbolic value – like all performances, how it is carried out, and how it is received, can be critical. One of our goals is to explore and, if possible to explain, the logic of the behaviour in a social context. By so doing, we follow David Garland's (1990: 277) description of 'theoretical work' as that 'which seeks to change the way we think about an issue and ultimately to change the practical ways we deal with it'.

In our view, it is essential that we try to understand the perspective of the person who engages in violence if there is to be any hope of prevention. Furthermore, we will present situations in which we found it impossible to divide the participants neatly into camps of 'perpetrator' and 'victim'. Indeed, we argue that approaches that begin with distributing blame block useful paths by which occasions of violence might be explained. To explain why violence occurs is not to 'blame the victim', but to alter the focus from blame to the search for understanding the structures, mechanisms and decisions – in short, the context – from which violence emerges.

Is violence necessarily irrational? If a rational response to a dispute entails dialogue in which both parties agree not to harm the other in any way and to pursue an agreement through marshalling evidence and working in collaboration to find mutually beneficial outcomes, then any use of force is, by definition, irrational. If by rational we mean any action that furthers the self-interest of the individual, then the use of injurious force can often qualify as rational. In their research Sparks *et al.* (1996) assumed that prisoners act as agents, on the basis of conscious decisions. They explained prisoners' behaviour by 'exploring the implicit knowledgeability or rationality of their actions' (ibid.: 81). The research on which the present book is based was carried out in a similar spirit.

A distinction is sometimes drawn between instrumental (or purposive) uses of violence and expressive (or cathartic) uses. We have not pursued this line of thinking. Instead, we have tried to investigate how the use of injurious force fits into the whole process of the interaction between prisoners, reserving judgement as to whether the act of harming the other party was rational or not.

Designing a new analytical framework

Looking at violence can be a bit like gazing through a kaleidoscope. From a psychological perspective, the emotions that drive people to harm others – fear, shame, anger or frustration, to name a few – provide an image of violence that defines it in terms of characteristics of violent people and fits the notion of an irresistible drive. Solutions are often based on altering the violent person's emotional patterns in response to stress. Turn the slide on the kaleidoscope, view violence from a legal perspective, and the picture changes. The images of violence are of behaviour that is technically defined (assault, rape, murder); evidence that is built up to prove the case against the accused; indices that determine the seriousness of the violence; an analysis of the intentions of the perpetrator; and solutions based on detection, punishment and deterrence. Social and political theorists provide yet another image. The focus is on the structures within which violence occurs. Violence is viewed from a 'macro' perspective, in terms of its functions within a particular cultural milieu.

No one is violent all the time. Explanations limited to the impact of social structure or psychology fail to answer why someone becomes violent in a particular situation. The circumstances in which a prisoner becomes violent form a vital part of the explanation of violence. Accordingly, we give serious attention to the decisions and intentions of people who use violence and to the interactions from which violence springs. Our 'conflict-centred' approach sets violence in the context of interpersonal disputes to investigate the circumstances and processes out of which violent incidents emerge. We focus on what the use of violence meant to the people most directly involved.

Approaching prison violence in this way has enabled us to suggest answers to the following questions:

- What is the likelihood of becoming a victim of serious crime inside prison?

- What factors increase the risks of being victimized?

- How does bullying relate to victimization and, specifically, to assault?

- What are the particular circumstances that lead to fights and assaults? In particular, what tensions between the interests of individual prisoners drive them into a dispute?

- What tactics do prisoners characteristically use when they find themselves in conflict with other prisoners? Under what conditions do these tactics become 'catalysts' to violence?

- What are the personal (and social) consequences of spending months or years in places where distrust and anxiety are normal?

- What effects do features of the prison social setting have in shaping conflicts between prisoners?

- What purposes does violence serve and when do prisoners believe that it is appropriate?

- What methods of handling conflicts do prisoners use that could prevent violence?

Exploring the intentions and interpretations of the person who used violence is essential to mapping the logic of violence. This approach, symbolic interactionism, was described by Herbert Blumer (1969: 73–4) in the following terms:

Since action is forged by the actor out of what he perceives, interprets and judges, one would have to see the operating situation as the actor sees it, perceive objects as the actor perceives them, ascertain their meaning in terms of the meaning they have for the actor, and follow the actor's line of conduct as the actor organizes it – in short, one would have to take the role of the actor and see his world from his standpoint.

We analysed behaviour as an interactive process. In this, individual prisoners' interpretations of the nature of their situations were central. We set fights and assaults in the context of the interactions that preceded them. Other studies have sought to identify persons with a propensity towards violence. Resulting policies have attempted to tackle the problem by identifying and controlling these 'violent prisoners'. In contrast, this book explains how violence arises from identifiable conflicts. Violence takes on particular forms, and is given distinct meanings, in the context of a prison.

The findings of the victimization study form the basis of our examination of the prison environment in Chapters 3–5. In Chapter 3, we map the frequency of crimes, such as assaults and robbery, which are committed by inmates against inmates. Victimization in prison is broader than this, however, for it encompasses non-criminal activities such as verbal abuse and exclusion. We argue that victimization is routine in prison and that the risks of being assaulted, threatened or exploited are sufficiently high to be a formative aspect of the prison social structure. Much victimization is mutual and we examine the victim–perpetrator overlap in Chapter 4. Fear and vulnerability are discussed in Chapter 5.

Against that backdrop, we draw on the conflicts study to explore how disputes between prisoners escalate into fights and assaults by analysing the roots of violent incidents in conflicts between prisoners (Chapter 6 and 7). Power plays a key role in prison society and in the interpersonal conflicts that arise between prisoners. This issue is discussed in Chapter 8. None the less, not all conflicts end in physical violence, and in the final chapter we build on all our work to outline pathways to safety, and present some ideas about how violence might be reduced in prisons.

Note

1 'Stewkley' and all other names for prisoners used throughout are fictitious, drawn at random from a list of English towns. The use of pseudo-surnames facilitates cross-references between stories and does not depersonalize the characters involved in the way terminology such as 'Prisoner A' and 'Prisoner B' would do.

Chapter 2

Methods and key concepts

Researching and writing about violence will never be a simple endeavor. The subject is fraught with assumptions, presuppositions, and contradictions. Like power, violence is essentially contested: everyone knows it exists, but no one agrees on what actually constitutes the phenomenon (Antonius Robben and Carolyn Nordstrom 1995: 5).

As noted in Chapter 1, this book synthesizes a large volume of information that was collected over the course of two funded research projects: the victimization study and the conflicts study, carried out between 1994 and 1999. Data were collected in diverse prison settings.

The victimization study was limited to males. It was conducted in two prisons for adults: Wellingborough, a Category C prison, with an average roll of 302, and Bullingdon, a local, multi-functional prison holding 625; and two young offender institutions (YOIs): Hunter-combe, with an average roll of 224, and Feltham, which held 825. The conflicts study encompassed four different populations: Long Lartin, a high security ('dispersal') prison, holding 404; Bullingdon (again), which had expanded to hold 844 prisoners; Eastwood Park, holding 255 women and girls; and Aylesbury YOI, holding 319.

The studies employed a variety of approaches. We were guided by the perspective of interpretive interactionism, that is, attempting 'to make the world of problematic lived experience of ordinary people directly available to the reader' (Denzin 1989: 7). The research methods of this approach include open-ended, creative interviewing; document analysis; life history; personal experience and self-story construction; and participant observation. These techniques were part of the methodological tool kit that we brought to our examination of prison violence, with a view to 'capture the voices, emotions, and actions of those studied' (ibid.: 10). There were also quantitative components to the research, including questionnaire surveys, which are described next.

The victimization study

The survey

Often, the study of prisoner culture has relied on limited periods of observation, interviews with small and non-random samples of inmates, and official data. While crime surveys have become methodologically sophisticated and widely applied in the community, they have rarely penetrated into custodial institutions. For this reason, before we began our work in the mid-1990s, there was little systematically gathered information about prisoners' experiences of victimization or their fear of crime.

Accordingly, we conducted a large-scale survey to determine the extent of crime in custody. Every inmate in the four institutions visited was approached in person by one of the authors and asked to complete a 12-page questionnaire which dealt with his personal experience of victimization in the previous month; whether he had witnessed the victimization of others; the extent to which he felt safe from being assaulted, insulted or having his property stolen; whether he would report any problems to staff; where in the prison he felt least safe; how he defined bullying and how he believed it might be stopped.

A small number of inmates failed to complete the questionnaire despite great efforts to persuade them to do so. This may have been for a number of reasons including lack of time, undetected literacy problems, suspicion of the research, doubts about confidentiality, apathy and reservations about the way the findings might be used. Several forms were spoiled. Some were torn to shreds, others were filled with abusive comments and one was retrieved from an inmate who was attempting to eat it. One adult prisoner announced that he would have nothing to do with the study, crumpled up his form and threw it out the cell window. It was retrieved from the rubbish strewn across the prison yard and found to be fully completed.

Overall, the response rate was highly satisfactory: 92 per cent of the young offenders approached agreed to take part and filled out a questionnaire (820/892). In the adult institutions, 87 per cent did so (722/827). Thus the overall response rate was 90 per cent. In addition a small number of questionnaires (15 young offenders and 9 adults) were returned partially completed with some useful information. These were included in the analysis which is based on a total of 1,566 returns: 650 from Feltham, 185 from Huntercombe, 518 from Bullingdon and 213 from Wellingborough.

The interviews

The victimization survey was followed by structured interviews with prisoners who had been identified as having had an experience of assault, threats of violence, robbery, cell theft, verbal abuse or exclusion in that particular prison in the previous month. Participants were asked to describe every incident in their own words, including where and when it had taken place, how many people were involved, whether weapons were used, what had led up to it, whether they had expected it to occur, what was said, whether a prison officer was told about it and what happened to the perpetrator. Victims also gave their views on how to prevent victimization. Finally, they were asked whether they had ever victimized other prisoners themselves.

In total, 61 prisoners who had been victimized were interviewed (27 adults and 34 young offenders; of whom 53 were white, 3 black, and 5 Asian). None of those approached refused to take part. Over one-third of interviewed victims ($n = 22$) were recruited from vulnerable prisoner units (VPUs). Segregation units were another fruitful source ($n = 10$), because, in institutions without a VPU, prisoners at risk are often held in the segregation unit until they can be transferred to another establishment. A large number of interviewed victims were resident on normal location ($n = 29$). Some of these were nominated by wing officers, occasionally within minutes of an act of victimization taking place. Others volunteered either by approaching one of the authors directly or by means of a plea written on the self-completion questionnaire.

Interviews were also carried out with prisoners who had victimized others. The purpose of these interviews was to learn how they structured their decision-making. Of primary interest were the selection of suitable victims, motivating factors and techniques of exploitation. Only prisoners who were currently active (i.e. had victimized others in the previous month) were interviewed. Thirty-one prisoners took part in this aspect of the study (28 young offenders and three adults). One reason so few adults were interviewed as victimizers is that the levels of victimization were much lower in adult institutions. Maturity may also have played a part, with older offenders less willing to suspend suspicion of outside researchers. Finally, preying on fellow inmates is an activity which adult prisoners generally condemn and consider to be juvenile and disruptive.

Seventeen of those interviewed were white, 11 black, one Asian and two were from other racial groups. The majority were selected because they were resident on a unit which had been established for identified 'bullies' ($n = 17$). These young men were questioned closely about the activities which had led to their removal from the wing. Two victimizers were resident on a VPU where they had been placed for their own safety. The remainder were on normal location ($n = 12$), and most were recruited through personal contact with the research team, usually made during the distribution of the self-completion questionnaire. A small number of those on normal location were referred by another interviewed victimizer. Only one inmate who had been identified as a victimizer refused to participate, even though strenuous efforts had been made to gain his co-operation.

Wherever possible the experiences which inmates discussed were verified by reference to the accounts of other inmates and staff, a scrutiny of official sources (such as wing observation logs, inmate files and security records) and checks of an inmate's story for internal consistency. On the whole we were confident that inmates had spoken to us candidly, even to the extent of telling us things which it was not in their interest to disclose. They seemed genuinely to appreciate the opportunity to give their side of the story.

The conflicts study

The survey

During the fieldwork, we conducted a survey to gauge the impact of violence in prison. Primarily, prisoners were recruited by opportunist direct approaches and asked to take part in an interview. Some were identified from adjudication records, staff referrals and recommendations from other inmates. Additionally, in the dispersal prison, Long Lartin, a letter was distributed to prisoners describing the purposes of the study and inviting them to participate. Because of the nature of the population, the opportunities to approach high-security inmates personally and individually were more restricted than elsewhere; for example it was not permitted for interviews to be conducted in cells.

A face-to-face questionnaire survey was conducted with 590 inmates, comprising 107 male young offenders, 151 female prisoners and 332 adult males. The questionnaire focused on the prisoners' experience of, and views on, prison violence, but also collected basic demographic data on age, ethnic origin, nature of their offence, sentence length, previous convictions, prior custodial experience and prison disciplinary history.

The prisoners were asked about their experiences of intimidation, participation in or witnessing fights or assaults, and whether they had been directly involved in conflicts with other inmates that had been resolved without violence. They were also asked how they perceived the level of assaults, the prevalence of sexual assault and self-harm, and more general attitudinal questions about their views on violence in a prison setting. The survey typically took about 30 minutes to complete, although some lasted more than 90 minutes. It allowed us to identify those inmates who had recently been involved in conflicts whom we interviewed again in greater depth.

The interviews

The in-depth interview, lasting around 90 minutes, was carried out with 209 of the inmates who had been surveyed. All acknowledged recent involvement in a violent (or potentially violent) incident. They were asked over 100 questions about the incident. Practical requirements of confidentiality, transfers to other prisons and the release of some prisoners meant that potential respondents were sometimes lost. However, only six inmates whose participation in an incident was known to the researchers declined when they were approached directly for an interview. These interviews covered a total of 141 incidents: 40 at Aylesbury, 37 at Bullingdon, 40 at Eastwood Park and 24 at Long Lartin.

Of the 209 participants, 132 had used injurious force. Of the 141 incidents, 57 were fights (in which both participants used injurious force) and 34 were assaults (in which the use of force was unilateral). In three incidents it was not possible to determine whether a fight or an assault had taken place, as the participants' accounts (or others involved such as officer witnesses) flatly contradicted each other: one alleged an attempted sexual assault which the accused completely denied; another alleged a beating by his two cell mates, both of whom denied any physical assault took place; and one prisoner said she had assaulted another but the officer involved said he intervened before any physical contact took place. This breakdown is shown in Table 2.1.

Among the remaining incidents (47/141) some involved an element of physical contact but we did not judge these to amount to a fight or

Table 2.1: Type of incident and number of participants interviewed

	Fight	Assault	Neither party used injurious force	Use of force disputed
One	15	20	43	1
Both	42	14	4	2
Total	57	34	47	3

an assault. Examples of such incidents included an inmate being jostled on the stairs as someone else ran past her; an incident between friends involving one poking the other in the leg with a screwdriver; two inmates holding on to a broom handle in order to wrest it from each other; an inmate having her trousers pulled down and then each of the participants aiming kicks at the other; and an inmate being pushed with the aim of making her trip over.

In Aylesbury there were three times as many fights as assaults (21 versus 7). In the local prison (Bullingdon2) there were twice as many (18 versus 8) and in the women's prison (Eastwood Park) and the dispersal (Long Lartin), the proportions were even (12 versus 13; 6 versus 6).

For each incident, the aim was to build a complete picture of what happened, and any background circumstances, by hearing from the prisoners directly involved, a witness if possible and – where relevant – the reporting officer and adjudicating governor. We interviewed 51 witnesses. Most were bystanders in the sense that they were physically proximate to the action and could have intervened. The witnesses were asked to give their views on how the trouble started, who was involved and who threw the first punch. Their contributions helped to clarify the sequence of events, especially when there was a discrepancy between the accounts of those most directly involved.

While this was the ideal coverage of an episode, there were incidents about which it was possible to gain only one participant's perspective, or where no witness was available. When a fight or assault had come to the attention of staff and the participants had been subject to the prison disciplinary system, the names of the inmates were a matter of record. Inmates involved in 'unofficial' incidents, which were unknown to staff and consequently had not been punished, were less likely to reveal the names of their counterparts, so accounts of these incidents were more likely to remain incomplete. At the dispersal prison, we had the most difficulty identifying both parties and we were able to interview both participants in only two of 12 incidents. The chief obstacle was that while inmates were happy to give their own side of the story, they would not name the other participant for fear of being seen as informers.

A complete incident was not necessarily one that was known to staff. A note was made whether the incident was official (i.e. resulted in an adjudication); known to staff, but handled informally; or unknown to staff. Officers knew about most – but not all – of the incidents investigated. However, they rarely knew the full story.

The interviews began with the participant's brief description of the incident, then gathered information about the circumstances that led to the use of force, including the role of peers or witnesses, whether weapons were used, the nature of the relationship between participants, the interests that divided them, the role of staff and the effects of any adjudication. A key tool that we developed for these interviews was the 'Escalator', an innovative framework for breaking down an interaction into its component parts (Alternatives to Violence Project 1996).

Interviewees were shown a schematic diagram indicating a series of steps and asked, 'What was the first thing that happened?' They were then able to pick up the story and to relate the sequence of events in far greater detail than they had been able to provide in earlier descriptions. After the sequence had been completed to their satisfaction, participants were referred to specific points in their accounts and asked supplementary questions about their interpretations, their impressions of their counterparts' intentions, their emotional state and the opportunities they saw for possible prevention. A number of completed escalators are presented in the Appendix. A particular benefit of using escalators to record personal accounts was the ease with which we were able to juxtapose one account against another. Often one person provided information that was lacking in the other's perspective (for a more detailed account of this aspect of the methodology, see Edgar *et al.* 2002).

The escalator made it possible to organize prisoners' accounts in a systematic and chronological framework. Comparing the diverse narratives of many of these situations revealed the reciprocal nature of the interactions. The rich detail in the participants' personal accounts opened the 'geometry' of conflicts to analytical exploration. The escalator structure enabled us to identify the patterns of thought and behaviour by which violence was introduced into the process of managing conflict. It uncovered the reasons someone turned to violence, thus generating more complete explanations of why the violence occurred.

The combination of brief description, direct questions and escalators provided three different pictures of the same sequence of events. This enabled us to interpret conflict situations from the perspective of those who were directly involved, and to recreate the context from which violence emerged. Our goal, in every incident, paralleled what Norman Denzin (1989: 33) termed a 'thick' description, namely:

(1) It gives the context of an act; (2) it states the intentions and meanings that organize the action; (3) it traces the evolution and development of the act; (4) it presents the action as a text that can

then be interpreted. A *thin description* simply reports facts, independent of intentions or the circumstances that surround an action.

Such descriptions are the basis for authentic understanding. They allow the reader to 'share vicariously in the experiences that have been captured' (ibid.: 83). If done properly, this, 'establishes the significance of an experience, or the sequence of events, for the person or persons in question . . . the voices, feelings, actions, and meanings of interacting individuals are heard' (ibid.). We set out to create an understanding of what actually happened in ways that would be suitable for theory building as well as acceptable to the participants.

Direct observation

Many hundreds of hours were spent informally in each of the institutions studied. The researchers were a visible presence on wings throughout the day, particularly during meal-times and association. Wherever possible we mingled freely, occasionally played games, had a cup of tea in a cell or chatted with groups of inmates waiting to use the telephone or wherever they congregated. We were always prepared to discuss our intentions at length, sound out general views and enlist inmates for individual interviews at more convenient times. In one institution, the researchers were not allowed on to some of the landings unless an officer was present. This condition hampered the research because it limited the opportunities to have the sorts of informal conversations which often generated useful information.

The researchers' direct approach met with considerable interest on the part of inmates, who could see the relevance of the work to their daily lives. Only on rare occasions did anyone respond with outright hostility. On some wings a prisoner, or small group of prisoners, 'adopted' the researchers. Their contribution to the project was great, as they facilitated introductions to other inmates and by their public acceptance encouraged support for the research.

In the victimization study 111 staff were interviewed to discover how frequently inmates informed them about victimization and how they responded when complaints were made. Time was spent during the fieldwork on a variety of specialist and non-specialist wings, and every effort was made to ensure that a broadly representative sample of staff was recruited. In the conflicts study, 58 staff were interviewed. All had witnessed a fight or assault, were reporting officers or were otherwise directly involved in an incident. While valuable, the staff perspective is beyond the remit of this book, the specific focus of which is the attitudes, beliefs and interpretations of prisoners.

Although most of the information we discuss in the chapters to follow came directly from surveys and interviews, we do not wish to underestimate the learning process each of us enjoyed through the hours we spent in the company of prisoners. We cannot put it better than Sykes (1958: 136), who described the value of such an approach as follows: 'This matter of circulating in a social system to record an event from many different vantage points may not warrant the dignity of labelling it a method of research, but it proved to be the key to the society of captives.'

Defining terms

Before proceeding it is important to explore the meanings of some of the key terms that are fundamental to understanding prison violence. These include the roles of victim and perpetrator, and the concepts of violence and conflict.

This book views violence through two lenses – as victimization and as conflict. Seeing violence as victimization defines it as a harm and leads to explanations based on the extent of the problem (such as rates of assault, threats or robbery). Seeing violence as an outcome of conflict focuses on how prisoners conduct disputes over competing interests, values or needs. The emphasis is on the tactics used in disputes, the interpretations each party makes and the power balance between the two.

Victim and victimizer

There is sometimes a naïve assumption that assigning the status of victim is self-evident or unproblematic. We interviewed prisoners about their experiences as victims or victimizers. Although the vast majority of victimizers could equally have discussed recent experiences as victims, the analyses of the interviews were performed on the basis that for certain purposes it was useful to consider these as two analytically distinct, if overlapping, groups. The degree, and significance, of overlap between the roles of victim and perpetrator is discussed in detail in Chapter 4.

The definition of the category victim was further informed in the victimization study by our examination of the behaviours that increased the risks of being victimized (victim facilitation is explored in

Chapter 4). To take a stark example, sometimes it transpired that the prisoner who was assaulted had earlier been trying to rob the person who attacked him. He became a victim of assault primarily because he had attempted to be a perpetrator of robbery. These situations inspired an understanding of the roles of victim and perpetrator that saw them as transient and conditional. In the conflicts study, where the focus was on interpersonal violence, the distinction between perpetrator and victim became still less helpful as an explanation of prisoners' roles. This refinement in our understanding occurred over the course of the two research projects.

Similarly, the concept of bullying proved elusive. Despite the widespread use of the term by psychologists, we recognized at an early stage that it was inherently contentious, ambiguous and of limited utility. It was relevant only to a narrow range of behaviours that occurred in particular types of relationship (see further, Chapter 4).

Violence

As a concept, violence is slippery. It evades easy description and fixed definition. From an ethnographic perspective, Robben and Nordstrom (1995: 5) have suggested that, 'Vested interests, personal history, ideological loyalties, propaganda, and a dearth of firsthand information ensure that many "definitions" of violence are powerful fictions and negotiated half-truths'.

Tony Coady (1986: 4) suggests that there are three types of definition of violence, which he labelled 'wide', 'restricted' and 'legitimate'. The most influential example of a wide definition is structural violence, which extends the term 'violence' to cover a range of social injustices and inequalities. Following Johan Galtung's (1975) original description, if a child dies of malnutrition in a nation where others can afford to pay £50 for a bottle of wine with their meal, the child's death represents the violence of social injustice. Structural violence, like institutional racism, can be perceived by its outcomes. However, in any given case it is difficult to trace the route from structural cause to harmful effect.

'Restricted' definitions concentrate on positive interpersonal acts of force, usually involving the infliction of physical injury. For example, Goran Aijmer and Jon Abbink (2000: xi) define violence as the 'Contested use of damaging physical force with possibly fatal consequences and with purposeful humiliation'. We would dispute every element of this rendering. Uncontested actions can be violent, physical force is not always present and humiliation is not necessarily intended.

23

'Legitimist' definitions incorporate a reference to an illegal or illegitimate use of force. An example would be David Riches's (1986: 8) view that violence is 'an act of physical hurt deemed legitimate by the performer and illegitimate by (some) witnesses'. In such definitions violence is the assertion of power. It is always contested. This approach has the benefit of recognizing how central moral issues are to the definition of violence. According to Riches, every use of force creates a demand for legitimization. However, we depart from this perspective on empirical grounds, because sometimes in prison all the parties to a conflict regard the violence as legitimate. For example, it is not uncommon for prisoners to concede that others are entitled to use force against them in the case of an unpaid debt.

Another type of definition, not mentioned by Coady, sees violence as a drive. It is inexorable and insatiable. An example of this school is René Girard (1977: 2) when he suggests that 'when unappeased, violence seeks and always finds a surrogate victim. The creature that excited its fury is abruptly replaced by another, chosen only because it is vulnerable and close at hand'. This does not fit with our observations and what prisoners told us.

As Robben and Nordstrom imply, every participant and witness brings a unique perspective, agenda and interpretive framework to stories of violence, with the result that the search for a simple objective conclusion is often futile. Violence makes statements and it is our job to decipher them, to learn what they say, amongst other things, about honour, reputation, power, identity and social context.

To illustrate the complexity of the meaning of violence in our research, consider the following. During the violence survey, prisoners were asked: 'Have you ever been the victim of a sexual assault in prison?' Males answered without hesitation. There were no problems of comprehension. However, when we asked females it became evident that the concept of sexual assault in prison was more nuanced than we had anticipated. Women asked us whether we meant them to include situations in which other inmates had forcibly removed drugs hidden in their vaginas (a practice known as 'de-crutching'). Some of the women were unsure whether this behaviour constituted a sexual assault.

At the outset we thought of incidents as being either violent or non-violent and began by conducting the interviews accordingly. It soon became clear, however, that this simplistic division was untenable, given the range of conflicts that were described. There were instances of extreme psychological violence, intimidation and armed threats. Sometimes inmates were in serious fear for their physical safety and were unquestionably harmed despite the fact that no physical force was used. Consequently the simple dichotomy was rejected and all incidents were seen as being part of a continuum with simple verbal disagreement located at one end and extreme physical injury at the other.

Incorporating the philosophical, political, anthropological and sociological literature with our fieldwork experience we have developed a working definition of interpersonal violence that includes five fundamental elements. This conception is neither 'restricted' nor 'legitimist'. For our purposes to be considered violent an act must be: intentional; harmful; personal; meaningful; and seen as part of a process.

Conflict

The term conflict covers an enormous range of interactions between individuals, groups and nations. In any conflict there is a clash of interests, values or needs between at least two parties who harm each other and whose actions are determined by reciprocity. The understanding of conflict we use in this book blends ideas from the theoretical literature with the descriptions of disputes provided by prisoners.

John Burton (1990) suggested that *interests* refer to aspirations, including, for example, opportunities, roles, economic, political or social goals, or any material goods. Interests initiate competition: if party X wins the material good, then party Y cannot have it. Burton further defined interests by setting them apart from values and needs. Interests are negotiable and can be traded, as two parties can agree on a distribution of material goods which is fair, though neither party gets everything they wanted. Finally, over the course of a conflict each party can change their central interests.

Values arise out of particular cultures. They help to determine how a party will pursue their aims in a conflict. Individuals sometimes invest their sense of identity in the particular values of their culture, even to the extent of being willing to die for them. Equally, values can change over time. Within a conflict, each side judges the other's conduct by its own norms. Just as material interests can spark a conflict, so can values.

Needs, unlike interests, are not negotiable. So long as the social structure or the other party blocks the realization of these needs, conflict will be unavoidable. In his early work, Burton (1979) listed nine basic human needs: consistency in response, stimulation, security, recognition, distributive justice, appearing rational, meaningful responses, a sense of control and defending one's role. He stressed the importance of these underlying needs in responding to conflict, arguing that so long as they are unfulfilled, any settlement of a dispute is likely to be transient. Imprisonment routinely blocks prisoners from fulfilling these needs. Therefore prisons will be high-conflict settings.

Hubert Blalock (1989) argued that the defining element of conflict was that the parties applied 'negative sanctions' against each other. He claimed that the development of conflict is always a *reciprocal* process, involving not just both parties' actions, but a dynamic loop between them. Blalock (ibid.: 70) described the arms race in the following terms:

> The basic idea is that nation X reacts to increases in Y's armaments levels by increasing its own arms, this in turn leading to an increase in Y's levels ... Each nation is also subject to certain limitations on its budget, however, and there also may be other internal factors within each nation that affect its level of 'fatigue'.

Logically, the decisions that each nation makes about its defence expenditures are dependent on the decisions of its counterpart. Blalock claimed that reciprocity is central to conflicts whether they are neighbourhood disputes or arms races between countries. Fatigue might indicate psychological exhaustion for individuals rather than the resource depletion that can affect nations. In either case the basic principle remains that conflicts escalate as each side mobilizes its resources in response to the perceived aggression of its opponent.

Thinking more widely about the possibility of reducing violence through managing conflict there may be a number of valuable clues in the 'pure sociology' of Donald Black. In his book, *The Social Structure of Right and Wrong*, Black (1998: xxiii, emphasis in original) stakes out his territory in no uncertain terms:

> The handling of right and wrong, known in sociology as *social control* or *conflict management*, occurs throughout the social universe, wherever people intermingle. It includes phenomena as diverse as litigation, violence, mediation, gossip, ostracism, psychotherapy, sorcery, sabotage, and suicide. It occurs unilaterally (by one party against another), bilaterally (between two parties), and trilaterally (by a third party). It involves groups as well as individuals – lynching and rioting as well as fist-fighting and wife-beating – and covers everything from a glance of disapproval to the bombing of a city.

Within Black's scheme all conflicts can be pinpointed within a social space characterized by several dimensions. Every conflict, in other words, has a 'geometry'. The co-ordinates include, for example, the vertical – is it directed downward (against an inferior), upward (against a superior) or laterally (against an equal)?; the horizontal – how are people related to each other (degrees of intimacy); and the corporate – the capacity for collective action or organization. We return to Black's theory in the final chapter, when we suggest pathways to prevention.

Prison violence viewed as conflict

This book advocates a new way of looking at prison violence, setting fights, assaults, intimidation, harassment, degradation and humiliation in the context of conflict. Taking into account the competition over interests, the underlying needs, the mutuality of harm and the reciprocity of conduct, we analyse violence according to six dimensions:

1. *Interests* Participants were asked, 'What were you hoping to achieve?' Their replies – together with information provided in other sections of the interviews – enabled us to make explicit what each person wanted out of the situation.

2. *Relationships* were analysed in part in terms of the social distance between the parties: were they total strangers, mere acquaintances, close associates or friends before the conflict began? Our focus on relationships also revealed the importance of third parties, in the form of peer pressure, uninvolved spectators or mediators.

3. *Catalysts* refer to the tactics used in conflict that exacerbated the tensions between the parties and increased the risk of a physically violent outcome.

4. *Interpretation* Each person relied on interpretation to define the conflict. They drew inferences about the intentions of their opposite number based on their behaviour. Interpretation functioned to mediate interests, catalysts, relationships, purposes and the social context.

5. *Purposes* were deduced from the reasons given by prisoners who had used injurious force. The term refers specifically to the objectives of prisoners who harmed their peers.

6. *Social context*   Prisoners as individual agents made decisions based on the structural constraints imposed by the prison social setting. An advantage of the research design is that it facilitated comparisons between different types of institution.

Each of these dimensions provides important information about the genesis, development, conduct and outcomes of inter-prisoner conflicts. We found that they formed the basic components of every conflict and each inter-related with the others. We have much sympathy for definitions of conflict as a competition over interests or values, marked by mutual harm. However, in this book we emphasize that violence emerges as a basic component of conflict and that conflict must be viewed as a dynamic process. Thus, while accepting the value of the traditional approach, we believe that our tightly defined geometry of conflict more fully describes the framework within which prison violence can be explained.

Chapter 3

The extent and nature of victimization

> The population of prisoners does not exhibit a perfect solidarity yet neither is the population of prisoners a warring aggregate. Rather, it is a mixture of both and the society of captives lies balanced in an uneasy compromise (Gresham Sykes 1958: 83).

The survey carried out as part of the victimization study was designed primarily to gauge the extent to which prisoners were subjected to intentionally harmful behaviour, which we delineated in terms of six different types: insult, exclusion, theft, robbery, threat and assault.[1] The findings from this survey show the dangers of the prison environment; confirm that some types of victimization are so frequent as to be routine; and suggest that prisoners have good reason to be distrustful of the intentions of their peers.

We discuss each type of victimization in depth, first by reporting on the extent of the problem. We then turn to information provided by interviews with prisoners that shed light on the circumstances in which the victimization occurred. In the next chapter, we examine more specific issues, such as the links between victimization and bullying, the characteristics of prisoners who victimize others and implications for understanding the roles of victim and perpetrator.

Rates of victimization

Table 3.1 summarizes the main findings about the extent of victimization. This table is based on the number of individuals who reported having been victimized and not on the number of incidents of victimization. Victimization was frequent, particularly among young offenders, of whom 30 per cent had been assaulted and 44 per cent threatened with violence on at least one occasion in the previous month. For adults the respective figures were 19 per cent and 26 per

Table 3.1:   Been victimized at least once in previous month (per cent)

	Feltham	Hunter-combe	All young offenders	Bulling-don	Welling-borough	All adults
Assault	32	26	30	20	17	19
Threats of violence	46	40	44	27	25	26
Robbery	11	8	10	5	2	4
Cell theft	28	26	27	30	42	34
Hurtful verbal abuse	58	51	56	26	26	26
Exclusion	20	12	18	7	7	7

cent. To state this in another way, in a young offender institution with a population of 500, there would be at least 150 assaults in an average month. Further, given that some prisoners were repeatedly assaulted, this is a minimum estimate. Although many of these incidents were undoubtedly minor, the rates of assault demonstrate a level of harmful activity which is frustrating for staff, frightening for many inmates and potentially destabilizing for regimes. No more than 10 per cent of those who had been victimized in any way said they had made a written report (see Chapter 9, for a fuller discussion on the problems arising from the tendency of prisoners to hide victimization from staff).

This routine victimization shapes the social ethos of prisons and young offender institutions. The potential for assault, theft and verbal abuse shifts attitudes about the boundaries of acceptable behaviour. Custody can be damaging in gradual, subtle ways which are all the more pernicious for being intangible and difficult to measure.

The survey also calculated rates at which prisoners victimized others. The extent of self-reported victimizing is shown in Table 3.2. Over one-third (39 per cent) of young offenders said they had issued a threat of violence in the previous one month and a slightly smaller proportion (32 per cent) said they had assaulted another prisoner. The levels for adults, although lower, are still worthy of concern – one in five adults (19 per cent) reported that they had threatened another prisoner with violence on at least one occasion in the previous month, and 16 per cent admitted to assault. There was a broad concordance between the proportions reporting experiences as victims and as perpetrators, except for cell theft.

A tiny minority of inmates was prepared to admit to stealing from cells. The ratio between self-reported admissions of theft and the

Table 3.2: Victimized others at least once in previous month (per cent)

	Feltham	Hunter-combe	All young offenders	Bulling-don	Welling-borough	All adults
Assault	34	26	32	18	11	16
Threats of violence	39	39	39	20	17	19
Robbery	13	6	11	5	5	5
Cell theft	10	2	8	3	2	3
Hurtful verbal abuse	44	43	43	16	14	16
Exclusion	14	11	13	4	1	3

number who believed they had been stolen from suggests that the prisoners understated their involvement in this particular type of victimization. For example, in the adult institutions 197 prisoners (34 per cent) reported having had property stolen in the past month while only 15 admitted to taking others' property (3 per cent). Similarly 157 young offenders (27 per cent) said that their property had been stolen, while only 44 stated that they had stolen from a cell (8 per cent). It is telling that although inmates showed no reluctance to acknowledge and describe the assaults, threats and robberies which they had carried out, they drew a clear distinction between such activities which are considered acceptable in some circumstances, and cell theft which was universally condemned, even if widespread.

Functions and contexts

From the 91 in-depth interviews conducted in the victimization study, we gained a deeper understanding of the range of activities within each of the six types of victimization. Our purpose in describing them here in more concrete detail is not to provide a comprehensive explanation of the behaviour so much as it is to sketch the ways these activities shape the world of the prisoner.

Verbal abuse

Insults and strong language are commonplace in prisons and YOIs. Prisoners knew that this behaviour was widespread, but many played down its impact, insisting that such banter was fun:

> If someone was being too mouthy or too quiet they were called to the window and slagged off: 'Wanker', 'Dickhead', 'Prick'. It was nothing special, routine. It's harmless fun, slagging someone off.

> It's just joking about, really. You say things about their mum and that. It goes on all the time. It's just a laugh.

The survey focused on the extent of verbal abuse that genuinely made the recipient uncomfortable by stressing that prisoners were being asked to think about 'hurtful' names they had been called or insulting remarks that had been made about their families or girlfriends. The damaging potential of abusive comments directed at mothers and loved ones seems to have an eternal character. Describing the situation 70 years ago in the USA, Clemmer (1940: 91) quoted a prisoner's observation that 'Instead of cursing one direct, they talk about the mother, sister, wife, or sweetheart of the other. This one thing alone, has caused more fights among prisoners than any other cause during my five-year term'. Such observations from the classic works of prison sociology show how much of prison culture is common across jurisdictions and over time.

Hurtful insulting language was much more common in YOIs than in adult establishments (as, indeed, were most types of victimization). In the previous month, over half (56 per cent) of all young offenders had borne the brunt of comments which they felt to be offensive and upsetting, compared with a quarter (26 per cent) of adults (Table 3.1). Of all those who were victimized in this way, one in three were repeat victims.

These rates establish that this type of victimization was routine. Comments about verbal abuse by the prisoners interviewed also suggested that it was an accepted part of prison life: 'I'm used to it – it's that way on every wing.' Although an everyday activity, it was none the less true that insulting language was often intended to wound the recipient, ridiculing them publicly in ways that the recipient felt was humiliating. The claim that 'slagging off' others was 'just joking' indicated the possible influence of techniques of rationalization and harm minimization. In contrast, the prisoners' descriptions of being insulted stressed the hurtful nature of the behaviour. As Bion of Smyrna observed, 'Though the boys throw stones at frogs in sport, the frogs do not die in sport but in earnest':

> At night-time out the window, or at work. 'Your girlfriend's a slag. Your mother's a slag.' I just cannot take it. I can't cope when they call me names. They get kicks out of it.

They start on someone just to join in and everyone is having a laugh except the victim.

The purposes of insulting others varied. For example, insults were frequently used to test the other person's strength of will. This could be useful in targeting weaker inmates for exploitation:

When new people come on, they've got to find their place on the wing. They'll say jibes and see how you react. If you go quiet, that's not a good thing to do.

They shout out things about your family and if you don't shout back and get the better of them, they keep doing it.

Verbal abuse was also used to try to break the other person's spirit. The person making the remarks goaded the victim, playing on any perceived weakness:

In Education when I first came in people kept taking the piss out of me and my family. One day a letter from my sister was taken from my coat and read out to the class. When I came back into class everybody was laughing at me. Sister's letter was affectionate so they took the piss. They laugh about my clothes as well. Eventually they stopped when I threatened to fight one. They still take the piss but I say nothing back so they think they can get away with it and continue it.

Verbal abuse also functioned as a tool of victimization by isolating the victim from his support base. Prisoners who were successfully isolated were confirmed in their vulnerability. Hence, insults were used in conjunction with exclusion to gain dominance over weaker prisoners.

Inmates who thought that their response to insults was being assessed by others often felt a need to retaliate in kind. Particularly amongst young offenders in front of witnesses, an insult could lead to verbal sparring:

On the servery, I gave this inmate a yoghurt. He came back and said he hadn't got one. I said, 'Shut up you black bastard, you mouthy pratt'. I never say anything about other people's mothers since mine died. But he started on me. No one talks to me like I'm an idiot. You got to deal with that at once. He started giving it the big one, so no one does that to me.

Insulting others was a risky activity, particularly when the other prisoner was provoked. We had the impression of a common progression from insults, through an exchange of threats, to fights. One interviewee told us of a dispute that would have led to a fight if others had not intervened:

> I had remand trainers on. Big geezer came in and was taking the piss out of my trainers. I said, 'You ought to look at your own, mate'. He said, 'These boots will be kicking your head in a minute'. Then someone came in and prevented us fighting.

Insults were also linked to violence by the damage labels could do to one's reputation. Common terms of abuse included 'nonce' or 'beast' (sex offender), 'fraggle' (mentally disordered offender), 'muppet' (vulnerable prisoner; inadequate) and 'grass' (informer). Unless the victim could demonstrate that he did not fit the label, other prisoners might accept its validity and ostracize him.

Given the widespread antipathy towards sex offenders and informers, to be identified as such (even without foundation) put an inmate at risk of attack (both physical and verbal) from other prisoners:

> I was in a cell with three others. They wanted me to go. One was saying, 'I want to suck you'. Another was saying, 'He's gonna rape you'. I told him, 'Stop it. Leave me alone'. Then they started calling me queer. One goes, 'You know what we do to poofs? You nonce kids'. They said they were going to tell everyone that I was a nonce.

In rare cases, insults took the form of racist abuse:

> Five or six London boys come in. There was a bit of tension. They started shouting, 'Paki bastards!' We confronted them. My mate went up to one in the shower. 'Did you say, "Paki?"' Guy said yes, so my mate steamed into him.

Despite the harm that verbal abuse could cause, or lead to, prisoners who suffered it suspected that staff, too, regarded it as a trivial event. As one prisoner remarked:

> Yesterday, at bang-up, somebody came round my door and said, 'Your mother is a slag and I have been shagging her every night'.

Q. Did you report it?
What's the point? 'I'm being insulted, officer!' He would just laugh.

Cell theft

Cell theft was the only type of victimization that was reported more frequently by adults than young offenders. While 27 per cent of young offenders reported having had property stolen from their cells at least once in the previous month, 34 per cent of adults claimed that they been victimized in this way. Fewer than one in 13 of either age group had been repeat victims of theft in the previous month (perhaps because they had little left to steal).

As already mentioned, cell theft was the form of victimization that prisoners were least comfortable talking about in the role of perpetrator. Many of the victimizers interviewed in detail expressed strong disapproval of the activity:

> Horrible. Bang out of order. It's generally considered that to burgle on the out is okay. But in here we're all in the same situation. There's no reason to steal off my neighbour. Radios and Walkmans only go missing as a form of bullying. But little shit, tobacco, that's peter-thieving.

None the less, the fact that over a quarter of all the prisoners in the survey reported that they had experienced cell theft in the previous month suggests that this, too, is quite routine in prison. The risk of theft is one reason that people in prison must maintain vigilance against being exploited by those around them.

Prisoners generally felt fatalistic about cell theft because the identity of the perpetrator was usually unknown. Furthermore they were largely dependent on staff to defend their property and keep their cell doors locked. For these reasons many simply resigned themselves to the inevitability of such losses, which were seen as part of the hazards of prison life:

> I bought half an ounce of Golden Virginia [tobacco]. It got taken out of my cell. I asked my cell mates who took it, but they said they had no idea. I didn't tell staff cos I didn't think it was serious enough.

> When I went down for meals I had stuff stolen. It was just pad theft. It wasn't just my cell. [We're] very vulnerable because

officers are not patrolling the landings during meal times. You can't lock your doors every minute.

Cell theft was sometimes purely opportunistic – the perpetrator saw an open cell door and quickly took what he could: 'I knew this other inmate stashed his phone cards. I saw where he stashed them. When he went on a visit and the door was open we went in and did it.'

Sometimes cell theft appeared to be petty: 'After work I came back to my cell. My juice, stamps and some burn [tobacco] was gone. Someone told me who it was, and he is off the wing. But I'm not going to get him back. It was trivial and it's in the past.' In other cases, the victim's interpretation of the episode and subsequent events suggested it was not coincidental that he had been the victim of theft:

> I moved cells, got told to leave door open all day as I was a cleaner. When I come back in the evening, all my stuff was gone. Everyone told me who took my burn. He said, 'What are you going to do about it? If you're roasting, then go to sleep'. That's when I found cigarette butts and spit in my bed. It was horrible.

Thus, cell theft was not often the random offence it is portrayed to be. The targeted nature of thieving was brought out by the differences in the rates of theft among the prisons. The rate was highest (42 per cent) at Wellingborough, where the population was serving the longest terms and was the most settled. The high rate of theft among a stable population suggests that property would be taken if the victim was considered 'suitable' in the sense that he could be offended against without fear of retaliation. In this establishment, the cell thief would have known whose cell he was in and would have been able to assess the probability of retaliation: 'It was petty. They took my socks and my shampoo and some of my valued pictures. It was the beginning of the harassment. They took my stuff because I had refused to have heroin brought in for them.'

Exclusion

By exclusion we refer to situations in which one had a right to take part in some activity – such as watching television, using the telephone, playing a computer game – but was forced by another prisoner to give way. Two equals could argue about whose turn was next, but exclusion was used to prevent someone considered to be of lower status from any right to participate. Excluding another prisoner typically entailed other types of victimization, for example, threats or even assaults were used to prevent someone from taking his turn at the pool table.

Self-reported rates of exclusion were comparatively low (18 per cent of young offenders and 7 per cent of adults). Although less frequent than other forms of victimization, social exclusion within a prison can have wide-ranging and harmful ramifications. Many of those who had been excluded repeatedly began to avoid situations in which they could be ostracized. Almost one-third (30 per cent) of all those who had been excluded reported that this was a regular occurrence. Those who were excluded (or robbed or insulted) were likely to be regularly victimized in these ways. Levels of repeat victimization were much lower for those who were assaulted, threatened or stolen from.

Even so, it would be logical to assume that the self-reported rates understate the extent of exclusion. If someone knew that their attempts to play pool or table tennis would be rebuffed, it was futile even to try to do so. As such, the experience of being excluded could have long-lasting effects, forcing a change of lifestyle in order to avoid situations of potential conflict:

I don't go on association or anything. Don't leave my cell at all because if I do I get water thrown on me and people slap me and call me names.

I don't get a chance to play games. Get pushed off it. At evening meal time, we were standing at the gate, first in the queue. We got pushed out of the way. I've been told not to use the phone, but I've got to keep in touch so I risk it. Now I've been told not to use the shower.

A pattern of exclusion over time sometimes led to an inmate being cut off from all possible allies. By virtue of being ostracized, an inmate was publicly identified as vulnerable, thus increasing the risk of other types of victimization. Excluded prisoners inferred their lower status in a variety of ways. One commented: 'In the dinner queue I always seem to start off first and get served last.'

Like verbal abuse, exclusion could be very damaging to the victim's self-esteem. Unlike insults, however, there was little possibility that the victim of exclusion could retaliate in kind. Like robbery, exclusion was accomplished by a show of superior strength, proving to the victim his insignificance. But the primary goal of robbery was more likely to be material gain. As stated above, incidents of exclusion often arose over access to resources, just as assaults were sometimes the result of such conflicts. It could be argued that, where conflict arose over a shared resource, those who gave way rather than resisting through negotiation or force were by definition victims of exclusion.

Robbery

The survey asked respondents to say how many times another prisoner had demanded their canteen goods. The wording was intended to cover any incident in which one prisoner was forced to surrender his property due to menaces from another. By definition, robbery involves both a threat and an attempt to steal. It is regularly accompanied by verbal abuse and sometimes by a serious assault. It is a complex form of victimization.

Robbery is often thought to be the essence of victimization in prisons, although the self-reported levels were comparatively low. Ten per cent of the young offender sample said they had been robbed at least once during the previous month. Here again, the rates were much lower in the adult prisons (4 per cent). Around one in three robbery victims had been robbed more than once.

Despite the comparative infrequency of this type of victimization, a small number of prisoners felt that it, too, was routine: 'Everyone gets taxed in here, except the blacks and the big guys.' 'Taxing' is the term used to describe robbery in English prisons. Although a range of activities are included within this definition (see 'Trading', below), the term 'tax' confers a false legitimacy upon the behaviour by drawing a parallel with revenue collection by the state. One victim described an incident in which the would-be robber alluded to another legitimate means of income:

> A prisoner came in the cell and demanded half an ounce of burn from each of us on next canteen day. Cell mate gave him a half ounce. He said to me, 'Where's the half ounce you owe me as rent for staying on my landing?' I told him he could buy it from the fucking canteen and if he wanted to get his half ounce he could come in and batter me but he still wouldn't get anything. He left the cell, came back the next day and said sorry, he hadn't realised I was Scottish and he was, too, and it wouldn't happen again.

Victims and victimizers described a range of techniques. Sometimes robbery was carried out with the support of others, sometimes the perpetrator acted alone. In some of the incidents victimizers reported to us, force was kept in the background, as a veiled threat; in others we were told of attacks causing injury. The target goods ranged from the trivial, such as cigarettes or biscuits, to valued possessions such as radios or cannabis. And, of course, anything obtained through a robbery could be traded on for something else.

Living in a materially deprived setting, there were temptations to improve the quality of one's life at the expense of others, even if doing so required the use of force. Further, while prisoners disapproved of cell theft, there was perhaps less stigma attached to strong-arming a weaker prisoner to take his possessions. As a young offender commented: 'When you ask for something, as a criminal, you think automatically, "Shall I take it off him?"'

Some robbers were systematic. A young offender described how he and his accomplice checked the lists held in the wing office to see which prisoners were getting visits: 'Always visits – either in visits or when people came back from a visit. We would search someone and take their stuff. "Sort us out, mate. If not, you'll get battered."' Such predators would target prisoners they believed would be compliant. The following example shows how a victimizer could intentionally develop an arrangement by which he could 'tax' a victim routinely: 'You give somebody one-quarter. They give you half. You know they're terrified. They know what you're up to. You say, "Next week, I want an ounce". No trade. You've got them.'

The most systematic and serious 'taxing' in the prisons we studied was drug related. Illicit drugs were the ideal item to steal because victims would be unlikely to report their loss to staff. Indeed, the purpose of taking other goods was often to trade them for drugs. The remote probability of an official response encouraged robbers to act without fear of the consequences. Young offenders were particularly forthcoming about situations in which they robbed others of their drugs:

A little boy came through. We had just come into the prison and were really roasting. He told us he had got a quarter of weed and an eighth of hash. He should not have told us that, but he did. We threw him in the showers. I said, 'I'm taking that'.

People on drugs behave in a nasty way, agitated and bad-tempered when drugs are in short supply. You can't complain though if you're bullied because of taking drugs, because you shouldn't be taking them.

Threats

To some extent, threats are a matter of interpretation. Tone of voice, context, body language, the reaction of onlookers, mood – all play a part in how each party regards the words used. The same remarks might be perceived as deeply coercive menaces or taken entirely in jest, depending on the persons involved and the context in which they are made. The onus is on the prisoner to whom threats are directed to decide to what degree the other wilfully intends to cause harm.

The rates reported in Table 3.1 refer to prisoners who believed that the threat was genuine; the risk of harm was real. To minimize the chance that inmates would include trivial verbal exchanges, we asked the prisoner to focus specifically on threats of violence.

A large number of the prisoners surveyed reported having been threatened with violence on at least one occasion in the previous month. This was true for almost half of the young offender sample (44 per cent) and about one in four of the adult prisoners (26 per cent). One in seven of all those who said they had been threatened with violence reported that this had happened 'occasionally' or 'regularly' during the past month. Clearly, threatening behaviour was a routine component of interactions in prison.

The purpose of threats varied. In some circumstances they seemed to be the most convenient way to express anger. In this regard, threats sometimes functioned to 'wind up' the other person, to provoke a fight which the perpetrator could justify:

> I collected my food from the servery and another inmate had put a big snot on the back of the spoon. I called the guy to the window. 'I'm going to pull your head off next time I see you.' I was fucking furious when I found it. I was climbing the walls with frustration. I arranged to meet him in the shower for a fight.

More often, threats aimed to force someone to do something against their will. Threats were used in conjunction with other forms of victimization, such as insults, or exclusion. Coercive threats were also aimed at forcing weaker prisoners to do jobs, such as bringing drugs into the prison. This use of threats was known as 'tasking': 'There was a gradual build-up of pressure and threats; intimidation, notes under my door. They know I've got money so they tried to pressure me to bring in smack [heroin].'

By definition, of course, attempts at robbery must involve a threat. A young offender described how threats were sometimes issued in a speculative attempt to obtain drugs:

A geezer came back off a visit. I told him to sort me out some puff. He said he would but when we locked up he refused from behind his door. I said, 'Give me the puff'. He refused. I said, 'I am going to kill you if you don't pass it under'. I went back to his cell next morning with a pool ball in a sock to sort him out, but he was gone. He'd handed his puff over to the officers and was fraggled off the wing.

Some threats were used to enforce payment of debts:

I was waiting at the gates to get my canteen. He called me. I went up to him and he reminded me to get his stuff. 'If I don't get my stuff I'm going to batter you'. I knew he weren't messing about. He's in for killing someone. He's a serious geezer. Every week before I paid in time. This was the very first time I couldn't pay. When I got my canteen I realized I hadn't enough money.

But it would be inaccurate to think of threats as predominantly used by stronger inmates to coerce weaker ones. Threatening behaviour was often mutual, and there was a substantial overlap between the perpetrators and the victims of threats: 'When someone goes on a visit, you tell them, "Bring me back something". Sometimes they give it freely, but most of the time, by threats. I threaten them to bring them to the window. It happens to me, too, when I go on visits.'

Threats were used as weapons by both parties in arguments as a way to win the dispute without resorting to physical violence. A young offender described his decision to issue a threat rather than assault a co-worker who was arguing with him:

There's this prick at work. He's very mouthy. He is low in the pecking order. He knows that, but continues to mouth off. We had an argument. Because the staff was there he started mouthing it, knowing I couldn't do anything. I said, 'Wait till we're back on the wing. I'll kick your fucking head in'. I was trying to get him to back down there and then.

In these situations, if the other backed down, the prisoner who issued the threat did not need to follow through:

He bumped me. He thought I was an idiot. I said, 'You bump me, I'll knock you out, thug. Don't say no more. We'll sort it out tomorrow'. I held off. There was people laughing at him. When I bumped him back he didn't back it, making him look like a cunt.

On association, I went to get some water and he nicked my seat. He was taking the piss. He started chatting shit. I said, 'What the fuck you going on? Don't take the fucking piss!' And then he backed down.

Despite the everyday nature of the threats reported by the prisoners their power to lead to violence should not be underestimated. Within every credible threat is the potential for physical harm. The link was often created in the reactions of the person being threatened, as illustrated by this comment by a young offender: 'If someone say they are going to stab me, I go and sharpen my toothbrush.'

Assault

We shall discuss the circumstances that lead to fights and assaults in prison in greater detail in later chapters. Our aim here is to consider how frequently such behaviour occurs and discuss how the risk of assault shapes the prison socal context, specifically by illustrating a range of situations in which it occurred.

The prison disciplinary code distinguishes between fights and assaults, viewing the former as mutual and the latter as attacks by one on another. However, this distinction was not made in the self-completion questionnaire, as asking people to report whether they had fought (mutual responsibility) or been attacked (blaming the other party) would run too great a risk of generating biased responses. Prisoners were simply asked to state how frequently in the past month they had been hit, kicked or in any other way assaulted by another prisoner.

Here again, the proportions of young offenders (30 per cent) and adults (19 per cent) who replied in the affirmative suggest that physical violence is routine in prison. One in 10 of those who reported being assaulted had been assaulted 'occasionally (once or twice a week)' or 'regularly (almost every day)'. The wider definition we used may explain why the levels of assaultive behaviour reported to us were higher than the 9 per cent of prisoners in the National Prison Survey who said they had been assaulted by another prisoner in the previous six months (Walmsley et al. 1992).

While it is true that some of these incidents might have been 'minor' – regarding either physical or emotional consequences – such low-level routine violence would necessarily have a destabilizing impact on the 'good order' of prison communities.

The interviews featured a wide range of physical attacks: from minor slaps to life-threatening wounding; from spontaneous aggression to chronic beatings; fights between equals or unilateral attacks by a stronger on a weaker prisoner; involving individuals or groups; and sometimes linked to other forms of victimization. Both the young offenders and the adults described fights involving serious injuries. Assaults arose from a variety of situations.

Some were directly related to the victim's offence. One prisoner said he was routinely harassed, although he was already on a vulnerable prisoner unit: 'At the gate, waiting to go out for dinner, about eight others charged up behind me and pressed me against the gate. They kept on crushing me into the gate. They said, "That's had you, nonce". I think I cracked a rib. I was in pain all last night.'

The view was sometimes expressed that a prisoner had to establish his status by fighting. Although common in prisons, this notion oversimplified the complex influence of relationships in the circumstances leading to assaults as we discuss in Chapter 6. One inmate was explicit about how he fought to defend his reputation:

This geezer had busted my nose in a fight – hit me from behind. Because he had busted my nose, people were thinking he was tougher than me. Weeks later I was out on my landing cleaning my cell. The geezer who broke my nose came on the landing. I went up to him from behind and knocked him to the ground. Then I jumped on his head. I could have PP9'd him [hit him with a battery] or used a razor on him. But I wanted it to be just fists.

Another interviewee believed that his credibility had been compromised by the allocation to his cell of an inmate he considered inferior. In order to force the other prisoner to move out of the cell he attacked him viciously: 'He had an attitude problem. He came in, started lying and everything. We just didn't connect. He was all mouth and no action. At night, he kept turning the lights on and off. I hit him with a broomstick. I hit his face, his back, his head.'

An assault could also function to enforce payment of a debt: 'Someone owed me an ounce of burn. I got him in a corner on association, and told him, "Give me burn or I'll slap you". I hit him. He had bruises to his arms and legs. I told him if he grassed me up I would do him.'

A few of the prisoners we interviewed offered their opinion that fights which were mutually initiated could relieve tension. We were told of fights that had established a bond between the two foes:

I threw a lighted cigarette at my cell mate, cos he was irritating me. He came at me with a piece of wood, hit me over the head. I took it from him and hit him over the head. Then we shook hands, and no hard feelings. That's the best thing to do; innit?

Although it is possible that a particular fight could lead to an increase of mutual respect, physical violence tended to lead to a deterioration in the relations between those involved (see below, Table 6.1). Indeed, the notion that fights could lead to bonds of friendship contradicted another axiom of prison life. Some inmates espoused the principle that if one is wronged there is a duty to retaliate. It was widely believed that an inmate who failed to take revenge might signal vulnerability to others. For this reason, in some prison contexts, it was crucial that the prisoners who were assaulted got revenge. Following this reasoning, each counter-assault would rachet up the stakes. Retaliatory strikes were among the most serious of the assaults we learned about. (Prisoners' justifications for the use of injurious force are explored in greater detail in Chapters 6 and 7.)

> Some guy was running off his mouth to me the previous night so next day I went up to him and told him to come in the TV room to sort it out. I said, 'Don't run your mouth off at me', and then threw a couple of punches to his face. Then I went to play pool. A couple of minutes later, I saw him coming towards me. He had a piece of glass in his hand which he cut me on the face with. I swung at his head with the pool cue and missed and then chased him back to his cell where he locked himself in.

Sometimes the 'victim' played a very active role and it was an open question who victimized whom.

An argument at the windows after evening lockup was carried over to the next morning. The prisoner who was interviewed explained that he had warned the other prisoner not to be 'mouthy':

> Next morning, I went to his cell to sort him out. When I saw him, he looked like a fraggle so I thought there would be no point in beating him up. I turned to walk away, but I was hit from behind. I turned and punched him back and knocked him out. He reported it and said I had bullied him.

A second prisoner described a situation in which a cycle of retaliation racheted up the level of physical violence:

It started in the gym when I hit him. He came in my cell and stabbed me. I broke his nose. Later, seven or eight of his mates came and threatened something nasty was going to happen.

In assaults, the line between self-defence and retaliation was thin. Some incidents seem to have begun as games designed to pass the time. Play fighting, for example, could escalate into something more serious. It should be noted that most incidents of this kind that were reported to us took place in four-man dormitories, which seemed to encourage harmful behaviour of this kind. The next example shows that prisoners could be assaulted regularly and suffer significant emotional harm despite a lack of serious physical injuries:

My cell mate flips and starts trying to beat me up. He puts me in a headlock, slaps me, punches me. He says, 'I'll do time for you'. At first I thought he'll get bored of it, but he thinks it's funny. He'll run across and jump on my bed and pull the sheets off when I'm trying to sleep. He thinks he's Jack the lad. He's making me hurt inside and I can't put up with it.

Another episode shows how serious assaults could emerge with explosive speed from minor play fighting. A small number of victim-izers said that they enjoyed such violence. In the following example drug use and the dormitory setting clearly aggravated the seriousness of the offence, leading the attackers to behave in increasingly damaging ways. It is important to point out that, although there was a sexual element in this case, sexual assaults were rarely reported in the institutions studied:

There was four of us in one dorm. One come off his visit with some cannabis. He shared it out. We started pillow fighting. He showed he was the weakest. All three of us set on him. We had books stuffed in the pillows. It turned nasty and we were punching him. It started as a joke, but it got serious. My friend held him down on the bed and I put a pillow over his head and held it. And he was crying and we started hitting him. I said, 'If you don't stop crying we will do it for real'. I put the pillow back on and held it for longer. My friend got a broomstick and put it up his boxer shorts. If he had done something to resist it would have ended right there. If he had tried to stand up for himself, then things might have been different. But he just stayed still and the other boy shoved it up his arsehole. I don't know why we did it.

> In the dorms, people get bored and look for entertainment and fun. Unfortunately, it is the weak who are the entertainment.

As this incident suggests, assault was often linked to other types of victimization. There is a logical link between robbery and assault: if the intended victim tries to resist, the would-be robber might need to use force to demonstrate that his threats were genuine. But sometimes, assaults seemed to be incidental to the main objective, which was to obtain the goods: 'He wouldn't give me any fags so I went to his cell, slapped him, and took them. He ran down and put some pool balls in a sock. One of my mates saw him and took them off him so the fight didn't get any more serious.'

Conversely, prisoners sometimes resisted robbery attempts with physical force:

> Someone said, 'Where's my burn?' I didn't owe him anything. 'What are you on about? I don't owe you anything.' He didn't say anything – threw a cup of tea over me and started hitting me. An officer saw the fight developing and stopped it. We both got nicked and put in front of the governor. I lost my job and got seven days added. I was told if I hadn't fought back I wouldn't have been nicked.

> I was in the shower. One bloke stood with his foot against the door; the other went through my clothes and found nothing. He told me to give him all my cigarettes, matches and Rizlas [cigarette papers]. I said, 'No. Who do you think you are?' Then he spat at me. When I got out of the shower they had left the room. That evening four or five come to my cell. One put his hands round me throat. I kneed him in the nuts.

These examples suggest that assaults could arise over the nature of a prisoner's offence, following arguments about material goods, for self-defence in response to assaults or attempted robberies, as a means of resolving differences or to relieve boredom.

The victimization study did not attempt to collect information about injury. In the conflicts study, we gathered reports from participants in fights and assaults about the injuries they had sustained. As this was not a random sample, caution must be taken in extrapolating from these data. Of the 91 fights or assaults, there were two in which no injuries were reported, and in one case no information on injuries could be obtained. The remainder were classified on a three-point scale, according to the harm caused. Level one were the most serious, involving broken bones, stitches, hospitalization, scalding or burning involving blistering. Level two were of intermediate severity, involving bleeding, swelling, bites, black eyes, bruising and scalds or burns not resulting in blistering. Level three were minor – lumps, bumps, superficial cuts, grazes, abrasions.

The distribution of injuries between the prisons is shown in Table 3.3. The proportion that were serious was highest at Long Lartin (25 per cent) and lowest at Eastwood Park (9 per cent). Intermediate rates were found at Aylesbury (11 per cent) and Bullingdon (15 per cent).

Table 3.3: *Injuries sustained in violent conflicts (per cent)*

	Level 1	*Level 2*	*Level 3*
Aylesbury ($n=27$)	11	48	41
Bullingdon ($n=26$)	15	31	54
Eastwood Park ($n=23$)	9	22	69
Long Lartin ($n=12$)	25	17	58
Total ($n=88$)	14	32	54

In a later section we discuss the range of trading relationships in prison, some of which involved physical violence. In the following chapter, we give more attention to the shifting roles of victim and perpetrator, particularly in the context of fights and assaults. Finally, we refer the reader to Chapters 6 and 7 where a conflict-centred method is applied to the problem of interpersonal violence.

Sexual assault

The victimization survey did not specifically measure the incidence or prevalence of sexual assault, because this had not emerged as a relevant issue during the pilot study, literature review or initial soundings with prisoners, staff and other academics. This may appear somewhat surprising given that rape, or the threat or rape, is often seen as a defining feature of imprisonment, especially in the USA.

When Sykes was carrying out his research in the New Jersey State Maximum Security Prison at Trenton in the 1950s prison rape was a quotidian experience. Punks, fags and wolves were established parts of prison life. Going back even earlier, Clemmer's appendix of prison argot makes it clear that the terms 'jocker' ('usually the active party in homosexual behaviour') and 'punk' ('a young male prostitute, the passive agent in pederasty') were widely used in the 1930s. Prison rape has been the subject of extensive litigation, lobbying and academic interest in the USA (for a wide-ranging review, see Sabo *et al.* 2001). In prisons in Britain there are lots of terms for sex offenders, homosexuals and the mentally ill but there does not appear to be an argot for the participants in prison sexual violence. This lack of a developed slang suggests that such activity is uncommon. There are fleeting references in the academic literature. In their classic work on Pentonville prison, for example, Terence Morris and Pauline Morris (1963: 185, 188) noted that 'active and passive' homosexuality were forms of 'abnormal adjust-ment' to the prison environment, but they did not develop this point.

The in-depth interviews carried out for the victimization study revealed just two instances of self-reported sexual assault. Human Rights Watch (2001), in citing this study, queried why levels of sexual assault had not been measured more systematically. When the conflicts study was designed, specific questions on sexual assault were in-cluded. Hence, the relevant data from that research are introduced here to provide empirical evidence of the extent of coercive sexual activity in a range of English prisons. The 590 prisoners surveyed in the conflicts study were asked individually if they had ever been sexually assaulted while in custody; if they had ever witnessed a sexual assault; and if they had ever been threatened with a sexual assault. They were also asked their opinion on how often it happened.

Personal experience of sexual assault in prison was rare. Overall, 481 prisoners responded to the question. Eight (less than 2 per cent) said they had been sexually assaulted while in custody; 14 (3 per cent) said they had been threatened with a sexual assault; and a further 9 (2 per cent) said they had witnessed one – one inmate said she was a perpetrator and two said they had intervened to stop a sexual assault. Two male young offenders mentioned sexual violence in prison – one said he had been threatened with a sexual assault and one claimed to have witnessed one; but none of the male young offenders said they had been sexually assaulted.

Overall, 76 per cent said that sexual assault did not occur at all or that it was rare: 'I've never ever come across it; never heard of it happening.' Four per cent said they believed it occurred in other prisons sometimes or regularly: 'I don't reckon there is in here. You hear about it in other prisons. If someone in here went and fucked another bloke, he'd get his head battered'. Eleven per cent said they knew of it happening 'not here, but elsewhere': 'I've never heard of it. There's one geezer on another wing did it somewhere else.' Nine per cent could not answer the question.

Thus, the evidence from the victimization study – based on in-depth interviews with 91 prisoners (30 interviewed as victimizers and 61 interviewed as victims) was that sexual assault in prisons in England and Wales was rare. The data from the conflicts survey – collected more systematically with regard to this particular behaviour – confirmed the earlier study and showed that the rates were vastly lower than those for assault.

Our findings are confimed by a recent study published by the Home Office, which was based on 979 inmates, aged 15–17 years, this being approximately half the population of juvenile prisoners (McGurk *et al.* 2000). The interviews revealed that the incidence of sexual victimization was very low. There were three reports (0.3 per cent) of unwelcome involvement in sexual activity and the same number of seeing an inmate do something sexual to an unwilling inmate. Nobody said they had made somebody do something sexual against their will.

These low rates are striking when compared with the USA where it was claimed that '. . . sexual assaults in the Philadelphia prison system are epidemic' (Davis 1977: 269) and a quarter of a century later that 'The constant refrain of prison is sodomy' (Pinar 2001: 1069). According to Toch (1992: 188) '. . . rape is almost always threatened by prison aggressors and is always feared by the victims.' Again, our work shows that even the threat of sexual assault was rare in the prisons we studied.

Underlying these data was an important insight into the ways respondents interpret questions and the impact this can have on self-reported rates. As long as the respondents were male, the meaning of the sexual assault question appeared to be unambiguous. With the first few women prisoners interviewed, the hidden complexity of the question became manifest, as mentioned in Chapter 1. Before they could tell the researcher how frequently they had come across the behaviour, they wanted to know whether forcefully depriving a woman of drugs she had hidden in her vagina 'counted' as sexual assault. Some of the women surveyed regarded the behaviour in this way and some did not. An experienced staff member at the female prison explained:

> Sexual assaults? I'm not really sure, but they do a thing that is awful. It's called 'de-crutching' and they do it if they think someone has drugs. In three years I've only heard of it once. I think it doesn't happen very often because I think that most women would give it up. I don't believe it does happen very often because there are inmates on the wing who tell me when bullying happens and would tell me if it was going on.

When one prisoner was asked if she had ever witnessed a sexual assault in prison she confessed having taken part in one herself: 'Yes, I did it myself. I was encouraged to de-crutch someone. About two weeks ago.' Asked to elaborate she revealed:

> I feel really ashamed about it now. I was clucking (in need of a fix) and she promised me from over the windows and she said she'd bring it to association. But then she'd given a bit to someone else and by the time it came to me she thought there wasn't enough left. I warned her but she wouldn't give it to me. Now I feel terrible. I know it's an assault, rape, everything. I've asked God's forgiveness. Every time she comes round me I go red. She tries to laugh it off but I'm really embarrassed. I wouldn't do it now. I was clucking and really ill and she had promised me. I got all excited knowing I was going to get a bit of heroin and these butterflies – all that and then to say no.

Trading

The inclusion of trading in a chapter on victimization requires some explanation. Whilst this was routine activity, it did not seem that the majority of trading – or even a substantial proportion of it – was direct victimization. On the contrary, the norm for trade appeared to be mutually agreed exchanges on good terms. However, exchanges of material goods always held the potential for exploitation, and it is for this reason that we discuss trading here. We first describe the incidence of trading, then explore its role in interactions between prisoners.

Borrowing and lending were widespread. Property changed hands routinely, despite the official prohibition against trading. The ways in which exchanges were made can be set on a continuum, depending on the terms (fairness) and the extent to which the deal was freely chosen by both parties (coercion). Whilst many prisoners shared tobacco, swapped cassette tapes or bartered possessions they no longer needed, other exchanges came about through coercive force. Figure 3.1 shows the continuum of ways that goods change hands in prison, from free exchanges to robbery with assault.

Adults who borrowed were more likely than those who did not to be victimized. Trading (usually in tobacco, phone cards or drugs) was more common on sentenced wings and among inmates who had spent some time in the institution. Large-scale lending on a remand wing would not make good business sense because of the possibility that a

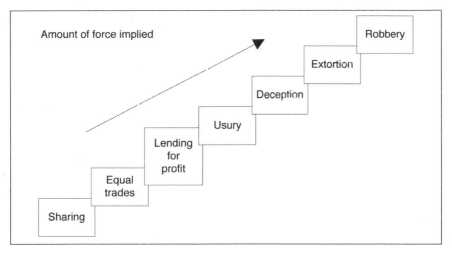

Figure 3.1   Prison trade: from sharing to taking.

debtor might go to court one day and not return (for example if granted bail or given a non-custodial sentence). The recovery of a debt would be difficult in such circumstances. Similarly it takes some time before an inmate's creditworthiness can be established – in the more stable population on a sentenced wing this is more likely to have occurred.

The following quotations give examples of these exchanges to demonstrate the increasing unfairness and influence of physical force on the exchange of property. The interviews carried out as part of the victimization study uncovered a wide range of situations in which exchanges of material goods played a part in the victimization of one or both parties. Although many prisoners shared their goods with others, 'lending for profit' was a fairly specialized role because the trader needed to have the credibility to enforce payment of a debt, and sufficient supplies to meet demand. The next example illustrates both lending for profit and deception:

> A lad on kitchens duty decided he wanted my tobacco. He knew I lend out and he was roasting, so he had to come to me. He asked, 'Are you lending burn?' I told him yes. I loaned him a half ounce for an ounce back. When I went to collect he refused to pay up and I lost.

Inmates could also make use of accepted trading practices to exploit others. Trading held great potential for the development of bullying relationships. A victim might voluntarily enter into a trade at 100 per cent interest per week, which was an accepted rate amongst some young offenders. Yet, victimizers told of how they would manipulate terms to their advantage: 'I would buy an ounce and lend a quarter. Then I would meet people who aren't clued up, sell them "moody" [under-weight] quarters for halves.'

If the debtor could not repay a debt, the lender might feel justified in forcing the issue and the debtor would have good reason to fear for his safety: 'You know when you don't get paid back you can't go to the Governor and say, "I loaned him five burns". You got to punch him.'

However, the assumption that unpaid debts necessarily required traders to mete out physical punishment was based on a misunderstanding of the demands of the role. Established traders would not want to bring the attention of staff to their activities. In addition, potential customers could be put off if they believed a trader was often violent to prisoners who borrowed. Confident traders had an interest in finding ways to recover debts that did not involve them in the use of physical force. We asked one trader if he believed it was necessary to use force if the debtor did not repay:

> It depends. They might have got themselves so that they can't pay back. But you know they've always been good before; they're not taking the piss. You give them a second chance. Maybe they pay a little now, leave some for next week. But if they are taking the piss, you can tell. That's where your rep comes in. You put on the psychological pressure; or you take something else as payment.

In situations of unpaid debts, the level of repayment that was acceptable was sometimes determined by the superior strength of the lender: 'Another inmate owed me an ounce [of tobacco] so I walked into his cell while he was there and took a Walkman and a radio.' This victimizer drew a sharp distinction between debt collection and cell theft:

> One thing I don't like is taking things from people's cells, as we're all in the same boat here. I don't like peter thieves. If I take something from somebody's cell, I make sure they're there when I take it.

> I had borrowed phone cards from somebody else and had paid them back. But the guy I had paid back was released and told

somebody else on the wing that I owed two phone cards and he could collect them even though I didn't owe anything. He kept demanding them and he threatened me. I said I didn't owe him any.

One prisoner explained that his understanding of any exchange could shift from a trade to a robbery, depending on the reaction of the other prisoner: 'If he had a Walkman, I would propose a deal. If he says no too often, he is being awkward. If he goes, "No matter what, I'm not giving it", then I might take it by force.'

We have already discussed robbery in detail. Here we use two incidents, drawn from the victimization interviews, to illustrate the continuum of force presented in Figure 3.1. Robbery, by definition, was an exchange of property that was clearly not fair, and required a high degree of coercion. None the less, the first example shows that it was often sufficient to allow the victim to infer a threat in order to accomplish a robbery. The second example, while more explicit, was also speculative:

I'd just rung the first couple of numbers to my sister. Some black geezer come over and hung up. I took the card and had it in my hand. They took me into the showers – all blacks – one stood near the door. 'Give us your phone card. We will pay you back.' He asked me nicely. I said no, but he kept insisting. He was all right. He said he could take it by force if he wanted. I gave it to him. I never asked for it back. I didn't have enough courage. I thought he would tell me to fuck off.

This new guy, just arrived, thought he was big. He came to my cell when I was banged up and tried to tax me. Demanded my drugs. 'Sort me out a couple of spliffs.' I said I didn't have enough left. He said to sort him out or he would knock me out.

The most extreme form of exchange (and the rarest) was when robbery was accompanied by an assault:

On the landing outside my cell, one person grabbed me by the throat and others were standing round. He punched me a couple of times. He wanted my canteen. He told me, when my cell was next open, I was to get all of my canteen and give it to him.

I had some burn, a lot, £20 worth. Everyone knew. They saw my canteen sheet. They went, 'Buy me this, buy me that; or I'll do you'. I was walking back from gym and I had a fight over it. He said, 'Sort us out some burn cos I'm roasting'. I said I didn't have enough. He said, "Don't lie. I've seen your canteen sheet." One geezer and a couple of friends attacked me in the main corridor, I got a few bruises, headache.

In conclusion, data from the survey on the extent of victimization demonstrate that the experience of being insulted, threatened or assaulted is routine in prisons. The evidence shows that inmates have good reason to perceive their environment as high risk. The perception of danger (and the actual risks of being assaulted or verbally abused) forms a key dimension of the social backdrop to conflicts between prisoners.

Some forms of victimization – insults and threats – are the norm in the sense that a young prisoner who refuses to engage in verbal sparring runs the risk of appearing deviant to those for whom verbally abusing others is an everyday pastime. Other behaviour – robbery, exclusion – while far less frequent, suggests to prisoners that they are in danger of injury or social isolation, and both these experiences can open them up to the possibility of sustained and systematic victimization. Prisoners know they must remain vigilant in anticipating that others will look for opportunities to exploit them. How they respond to the ever-present risks of being victimized is one of the determinants of how often they will be involved in violence. The reciprocal nature of victimization is the subject of the next chapter.

Note

1 Although a total of 1,566 questionnaires were collected as part of the victim survey, the analyses in this chapter are limited to the 1,182 inmates who had been at the institution for at least one month, the reference period for the victim survey (436 in Feltham, 152 in Huntercombe, 408 in Bullingdon and 186 in Wellingborough). Proportionately more cases were excluded from Feltham and Bullingdon as these institutions had more transient populations.

Chapter 4

Reciprocal victimization and bullying

The prisoner's world is an atomized world. Its people are atoms interacting in confusion (Donald Clemmer 1940: 297).

In this chapter we set out one of our key findings – the extent to which much victimization features an overlap between victims and perpetrators. When it comes to harming each other, prisoners are not atoms colliding in confusion, as Clemmer suggests in the above quotation. Their collisions are patterned; their violence is not random. It has an internal logic that can be deciphered.

Bullying

Bullying and victimization are closely linked, but there are crucial differences between the two concepts. To set the scene, our discussion of bullying leads to a proposed definition that incorporates the following key components: one individual establishes a position of dominance over another through intimidation and exploits their relative power over time. We first present the views of prisoners and staff as represented in both interviews and the victimization survey. We then explain our definition in further detail and conclude the section by addressing the differences and similarities between victimization as we use the term and the looser notion of bullying that is often found in the literature.

Prison psychologists have attempted to explore the extent and dynamics of bullying by adopting methods developed by Dan Olweus (1993) and Peter Smith (1991) for use with school children. For example, Graham Beck (1995: 59) provided the following definition: 'We say it is bullying when someone deliberately hurts, threatens or frightens someone either in order to take things from them or just for the fun of it.' Prisoners were then expected to indicate whether they had been bullied or had bullied others. However, the term carries strong moral connotations, and prisoners may have been reluctant to admit that they had been bullied (seeing that as an admission of weakness) or that they had bullied others (because the prison community disapproves of such behaviour).

The stark division between the roles of victim and bully is the most contentious issue in the bullying literature, according to David Farrington's (1993: 394) authoritative overview of the prevalence and dynamics of bullying and preventative strategies. To aid conceptual clarity we made our major focus six discrete types of victimization, without reference to whether they could be seen as bullying. It was our view that information about victimization could be collected much more reliably than data about bullying and that as a result preventative measures would be easier to design, implement and monitor.

However, it was inevitable that an analysis of prisoner victimization would identify situations which were defined as bullying by staff, prisoners or observers. The fieldwork carried out for the victimization research shed some light on the characteristics of such encounters. Equally, some of the limitations of the concept 'bullying' became much more apparent. We found that there was no clear consensus among staff or inmates regarding which behaviours might be considered to constitute 'bullying'. The same incident could be interpreted in widely different ways by the victim, victimizer, witnesses and staff.

Prisoners' views of bullying

Individual prisoners interpreted the word bullying in divergent ways with little consensus of opinion. Each type of victimization could be interpreted as an incident of bullying or not bullying, depending on factors other than the circumstances in which the victimization took place. Even the victims were by no means unanimous in their interpretation of similar experiences. Many beatings and other forms of victimization were not considered to be bullying, particularly if the assailant did not take anything from the victim. Similarly, robberies and threats of violence were open to a variety of interpretations: 'One boy in here has threatened me. He asked me, "Do you want a beating?" Then he came over and made as if he was going to hit me. This wasn't bullying. It was just a wind up.'

Still more problematic was the identification of a bully. The prisoners in the victimization survey did not present a coherent description. When asked to define bullying, many prisoners responded with a single pejorative word: 'wankers', 'prats', 'cowards', 'idiots', 'scum', 'wannabes'. Some prisoners focused on faults of character while others highlighted the supposed objectives of bullying:

Bullies are people that ain't happy unless they are making other people's life difficult.

Two different types – people could bully to be mean and people could bully to get what they want.

Others stressed that peer group pressure caused people to act like bullies or that bullying could be situationally determined: 'Not many people do it, but the ones who do are usually immature and feel they have to prove something. In some cases, a person gets bullied by a lot of people some of which aren't usually bullies.'

Prison staff's view of bullying

Prison staff were asked as part of the victimization study what they understood the term bullying to mean. About half limited themselves to bald descriptions of the typical forms which victimization may take or vague generalizations about the strong preying on the weak. The other half, however, focused upon what they believed were the purposes it served. The following aims were put forward (listed in descending order of importance).

Material gain/services

This was the most frequently cited explanation of what bullying involved, referred to by over a third of the staff interviewed:

Bullying is applying pressure on another person to get something from them or make them do something they don't want to do.

It's taking advantage of somebody's disadvantage. Pressurizing weaker and more vulnerable prisoners. Incorporates taking canteen goods and getting people to run around for you.

'Services' refers to coercing a victim into doing a task, for example, tasking another prisoner with smuggling drugs back from a visit. Staff believed that bullying to force someone to perform a service was one form of bullying for material gain. When services were mentioned it was always in conjunction with material gain.

57

To frighten or intimidate as an end in itself
In its extreme form this was considered to be pure malice. Intimidation was identified as an element in bullying by about one in ten of all staff interviewed: 'When a stronger person – physically or mentally – derives some kind of sadistic pleasure from imposing their will on a weaker person.'

Status/group solidarity
A very small number of officers believed that bullying was motivated by a desire on the part of the prisoner concerned to secure a privileged place in the prison hierarchy or to emphasize his solidarity with an inmate group: 'Someone trying to prove his ability to run a little gang.'

Control of scarce resources
A small minority of officers saw bullying behaviour as involving an attempt to control scarce resources such as the pool table or the telephone: 'In simple terms it's the big guy taking something off the little guy. But it can also be someone deciding which television programme to watch, which gymnasium equipment to use, etc.'

Some officers did not look at the purposes of bullying, preferring to answer this question by reference to the victim's state of mind, rather than the victimizer's intentions. The subjectivist point of view was espoused by a fairly large group and was much more common than factors such as status, control of scarce resources or group solidarity: 'Bullying is anything that makes the victim feel unsafe, threatened or uncomfortable and nervous, where he feels that he just cannot get on with his own sentence without looking over his shoulder.'

Three-quarters of the members of staff felt that it was possible to identify potential bullies. (The proportion was slightly higher amongst staff in young offender institutions.) Yet, when pressed for their distinguishing traits, they listed a wide range of characteristics. They tended to rely on behavioural patterns rather than physical traits. Only a few staff felt that size was a sign of a potential bully. Many who had stated that they could identify potential bullies could only expand by alluding to a 'gut feeling', or the development of intuition and special understanding which came with length of service. Although they could not list the characteristics of bullies, they believed they would know one if they saw one. There was no method of identifying bullies which appeared to be reliable and uniformly applied.

A suggested definition of bullying

In practice bullying might be obvious to the recipient of intimidating, exploitative behaviour, yet denied by the 'victim's' counterpart, and not apparent to a bystander. The subjective definition respects the extent to which the judgement about whether or not someone is being bullied rests with the possible victims: only they can decide whether they have been coerced into a relationship in which they feel dominated, and which they believe will bind them in the future. Yet, these very features arose in a sufficient number of interviews and discussions for us to hazard a working definition of the concept. On the basis of our discussions with prisoners and prison staff, we suggest that there are four defining features of bullying. We illustrate each with a descriptive quotation from a prisoner:

1. One individual establishes a position of dominance over another: 'When you push somebody into a situation that they have no control over, against their will.'

2. This position is created through a process of intimidation: 'When a person pressures other people with insults, threats of violence etc. into giving up personal possessions, running errands for them or simply just instilling fear into a person by intimidation through piss taking, picking on.'

3. The position of relative power is exploited: 'Bullying serves three purposes: personal gain i.e. canteen; it also prevents the bully from being bullied; and finally, it feeds the bullies' egos which are low due to being in prison.'

4. The exploitation persists over a period of time: 'Bullying means that if you know that the person is not going to say no then you do it all the time.'

Bullying, in this sense, requires a relationship, developed over time, with starkly defined roles between the two parties involved. Therefore, the problem with reducing levels of bullying is not so much that it is hidden – as it would be if it were a simple kind of behaviour that the parties attempted to conceal from potential witnesses. Rather, it is a relationship between two people which each may see and define in mutually opposing ways. Indeed, the term bullying is inherently imprecise because its interpretation is always subject to conflicts of interest.

By way of contrast, the concept of victimization refers to a defined set of behaviours which are clearly observable (in the sense that if one witnesses a prisoner striking someone with his fist one has seen an assault). It is therefore more easily measured and open to practical means of prevention. Victimization requires neither persistence nor a one-way relationship of dominance. But it also enables a dominant predator to form a bullying relationship. Later, in exploiting the victim, the bully routinely victimizes him. But much victimization occurs completely independently of a bullying relationship. This fact is seldom recognized in the wider literature. For example, the recent review by Jane Ireland (2000) shows no awareness of this crucial distinction.

Victimization can take many forms, ranging from petty physical assaults such as punches, slaps, and shoves, to serious wounding; verbal intimidation by offensive insults and threats; taking possessions by force or stealth; and exclusion from games or other inmate activities. However, one could experience any of these behaviours without feeling bullied, depending on the motivation of the perpetrator and the perception of the victim. The problem is not that a more precise definition of bullying is required. Rather, because bullying is susceptible to diverse interpretations, it is an unreliable concept for characterizing the range of harmful behaviours between inmates.

In stark contrast to the structured variety of types of victimization, definitions of bullying collapse into a single category a diversity of actions, which vary widely in terms of their seriousness, the factors which give rise to them, the motivations of the participants and the possibilities of finding means of prevention. A loss of detailed information is inevitable when imprecise definitions are used. From an analytical point of view therefore it is more productive to work with discrete and clearly defined behaviours, such as assault, robbery or theft. Our preference for the concept of victimization over bullying to understand the multifarious ways people can do harm to others leads to further thoughts about the concepts of victim and perpetrator or victimizer.

The victim's contribution to assaults in prison

Lifestyle choices influence an individual's level of risk. We need to consider more deeply the role of 'victim', and in particular to understand how a prisoner's behaviour can – perhaps unwittingly – increase his risk of being victimized. To illustrate how activities relate to the risks of victimization we will take assault as a model case. The 91 in-depth interviews conducted in the victimization study provided qualitative information about what behaviour contributed to the risk of assault. All together, these interviews enabled us to analyse 96 incidents in detail.

Robert Meier and Terance Miethe (1993) reviewed the history of attempts to describe the victim's contribution to criminal events. One such interpretation came from Marvin Wolfgang's exploration of the behaviour of homicide victims in Philadelphia. Wolfgang (1957: 2) used the term precipitation to refer to situations in which the victim of a homicide had been 'the first in the homicide drama to use physical force directed against his subsequent slayer'. David Luckenbill (1977: 177) presented an interesting account of homicide as a character contest, defined as 'a confrontation in which at least one, but usually both, attempt to save face at the other's expense by standing steady in the face of adversity'. The killings studied by Luckenbill were characterized by a common series of stages which began with a perceived affront and concluded with a commitment to engage in potentially lethal force. Generally speaking the participants forged a 'working agreement' that violence was a useful tool for resolving questions of face. In almost two-thirds of cases in Luckenbill's study, the transaction that led to death was initiated by the victim.

To examine the behaviour of prisoners in a way that sheds light on how their activities can increase their risk of being assaulted, the relevant factors need to be seen in terms of actions, attributes or possessions of the victim – not inferences the assailant made about them. Richard F. Sparks (1982) examined the role of victims more broadly, and came up with six different ways their actions or choices might make an offence against them more likely. These were: facilitation, precipitation, vulnerability, attractiveness, opportunity and impunity.

Looking at the first of these factors in more detail, facilitation refers to ways that actions might place one at *special* risk of being victimized. This does not mean *any* activity by which a particular assault might have been made possible. Assaults in prison sometimes occurred when the victim was taking a shower. However, showering is routine behaviour – this is not activity which creates a special risk for the eventual victim. Better examples of ways prisoners *facilitate* assaults upon them involve the lifestyle choices they make.

Michael Hindelang, Michael Gottfredson and James Garofalo (1978) wrote of the influence of lifestyle choices on the risks of victimization. In the wider society, young men increase their risk of being assaulted by engaging in heavy drinking late at night in urban centres. This option is not available to prisoners. However, prisoners can choose to enter into verbal sparring with others; they can decide that they are going to assault someone; they can look for ways of exploiting their peers; and they can involve themselves in the underground economy of drug trading. These activities foster a special risk of being assaulted and typify the ways that prisoners might facilitate an assault upon themselves.

Drug dealing might be seen by some to be the lifestyle choice most directly tied to the increased risk of being assaulted in prison. The desirability of drugs meant that using them increased the likelihood of assault by creating the opportunity for someone to try to take the person's drugs from them by force. Also, dealing in drugs – like all trade – created the potential for exploitation, which shortened the odds of assault. Yet, in the 96 assaults we analysed, only 13 were about drugs.

Trading more generally provides an example of a lifestyle choice which could facilitate assault, but by indirect routes. Trading was both against prison rules and commonplace. As such, the activity did not place the prisoner directly in danger of being assaulted. However, because it was against the rules, trading was also unregulated, giving rise to various possibilities for exploitation. When prisoners decided to exploit others, they clearly increased the risk they would be assaulted. The prisoners' decision to become involved in illicit activities, hidden from staff, created the conditions required for the victimizer to act with impunity.

The victimization survey revealed that assaulting others made being assaulted more likely. How did this work in practice? Obviously, the prisoner who assaulted another put himself in a position where, physically, he was susceptible to being hit back. In order to carry out the initial assault he had to place himself within reach of his intended victim. If the victim fought back, the initial assailant had directly contributed to his own assault. But, perhaps more important, a prisoner who assaulted another opened himself to an increased risk in at least three ways. First, the initial victim was likely to have allies who would seek revenge or – at the very least – the initial victim would have been given a motive to assault the perpetrator. Secondly, it is likely that some prisoners would recognize the assailant's willingness to fight and deliberately target him when they wanted to use an assault to improve their own reputations. Thirdly, by fighting the prisoner removed any ambiguity about his physical prowess and clarified his potential resistance to any future attack. After he fights, he ceases to be an unknown quantity.

A traditional approach to interpreting crimes of assault begins by defining one party as the aggressor and the other as the victim.

However, some of the assaults in the victimization study arose out of a shared willingness to resort to violence (see also Chapter 6, for a discussion of how conflicts are sometimes settled with force). In such incidents, the distinct categories of victim and perpetrator break down. When considering homicide, robbery or rape, to take three examples, there can be no ambiguity about which person was the victim. But in the aftermath of a fight between two prisoners of comparable strength, labels of perpetrator and victim are often ill-suited to describe the roles of those who took part. The role of victim includes ambiguities about the extent to which the person's prior behaviour contributed to their becoming a victim.

Implications for the category of victim

The foregoing discussion of ways in which prisoners contributed to their own victimization by their lifestyle decisions leads to questions about the concept of victim:

- Is innocence a part of the definition, or can someone who deliberately engaged in illegal activities still qualify as a victim?

- Can someone who was aware of the risks and who was subsequently assaulted be a victim if they failed to take preventive measures?

- In a fight (when the person who was attacked fought back) is victim status to be determined on the basis of who sustained the more serious injuries?

- In a fight, is the victim to be decided on the basis of who was wrong and who was right? Further, who makes this judgement?

The victimization study revealed that in three-quarters of the 96 cases analysed, the victim had made the attack more likely or had directly brought it about by his own actions. The contribution to their own assaults did not seem to arise through any intention to be assaulted. They simply participated in activities that carried risks, and they were motivated to do so by the potential rewards, including the intrinsic pleasures associated with the risk-taking experience. People outside prison also take part in risky activities; hang-gliding, bungee jumping, motorcycling or scuba diving to name but a few. They do so because of the meaningful benefits they get – not because they want to get hurt. Similarly, when prisoners act in ways which lead to their being assaulted they may nevertheless have good reasons for so doing. Stephen Lyng (1990: 851–2) introduced the concept of 'edgework' to explain why, despite general agreement about the value of reducing threats to individual well-being, '. . . there are many who actively seek experiences that involve a high potential for personal injury or death'.

'Overlap' and reciprocal victimization

The terms victim and victimizer suggest fixed roles. Our analyses of the survey data led to a deeper understanding of prison victimization. The roles did not signify completely distinct groups. Rather, the same individuals could be both victim and victimizer, even over a relatively short period of time (and sometimes in a single incident).

Indeed, as Figure 4.1 shows, for any single type of victimization, inmates could occupy roles of victim and perpetrator in five distinct ways. A and B threaten each other – their role is one of mutual or reciprocal victimization. C is a victim only. D was threatened by E and D threatens C, sliding between the roles of victim and perpetrator in different incidents. E threatens but is not threatened by others. F is uninvolved, neither threatened nor threatening others. A, B and D exemplify an 'overlap' in that they were both victimizers and victims of the same behaviour.

The extent of overlap between the categories of victim and victimizer varied depending on the type of victimization. These variations are shown in Figure 4.2 (young offenders) and Figure 4.3 (adults) which are based on the number of prisoners who had experience of victimization in the previous one month (see also Tables 3.1 and 3.2).

Perpetrators and victims of assault, threats and verbal abuse were not mutually exclusive groups. For example, 42 per cent of young offenders and 36 per cent of adults who had experience of assault in the past one month had been both victims and perpetrators. For threats

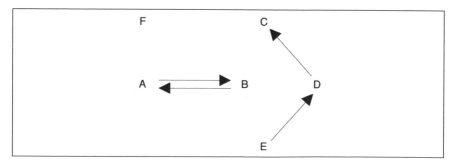

Figure 4.1   Possible victimization roles.

of violence the respective figures were 35 per cent and 27 per cent; and for harmful verbal abuse the overlap was 46 per cent and 26 per cent.

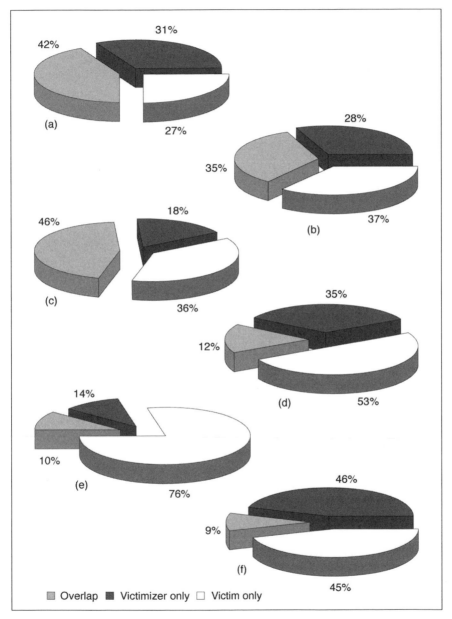

Figure 4.2   Young offender overlap: (a) assault; (b) threats of violence; (c) verbal abuse; (d) exclusion; (e) cell theft; (f) robbery.

The fact that threats and verbal abuse were very widespread – indeed, routine – is part of the reason that an individual prisoner was

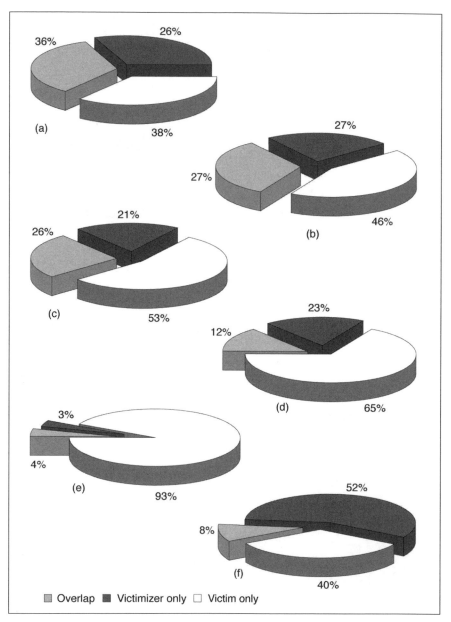

Figure 4.3   Adult overlap: (a) assault; (b) threats of violence; (c) verbal abuse; (d) exclusion; (e) cell theft; (f) robbery.

likely to be both perpetrator and victim of the same behaviour over the course of a month in prison, although not necessarily within the same dyad. But the frequency of the behaviour is not the whole explanation.

The overlap in certain types of victimization shows that the roles of victim and perpetrator are far more shifting than is often assumed. As Sykes (1958: 108) put it: 'Even those who are most successful in exploiting their fellow prisoners will find it a dangerous and nerve-wracking game, for they cannot escape the company of their victims.' Assaults, threats and insults often arise when the power balance between the prisoners involved is uncertain. But the overlap also suggests a brutalizing influence – that people learn to victimize others by being victimized themselves.

Yet, robbery, exclusion and cell theft were different in kind from verbal abuse, threats and assault. Generally speaking, those who were robbed did not rob others, those who were excluded did not exclude others and those who were the victims of cell theft did not steal from others. These types of victimization were more hierarchical. For young offenders and adults the degree of overlap was around 10 per cent.

The reasons only some types of victimization tend to be mutual emerge if victimization is seen as a developmental process. Few incidents of cell theft or robbery were truly opportunistic, and assaults or threats did not emerge spontaneously. It takes time for prisoners to assess a newcomer in order to anticipate his likely response to an attempt at victimization, for a new arrival to establish his credentials and for positions of relative wealth to become known. When these parameters have become established, victimization becomes more likely. Someone who set out to take property by force did not head for the nearest cell – he selected his victim, basing his judgement on the likely level of resistance he would encounter:

> A little boy came back from a visit with cannabis. I pushed him into my cell and shoved a pencil against his throat. I said I would stab him if he didn't give me the cannabis. Then I punched him and he got frightened and handed it over. I target his kind because I know he will give it up without problems. I find most people prefer to take the easy way and give it up instead of fight.

A prisoner who was robbed in this way was very unlikely to display the sort of ruthlessness required to rob others. Robbery and exclusion were behaviours that were clearly grounded in dominance (see Chapter 8 for a fuller discussion of the links between fights and assaults and the power balance between prisoners).

Robbery is usually non-random. Prisoners could be expected to know the identity of those who had robbed them. In the wider community, robbery is often seen as the quintessentially stranger crime. However, in a recent article Richard Felson, Eric Baumer and Steven Messner (2000) found that more than one in three robberies reported in the US National Crime Victimization Survey involved people who were acquainted in some way. They felt there were four explanations why an offender would target someone who could report them to the police. These were that the offender:

1. believes the victim will not report the incident to the police;

2. has a grievance with the victim and their primary motivation is revenge rather than material gain;

3. has inside information about the victim; and

4. chooses a convenient target without consideration of the consequences.

One interesting finding was that robbery victims were more likely to be injured by acquaintances than strangers. The explanation for this is that in stranger robberies the use of force was usually tactical and deployed in the case of non-compliance. However, some acquaintance robberies were carried out as a form of punishment. The robbery was staged as an opportunity to hurt the victim.

Once one's reputation had been established as vulnerable, a suitable target for victimization, it was very unlikely that one could cross over to become a robber of others without a significant change of context. Yet, in a social world in which hurtful banter was routine, anyone could engage in verbal abuse, regardless of his public image. Indeed, much verbal jousting took place at night, out of cell windows. This provides a degree of protective anonymity. Potential assailants did not always select someone they knew would be easy to fight – indeed, there could be good reasons for attacking a prisoner with a reputation as a fighter. And, logically, a physical assault could be mutual (fighting), whilst mutual robbery is virtually nonsensical.

The fact that cell theft should also show very little overlap between perpetrators and victims seems to counter the link between these types of victimization and dominance. However, as we argued above, theft was not the spontaneous and random offence it is sometimes assumed to be. There was some evidence that, despite its reputation as a 'sneaky' offence, cell theft tended to be carried out on those prisoners who were identified as too weak to retaliate if the thief was discovered.

As we have seen, prisoners were more likely to become victims of insults, threats or assaults if they had themselves engaged in these activities towards others. In addition, being victimized in one way could increase vulnerability in other areas. Few victims were subjected to only one type of victimization. Prisoners who had been excluded, insulted or had possessions stolen from their cells were much more likely also to have been assaulted, robbed or threatened with violence (see O'Donnell and Edgar 1996 for a statistical analysis of risk factors).

It would appear that those inmates who were ostracized by their peers and existed on the margins of prison life were victimized in part because they were so obviously vulnerable. Without allies and considered by others to be unworthy of association, they were easy targets. They were picked on repeatedly and in a variety of ways.

Prisoners were unlikely to report being robbed or threatened with violence. Hence officers might find it difficult to identify a prisoner who was enduring victimization in silence. However, cell theft was reported more often than other types of victimization (see Table 9.1) and exclusion by its nature took place in public. Both were reliable indicators that other forms of victimization were also being endured. When a prisoner was excluded from games or isolated at meal-times, it was also highly likely that he was being threatened, robbed, verbally abused or assaulted.

Victimization and prison roles

The overlap between victims and victimizers for assault, threats and insults suggests that being victimized in these ways does not necessarily fix the prisoner in the eyes of others as vulnerable. Rather, in some circumstances the roles can shift. In Lee Bowker's words (1980: 31), this switching of roles is akin to a 'macabre version of the game of musical chairs in which today's aggressor may become tomorrow's victim'. How can this be possible in a prison?

First, we need to consider the processes by which roles become established. A 'role' is a pattern of behaviour that can be defined and labelled because it is important enough and acted out consistently enough to be easily identified. Approaching the question of prison roles from the perspective of victimization alone distorts the wide range of roles available to prisoners by limiting them to two: victimizer or victim. No prisoner arrives with a mark on his forehead, stating 'victim'. So, how are roles defined? How do individual prisoners come to inhabit a particular role at a point in time? What are the implications of different roles for the prisoner's susceptibility to victimization? Peter

Berger and Thomas Luckmann (1967) discuss how roles are created and how people come to identify with them. In this section, we apply their insights to prison life.

Recalling our point about the developmental character of victimization, when two prisoners interact for the first time, each makes assessments of the other across a wide range of characteristics. Each develops – on the basis of their interaction – a sense that the other party fits into certain typical patterns of behaviour. Just a few of these typifications make clear the complexity of the factors the prisoner needs to consider in weighing up the other party, who is not yet defined as an opponent. From what Prisoner B can observe as they converse, he might size Prisoner A up as:

- an experienced prisoner, coming back after a spell outside, or naïve, a newcomer to prison;

- someone with ready access to drugs or someone with a need for drugs;

- linked to him through other offenders (potential ally), a stranger or even an enemy from a competing 'manor'; and

- someone whose type of offence signifies honour (armed robbers), anonymity (burglars) or shame (sex offender).

Three of the many characteristics the prisoner assesses have particular relevance for victimization:

1. Networks and alliances (is the prisoner popular in the sense of being able to rely on others to back him up?).

2. Physical prowess and willingness to use force.

3. Material wealth, including his capacity to use the official and illicit economies of prison to his advantage.

The prisoner will need to form a judgement about his counterpart on the question of victimization. Here, there are three options: B might be a vulnerable type whom A thinks he can exploit; a potential threat whom A should fear; or outside these two categories, as would be the case if A learned that B was a good friend of a friend. Prisoner A can match B's performance to one of these predefined roles.

Anthony Giddens's concept of structuration provides a useful interpretation of the process through which people, in interacting with each other, set routines that shape and define their mutual relationships. Giddens (1984: 331, emphasis in original) suggested that through routines, roles become meaningful as socially constructed facts. He described how three people with identified roles in a courtroom – a judge, a public defender and a district attorney – follow characteristic behavioural patterns:

> In order to 'bring off' the interaction, the participants make use of their knowledge of the institutional order in which they are involved in such a way as to render their interchange 'meaningful'. However, by invoking the institutional order in this way – and *there is no other way* for participants in interaction to render what they do intelligible and coherent to one another – they thereby contribute to reproducing it.

The theory that when patterns of interaction become routinized they not only choreograph the actions of the individuals concerned but also contribute to the perceived reality of socially constructed roles finds expression in a predatory interaction between two prisoners. A successful robbery tends to fix the robber in a dominant position and the victim in a submissive role. Equally, the interaction reproduces their roles and reinforces the sense amongst prisoners that taxing is a fact of prison life.

Yet, roles are also situated in particular social contexts. To take a blunt example, when you enter a library you might identify bookish people and more frivolous types; you would quickly be able to determine who were the readers and who were library personnel. You would be very unlikely to define the people in the library as either perpetrators or victims of violent crime.

Assigning an unfamiliar prisoner to a role is only half the picture. While A is assessing B and noting how his reactions fit into the pattern labelled 'one of us' or 'bully' or 'druggy', B is also assessing A. B is sending signals to A which convey the role into which he is placing A. The next step is the one by which A accepts the role into which he has been assigned. Berger and Luckmann write that as soon as the pattern of behaviour has ended, the person tends to distance himself from the confines of the role.

Identification with a role is complicated by the moral implications attached to it as well as the practical consequences. The typification 'dickhead' is built on a pattern of vulnerability. The word signifies submission to intimidation or exploitation. During a brief interaction in which A robs B, B wears the typification 'victim' but as soon as the episode ends, B would normally attempt to separate himself from the label. The practical ramifications of identifying himself permanently as a victim would be that B could expect others to target him in the future. This is akin to the notion of secondary deviance, in the sense that the victim identity is internalized and life is reordered accordingly.

Ironically, because of social disapproval, A also has reasons to dissociate himself from the role that matches his behaviour. The label 'bully' can mean robbing someone through shows of aggression. Prisoner A inhabited the role by demanding B's possessions and threatening to use force, but after the episode, A would normally deny that he was a bully. There is an important degree of plasticity in role playing.

In theory, the prisoner's capacity to slip into and out of roles diminishes over time as his personal proclivities manifest themselves, and as others around him fix him into particular styles of interaction – showing fear or respect to the 'predator', constantly turning to the 'trader' for goods or socially isolating the 'grass' by going quiet whenever he approaches. We have seen solid evidence of the enduring quality of labelling in that prisoners who are victims of some types of harm are also more vulnerable to other types.

However, it is important to bear in mind that each prisoner has a multiplicity of roles available and that their use depends on context. Prisoner A might be a bully at the time that another prisoner receives canteen, but he might also play the roles of 'engaged student' in education; 'dutiful worker' on the servery; and 'mediator' in disagreements between his allies.

This brief sketch of role playing prepares the ground for exploring the roles we found amongst victimizers. Before doing so, however, we return briefly to the work of Gresham Sykes.

Typology of victimizers

Sykes analysed prison argot to specify roles played by the prisoners he studied. His study took place in the 1950s in New Jersey, and therefore we should not be surprised to learn that the labels he found are not the same as those in use in contemporary prisons in England. However, his descriptions of the types of behaviour that match the labels are immediately recognizable and bear witness to the consistency over time and across cultures of coping strategies in prison. He argued that these argot roles provided 'a map of the inmate social system' (1958: 84).

Each role signified a strategy for coping with the demands of prison life, yet most of them could be viewed as set against the comradely ideal of inmate solidarity. Consider, for example, his descriptions of the 'rat' and the 'gorilla' (ibid.: 87 and 91):

> ... inmates argue fiercely that a prisoner should never give any information to the custodians which will act to the detriment of a fellow captive. Since the most trivial piece of information may, all unwittingly, lead to another inmate's downfall, the ban on communication is extended to cover all but the most routine matters ... The word rat or squealer is a familiar label for the man who betrays his fellows by violating the ban on communication and it is used in this sense in prison.

> It is possible for an individual prisoner to monopolize the scarce goods possessed by the society, to wrest from his fellow captives their few possessions, and thus soften the hurt of his material deprivation. In the argot of the inmates, an individual who takes what he wants from others by force is known as a gorilla ... He stands ready to use a knife or a piece of pipe, he faces a lone victim, and his demands are simple. And it is this blatant readiness for the instrumental use of violence that often sets the gorilla off from other inmates rather than his strength, size or constant use of force.

The 31 prisoners we interviewed as victimizers described a wide range of activities by which they had exploited or harmed their fellow inmates. Their accounts led us to characterize them according to four different types or roles. Although all four involved victimization of others, most diverged in some way from our definition of bullying.

Predators (28 per cent of victimizers)
These prisoners, like Sykes's 'gorillas', were persistent and calculating. They engaged in a wide range of victimization behaviours, with multiple victims. Enjoying a high profile on the wing, they were confident of their position and popular with staff. Their motivation was usually to obtain drugs or goods which would be exchanged for drugs. They spoke about their approach in the following terms:

> This happens to a number of people. They've come off a visit. I get them. I become abusive and threaten. Certain people you know they've got drugs. You are expected to share. If they don't share,

73

you take it. But only if you know they are a weak person you can intimidate.

Another prisoner said: 'Every day I go to every cell, 60 or 70 of them, and tell them to sort me out. No one refuses me. I smoke about an eighth of an ounce of draw [cannabis] on the out every day and the same amount in here.'

Traders or 'barons' (16 per cent of the victimizers)

Sykes's 'merchant or pedlar' is our 'trader': 'He does not share the goods in short supply, but exploits, instead, the need of others ... so selfish in his pursuit of material advantage that he is willing to thrive on the misery of his companions' (1958: 94).

Traders interviewed in the victimization study saw themselves as service providers who had a reliable stock of goods to retail at a profit. Their businesses were aided by the usual prison routine which allowed prisoners to visit the canteen (prison shop) only once a week. Many prisoners found it difficult to ration their consumption and were 'short' within days. The trader filled the gap, often providing half an ounce of tobacco or one phone card today for an ounce or two cards when the debtor received his next consignment of canteen goods. Tobacco barons are an enduring feature of English prisons, having been described by Morris and Morris (1963) in their study of HMP Pentonville. The interest rate was well known and widely accepted. Hence most traders did not attract the opprobrium that Sykes reported fell to his 'merchants'. If customers persistently failed to settle their accounts they would be denied further opportunities to borrow and the debt could be enforced with violence. However, traders were explicit about not seeing themselves as bullies (although staff might have considered them to be engaging in classic bullying behaviour):

> I used to go round picking up the plates and I took forty cigs with me. You set out your terms to give you a good profit. One cig might mean three back. I was doing them a favour. The officers knew about it. They let it go on. It wasn't bullying, it is business. They agree the terms when they take the burn.

A baron told us that his original motive in engaging in trade had changed over time in a way that had made his transactions more aggressive:

I started selling to make ends meet. You just don't want to be in need at the end of the week. But then you get a need to have more and more. You get greedy. I can see that now. I see how other barons work and think I must have been like that. When people don't pay back you get pissed off, you say, 'Pay up. Stop pissing about'.

Fighters (36 per cent)

These inmates, corresponding to Sykes's 'toughs', were regularly involved in incidents of violent victimization, usually threats and assaults: 'His assaults flow from the fact that he feels he has been insulted rather a desire to exploit others . . . Encounters with him are hazardous . . . he will fight with anyone, the strong as well as the weak' (1958: 103). The fighters we spoke to did not always emerge the victor. They were preoccupied with status and quick to take offence. Their desire was primarily for recognition rather than material gain or drugs, although these were fringe benefits of their behaviour. They were not popular with staff:

On association, playing pool, someone watching got on my nerves because he was taking the piss out of my shots. I told him to shut up. Threatened him, invited him into the showers, but he wouldn't go in. He shut up then and I continued playing. As there was screws there, couldn't do anything on the spot. Didn't fight him later cos he's a muppet. I don't back down. I would have whacked him with the pool cue.

Avengers (20 per cent)

These were people who had perpetrated acts of victimization, perhaps with serious consequences, which were clearly isolated events. Sometimes the incidents were the outcome of a feud between two individuals which had escalated in intensity. On other occasions they were a continuation (or the conclusion) of a conflict which had begun outside prison. These prisoners were interviewed as victimizers, but for them it was not a role into which they felt fixed. The common theme was that the incident was not part of a pattern of victimization. It was out of character:

The previous night he cussed my mum. I was furious. Next day when we were being let out of our cells I said, 'What did you say about my mum?' and punched him in the face twice before I was grabbed by officers and put down on the floor.

> He was leaning against a wall with his mate. He said he thought I was nothing. He said I was a wanker, and pathetic. I kicked him in the face and broke his nose. He wanted to provoke me into hitting him so this would give him a licence to beat the shit out of me. But I got my kick in first.

Referring back to the discussion of bullying earlier in this chapter, only the *predators* – about a quarter of interviewed victimizers – could rightly be considered to have engaged in bullying. *Traders* were not bullies because intimidation was not an integral part of their modus operandi. In trade, contracts are entered into willingly. Even the *fighters* could not be considered bullies as they had not established a relationship of dominance which they then exploited. This distinction is particularly important as, in some prisons, the difference between bullying and assault is not sufficiently recognized. *Avengers* were not bullies because there was no continuity in their behaviour. In other words of all the roles played by prisoners who victimized their peers, only a small subset could be considered to have taken place in the context of a bullying relationship.

How victimizers viewed the motives for their behaviour

Victimizers were asked in detail about what they felt had motivated their conduct. Six main reasons emerged: status, conformity, drugs, mutual antagonism, enjoyment and material gain. These motivations were universal in that they applied to the full range of roles which are outlined in the above typology.

Twelve of the 31 interviewed victimizers described their conduct in terms of status. In cases of assault or threats, some were instigated by prisoners who felt they lacked status; others by persons who felt they already had high status which was being threatened by the victim. One described a situation in which an attempt to rob drugs had been thwarted. When the deception was exposed the victimizer reasserted his authority through violence:

> A little black boy came back off a visit. I dragged him into my cell and asked him for his puff [cannabis]. He said he had none, so I tried to play it sweet. I said, 'All I want is a joint. Just pass me a joint under the door tonight'. He agreed to do this so I knew he had lied to me and had puff up his arse, so I gave him a good hiding. One of my pals had him in a headlock so I kicked him in the head twice. The side of his head was all bloated.

Victimization driven by a desire to conform took different forms. Some of the victimizers felt that their conduct was widespread, and hence not bullying. A second group were attempting to follow the model set by prisoners with higher status – they tried to conform through imitation:

> You may not want to be top dog but just his friend. If you want to be in with him you show you're tough by bullying – not trying to be top dog – just to be in with the crowd.

> I was in a dorm with three others. Every night everybody had to do 50 press-ups, 50 sit-ups, 50 handstand press-ups, 50 dips down from the door. If somebody doesn't finish they get beaten up with pillows by the others – very painful. One guy didn't finish so we started beating him – each person hit him 50 times and he sat on his bed and started crying.

A third group described their conduct in terms of defensive measures. They felt that the norms of the prison demanded that they victimize others in order to protect themselves from being victimized: 'In here you either bully or get bullied. It happens to everyone.'

Seven prisoners stated explicitly that their reason for victimizing others was to obtain drugs. In some cases, the desire for drugs led to threats and assaults. But drugs could also be obtained through trade, either by fraudulent means or by the use of possessions which had been gained through cell theft or taxing:

> To me, there shouldn't be drugs in the prison. If there is, I'm having some of it.

> I would pretend to be friendly, invite him back to my cell to make a spliff and then take it and beat him up and throw him out of my cell.

Six victimizers described situations which were marked by mutual antagonism. These were obvious cases of the victim–perpetrator overlap.

> If a boy hits me I can defend myself so there is going to be a fight.

> It was over his phone card. I beat him up after I used it up. Later I was playing table tennis. He came up and hit me with a pool ball right in front of an officer. I doused him with a mug of boiling

77

water. Burned him all down the side of his neck. The officer knew he caused the fight, so it didn't get reported.

Six inmates also stated that they victimized others because they enjoyed it. One young offender drew a distinction between taxing others for material gain and doing so for fun: 'I'm not in it for things. I only took a half packet of biscuits. I have said, "I want your canteen", and not took it. Just for the fun.'

Victimization as a defining characteristic of the prison setting

When violence is explored as a feature of prison life, fights and assaults are often introduced as a break in the social order, a threat to social stability (as we have described in the opening chapter). But prisons seem to cope with high rates of fights and assaults as a matter of course. Our discussion of the extent and nature of victimization has shown that fights and assaults are a logical outcome of the high risks of being threatened, hurtfully insulted or having one's possessions taken.

Chapters 3 and 4 discussed a wide range of behaviours by which prisoners harm other prisoners. The underlying crime rate in prison is unquestionably high. The routine nature of insults, the practice of isolating prisoners through exclusion, the risk of theft – prisoners experience these every day, either directly or vicariously. The diversity of prisoners' experiences of victimization provides the backdrop against which violence in prison finds its meaning.

Sykes argued that victimization amongst prisoners can be traced back to the material deprivations inherent in the loss of liberty. In his view, some prisoners were willing to exploit others merely to improve the quality of their lives inside. As he observed, the ultimate expression of this logic for the prison community was a war of all against all. Hence, Sykes counter-balanced the risk of victimization with the interest the prisoner community had in maintaining solidarity against their captors. This tension results in an uneasy and imperfect peace.

For the purposes of clarifying the links between prison violence and other types of victimization, the important issue is Sykes's assumption that victimization has a materialistic basis. Robbery, theft – even exclusion when its purpose is to gain access to the games tables or the telephone – are types of victimization that are deeply rooted in the material life of the prisoner. But there is no obvious link between insulting another prisoner, for example, and the improvement of one's standard of living. Not all victimization has a materialistic basis.

Assaults might be about debt, arguments over ownership or other materialistic concerns (see Chapter 6) but alternatively, assaults can be committed without reference to the material deprivations of prison life. Sykes's portrayal divides prisoners into two camps – the predators and the prey. In contrast, we have seen strong evidence that this distinction oversimplifies the roles open to prisoners.

Further light on the influence of victimization on prison culture comes from an implication of the victimization study we have not yet mentioned. The survey found that 46 per cent of young males had been robbed, threatened with violence or assaulted at least once in the previous month. Stated the other way round, 54 per cent had not been robbed, threatened or assaulted during the time-frame we examined. There can be little doubt that some of them had been assaulted, robbed or threatened earlier during their time in prison, or were victimized after our survey was completed. Also, a proportion of the 54 per cent had victimized other prisoners in these ways. None the less, there were certainly prisoners who were able to negotiate life in prison without victimizing or being victimized.

Violent victimization must be explored in the context of a social system in which insults and threats are commonplace and there are serious risks of being excluded, or having one's possessions taken by stealth or force. The threat of materialistic victimization cannot fully provide the sources from which assaults and fights emerge. A key link between the risk of victimization and the underlying causes of assaults is the prisoners' perceptions of prison settings as high-risk, dangerous places. Alongside the levels of crime in prison (self-reported) we must consider the dimensions of the fear of crime, and that is the topic of the next chapter.

Chapter 5

Fear and vulnerability

We have been looking at violence as something related to the characteristics of the inmates themselves, without taking into consideration the interaction between the inmates and the environment in which they live (William Nagel 1976: 57).

There has recently been a keen interest within criminological research in the subject of fear of crime – but the literature is almost entirely devoted to communities outside prison (see Hough 1995 for an account of the correlates of fear as revealed in community surveys). In his review of some 200 articles, conference papers, monographs and books written about fear of crime over the past 30 years, Chris Hale (1996) makes no mention of custodial institutions.

The rates of assault, threats, robbery or theft reviewed in the previous chapters imply that there are good reasons for prisoners to be fearful. However, this line of thinking assumes a straightforward link between the incidence of victimization and fear. This chapter explores how the perceived risk of victimization can be linked to assaults and fights. The concept of fear might help to explain why, when faced with a risk of being victimized, an individual prisoner decides to turn to violence.

In broad terms, fear of crime can be caused by direct experience of criminal victimization, in the sense of becoming a victim of assault, robbery, theft or other crimes; or by direct experience of 'incivility' – behaviour which may not be criminal but which is still socially disruptive and personally upsetting. In addition, fear of crime is influenced by vicarious experience of crime and incivility. Witnessing the victimization of others is likely to have an impact on the witnesses' expectation that they too will be victimized.

Martin Killias (1990) enumerated three general conditions under which people tend to become fearful: exposure to non-negligible risk; loss of control over the environment; and anticipation of serious consequences. All these conditions are satisfied in a penal setting. In a situation where the threat of harm is ever present, prisoners cannot control key aspects of their lifestyles. For example, they have little choice about how to spend their leisure time, when to associate or with whom. They have limited possibilities of escape and may lack an effective range of defences. Finally, the company of violent men and the widespread use of force as shown in the rates of assault and fighting demonstrate the need to take seriously all threats. As Sykes (1958: 102) expressed it: 'It is clear that violence runs like a bright thread through the fabric of life in the New Jersey State Prison and no inmate can afford to ignore its presence.' Thus, following Killias's conditions, there is good reason to believe that prisons will be high-fear environments. A theory of when involvement in conflict will lead to fear or anxiety is developed later and summarized in Table 8.1.

Other factors (again drawn from community studies) have been shown to influence fear of crime, as discussed by Stephen Farrall, Jon Bannister, Jason Ditton and Elizabeth Gilchrist (2000) who cite social psychological research carried out in Holland by Van der Wurff (1986) and his colleagues. The Dutch research identified four components of fear:

1. *Attractivity* – a person's sense that others might target them for victimization, because something about them or their possessions would attract predators; an example would be walking a city street with a large amount of cash in one's pocket.

2. *Evil intent* – the projection of criminal intentions on to other people in one's surroundings.

3. *Power* – this component brings together two aspects: the control the person has over their environment (similar to Killias's condition) and the extent to which others in one's vicinity are assumed to have the wherewithal to carry out their criminal intentions.

4. *Criminalizable space* – the person's assessment of the opportunities within a situation for others to commit crime.

These social-psychological factors were tested against demographic variables such as gender, age, level of education and income. Farrall *et al.* (2000) argued that these factors must be supplemented to provide a more comprehensive measure of fear of crime. They added variables such as victimization during the past year, time living in the area, health in the past year and whether local places (streets, shops, woods) were seen as dangerous.

Of course, many of the factors used by Farrall and his colleagues do not apply in prisons, although some of them can be translated into the prison context. 'Income' could be defined in terms of weekly earnings or spending at the prison canteen; and ratings about the relative safety of shops, streets and woods can be measured with reference to well defined spaces in prison, such as the showers, the corridors and the exercise yard (see below.) Similarly, the concept of 'criminalizable space', defined by Van der Wurff et al., applies directly to prisons; areas with poor supervision might – all things being equal – be considered a higher-risk area for crime than parts of the prison under direct staff surveillance.

Self-reported fear

The National Prison Survey found that 18 per cent of prisoners in England and Wales said they did not feel 'safe from being injured or bullied by other prisoners' (Walmsley et al. 1992: 53). A slightly higher proportion of Asian prisoners felt safe, but this difference was not statistically significant. The victimization survey established the extent to which prisoners felt fear in the prison setting. To put their self-reported fears in perspective, we refer readers back to the rates of victimization discussed in Chapter 3 and summarized in Table 3.1.

The self-report survey measured two key dimensions of the prisoners' sense of security: fear of being insulted and fear of being physically harmed. There was a sharp contrast between prisoners' *feelings* of safety and their *actual* risk of victimization. Despite the high rates of assault, theft and insults, a majority of prisoners said they felt safe. More detailed analyses were carried out that enabled us to draw two important distinctions: first, between criminal victimization and incivility and, secondly, between victims and witnesses. Experience of criminal victimization was measured by the frequency with which inmates either witnessed or were themselves victims of assault. Incivility was measured by the extent to which inmates had been insulted or had seen others bearing the brunt of hurtful verbal abuse.

The results of these analyses are shown in Tables 5.1 and 5.2, which are based on the 1,182 prisoners who had been resident in the institution for at least one month when the victimization survey was conducted. As one might predict, inmates with direct experience – particularly those who had been assaulted recently – were much less likely to report feeling safe than those who had not personally been victimized (see Table 5.1). This difference was marked – especially for

Table 5.1: *Fear and recent direct experience of victimization/incivility (per cent)*

	Feltham	Huntercombe	Bullingdon	Wellingborough
Not been insulted and feels safe from insults	70	82	77	76
Been insulted and feels safe from insults	63ns	66*	42***	53**
Not been assaulted and feels safe from assault	66	73	66	68
Been assaulted and feels safe from assault	47***	54*	41***	23***

Results of chi-square tests: ns, not significant; $*p < 0.05$; $**p < 0.01$; $***p < 0.001$.

Table 5.2: *Fear and recent vicarious experience of victimization/incivility (per cent)*

	Feltham	Huntercombe	Bullingdon	Wellingborough
Not witnessed insults and feels safe from insults	61	72	72	74
Witnessed insults and feels safe from insults	66ns	75ns	65ns	67ns
Not witnessed assaults and feels safe from assault	51	65	64	64
Witnessed assaults and feels safe from assault	63*	70ns	59ns	53ns

Results of chi-square tests: ns, not significant; $*p < 0.05$.

adults – and held true for all four institutions. The greatest discrepancy was found at Wellingborough where 68 per cent of inmates who had not recently been assaulted felt safe from the threat of assault while this was true for only 23 per cent of those who had been assaulted in the past month.

However, amongst young offenders, we found that a substantial number of those who had been victimized none the less said they felt safe. Two-thirds of those who reported having been insulted also stated that they felt safe from insults. Half of those who had been hit, kicked or assaulted stated that they felt safe from assault. In a similar vein, Richard McCorkle (1993) found that only 14 per cent of inmates considered prison very unsafe, despite the fact that a significant proportion of his sample reported being victimized.

Most inmates had, in the previous month, witnessed criminal victimization (assault) and incivility (verbal abuse). However, the majority reported feeling safe from insult and attack. In his lengthy review, Hale (1996) suggested that vicarious victimization was more highly correlated with fear of crime than was personal experience of being a victim. As he put it: 'Fear appears to be only weakly related to victimisation experience' (ibid.: 131). The reverse appears to be true for prisoners. The relationship between fear and vicarious victimization was not statistically significant. There was no evidence that prisoners who had witnessed victimization or incivility felt any less safe than those who had not. As Table 5.2 shows, the only statistically significant relationship was found in Feltham and this was not in the expected direction: those who had witnessed assaults felt safer from assault than those who had not.

The safety paradox

Fear of crime is notoriously a matter of perspective. One can live in an area or fit a demographic profile in which the risk of a particular crime is exceptionally low, yet still feel frightened of becoming a victim; just as one can face a high risk of crime, yet feel safe. In this light, Van der Wurff et al.'s (1986) psychological factors, such as feelings of attractiveness, attributions of criminal intentions and a sense of power, provide helpful insights into the personal attitudes that elicit a fear of crime.

Bottoms (1999) has identified a contradiction at the heart of prison life: the rule of force is pervasive in inmate society, but co-exists with high levels of perceived safety. He termed this the 'safety paradox' (ibid.: 269) and saw its explanation as a key task for researchers. In this book we consider this matter by examining how prisoners cope with pervasive insecurity. Bottoms listed five possible areas in which answers to the paradox might be found. We shall first briefly follow his points, then explore what evidence we have found that can shed light on this question.

His first theme is the lived experience of prisoners. A factor that might reduce fears is the length of time the person has been in the prison. Bottoms (ibid.: 270) commented: 'While most new prisoners (especially first timers) are disoriented and fearful on arrival in the prison, there is now substantial research evidence that over time they gradually work out ways of coping with this strange social world.'

The second factor that might clarify why so many prisoners feel safe is that they develop strategies for self-protection. McCorkle (1992) analysed these strategies in prisons in Tennessee. He narrowed the protective strategies to two: withdrawal from interactions with other prisoners and an aggressive stance. McCorkle found that the withdrawal strategy reduced the likelihood that one would be assaulted but increased the risk of being robbed or otherwise exploited. The aggressive approach reduced the risk of being robbed but increased the chances of being assaulted. We shall say more about personal protective strategies later.

A third factor cited by Bottoms is the balance between routines – which, being predictable, can lead to a sense of stability and order – and personal choice. While many descriptions of prison life focus on the loss of autonomy – what Goffman (1961: 50) describes as 'mortification or curtailment of the self' – inmates retain some power to determine their prison lifestyle (see Chapter 4) and how they relate to their peers (see Chapters 6 and 7). Bottoms (1999: 273) added:

> A crucial . . . question seems to be: Is it in fact possible to minimize one's participation in activities that risk violent victimization (such as striving for status or sub rosa trading) while at the same time also avoiding the potential label of 'vulnerable victim'? Clearly, this kind of 'tightrope-walking' will not be easy to accomplish, but how many prisoners in fact successfully achieve it?

The fourth factor is the tendency in prison societies to rely on private justice between prisoners in preference to turning to staff. While this attitude seems certain to lead to an increase in the level of assault, the norms that it is wrong to turn to staff, and that physical force, in these circumstances, is a legitimate option, might make assaults an accepted part of the routine. If the potential for violence is part of the expectations prisoners have of one another, and these expectations are consistently fulfilled, then it is possible that inmates may become resigned to violence.

Finally, the ethos, management style and staffing arrangements of an institution may promote feelings of safety and the sense of order.

These five factors can serve as a framework for thinking further about the safety paradox. What evidence do we have, from our two studies, that can contribute to a fuller understanding of why, when faced with substantial risks of being victimized, so many prisoners appear to feel safe?

As we have noted in Chapter 4, much victimization is mutual. This is especially true of assaults, threats and verbal abuse. Perhaps when there is a degree of overlap between being victimized and victimizing others, the fact of being a victim becomes a normal expectation and is therefore less disturbing. At the very least, behaviour over which the prisoner feels he has some control (such as assault, when it is mutual) would reduce the fears of being victimized in the sense of being passively controlled by someone else.

To some extent it might be true to say that having been assaulted or having directly experienced incivility may inure the victim. Although those with recent direct experience felt less safe than those without, it was still the case that many of those who had been recently assaulted felt safe from assault (e.g. 54 per cent in Huntercombe and 41 per cent in Bullingdon as shown in Table 5.1). Perhaps some of those who have been assaulted and learned that they can survive are less prone to fear.

It is also possible that having been victimized, inmates believe that they can modify their routines so as to make repeat victimization less likely. Alternatively they may adapt to a style of life where they are constantly at risk and get some satisfaction from it.

Familiarity has a role in reducing fear of crime. As prisons are small and enclosed communities, victimization is rarely perpetrated by complete strangers. This could have the effect of reassuring prisoners that they can try to avoid contact with those who they suspect might prey on them. Such a hypothesis is supported by the finding presented in Table 5.3 (see below) that prisoners feel safer when in their own private space (e.g. cell) or in structured/supervised public space (e.g. chapel, library, visits room) than when in public space where it may be difficult for them to control with whom they have contact (e.g. showers, reception, segregation unit). Ironically they were vulnerable in their own cells where they felt safest.

Furthermore victimization is sometimes considered legitimate by all parties, including the victim. This could be the case for example when payment of a debt is enforced with violence. In addition, the victimization of some categories of prisoner is considered to be appropriate. In our survey most inmates (56 per cent) agreed that 'grasses' (i.e. informers) 'deserved to be bullied'. An even greater proportion (72 per cent) agreed that sex offenders deserved to be treated in this way. An inmate who does not fall into such a category may not feel fearful even if genuinely at risk of victimization.

Inmate solidarity is another possible factor. The victimization survey found evidence that prisoners believed that if they were in difficulty other inmates would intervene to protect them. For example, three-quarters of the adults felt that other prisoners would 'sometimes' or 'always' intervene (74 per cent in Bullingdon and 78 per cent in Wellingborough).

The young offenders' faith in other prisoners differed significantly between the two institutions. In Feltham, 59 per cent agreed that other prisoners would 'sometimes' or 'always' intervene, compared with 75 per cent in Huntercombe. This confidence was confirmed throughout interviews with staff, victims and victimizers, and may help explain why inmates in Huntercombe felt safer (see Tables 5.1 and 5.2) and were less at risk (see Table 3.1).

Some inmates were confident that staff would come to their aid, and this could be another protective factor. Such a view was more common among young offenders, 37 per cent of whom felt that prison officers would always 'try to put a stop to it when someone is being picked on'. Half as many adults (18 per cent) shared this view. Adults were twice as likely as young offenders (31 per cent versus 15 per cent) to believe that staff would 'never' intervene.

When asked how helpful the officers in their institution were to inmates who were being victimized, half of those surveyed indicated that they didn't know (46 per cent of young offenders and 52 per cent of adults). Of those who felt able to express an opinion, 70 per cent of young offenders stated that officers were 'helpful' or 'very helpful'. Once again adult prisoners were much more pessimistic, with only 48 per cent sharing this view.

Relative safety

Bottoms did not pursue the notion that safety is relative. In general, our data show that prisoners felt safe in prison, but the question arises: in comparison to what? In blunt, statistical terms, what proportion of frightened prisoners would be sufficient to establish the point that prisoners in general do not feel safe?

The extent to which people in the community express fear of crime provides one point of comparison for levels of fear in prisons. Michael Hough (1995: 25) reported that 36 per cent of those who took part in the British Crime Survey said they felt 'a bit unsafe' or 'very unsafe' when walking alone on their street in the dark. This finding led Farrall *et al.* (2000: 399) to comment: 'It appears that the fear of crime is a social phenomenon of truly striking dimensions.' For prisoners who had not recently been assaulted the proportion feeling unsafe is very similar (Table 5.1). It would be useful to disaggregate the findings of community studies to see whether those who had recently experienced various forms of victimization, whether directly or vicariously, felt any more unsafe than those who had not. In this regard it is interesting to note that recent research by the Home Office has shown that the homicide rate was lower among prisoners than offenders under supervision in the community, 'thus lending support for the idea of prison protecting offenders from violent death' (Sattar 2001: 54).

The victimization study neglected to ask prisoners whether they believed they were safer in custody than they were at home. There is, however, evidence from the wider literature of communities in which people feel safe despite a statistically high risk of crime. Janet Foster (1995: 568), describing her study of an estate in the East End of London (which she called 'Riverside'), also identified a safety paradox: 'Survey data revealed that Riverside had crime rates comparable or higher, in the case of motor vehicle crime and burglary, than the [British Crime Survey] average for the least well-off or poorest estates ... [Yet] residents rarely mentioned crime as a "problem" during the ethnographic research.' Foster's work raised a number of parallels with prison life that suggest further factors to be explored in trying to understand the safety paradox. For example, she distinguished between general fears of crime held by people on the estate (such as they gained from the news media) and particular fears (about specific people or particular situations that arose on the estate). While her respondents sometimes told how they faced situations of present danger, they were clear that their feelings were partly inspired by the general fear of crime. She cited the experience of one tenant (ibid.: 570):

> [One night when] I come back there was a group of these coloured fellas downstairs. As I've got to the flats I've gone straight to the phone box, rung up [my husband] and said, 'come and meet me'. I was really scared. When I've got in I thought that was really stupid. I know most of them, they live on the estate. If I'd gone up to them and said, 'can you see me up because I'm really scared'?, they would probably have done. But you get paranoid because of the news and the papers.

Secondly, Foster showed that, for residents on Riverside, some forms of crime were routine, yet not widely viewed as crimes. For example, there was a thriving hidden economy. Foster's view was that the acceptance of such practices may have neutralized the residents' sensitivity to other criminal activities. In prison, as we have seen, illicit trading is rife and an assault for non-repayment of debt can be accepted as legitimate.

The way that residents on the estate engaged in, and accepted, hidden economic practices provides a good illustration of the importation theory of prison culture – namely, that people bring into custody the values and routines they know in the wider society. More broadly, it is possible that a common experience of being victimized outside leads prisoners to normalize crime inside and to feel less fear as a result than they would if, for example, they had lived in areas in which assaults were very rarely witnessed (ibid.: 571): 'Residents seemed to accept, or at least tolerate, a diverse range of offending, providing it did not infringe upon their individual privacy.'

A third possible parallel with prison culture from Foster's account of Riverside was that the demands of life on the estate meant that tenants had other, perhaps more important, concerns than crime (ibid.: 568): 'Statistical distributions do not provide us with any detailed picture of the experience of living within a community where crime is just one, and not necessarily the most serious, problem residents face.'

Similarly, despite the high risks of assault, theft and threat we found in prisons, it is likely that prisoners were equally – if not more – anxious about their families, their relations with staff, preparations for release and maintaining a reasonable diet.

Roger Hood and Kate Joyce's (1999) study of the perceptions of crime of three generations of working-class Londoners suggests dimensions of people's experience of risks outside that may reduce their anxieties about victimization in prison. Like Foster, they found widespread participation in the hidden economy. One respondent – from the '80s generation' – told them (ibid.: 155): 'I don't think I went round with anyone who wasn't involved in crime in some sense ... There were lots of people involved. It was definitely a culture, definitely. Like if people weren't nicking they were buying.'

They found a strong sense that informing the police about criminal matters was wrong (ibid.: 147): 'Anyone seen talking to a policeman was in danger of being called a "copper's nark". This indicates that there were activities to keep from the ears of the law and certain loyalties to (or fears about) those who were known to be engaged in criminal activities.' More directly relevant to violent victimization in prisons, Hood and Joyce described fighting traditions in the neighbourhoods, widely accepted violence which, for some, provided entertainment (ibid.: 145): 'Amongst those who undoubtedly would have been regarded as "rough", fighting was recalled by some as a pleasurable experience, as a gladiatorial activity which conferred masculine status and a sense of identity, but none of the participants referred to this as a "crime of violence".'

Drawing on this wider literature, it would appear that the feeling of safety comprises five elements that would also apply in prisons: crime as a normal part of everyday life; familiarity with people and places; territory – a sense of belonging, or, more accurately, of ownership of space; a sense of control over one's environment; and networks of support.

Foster stated that residents tended to accept the presence of offenders in their midst, in part because the ways of crime were not entirely unfamiliar to them. How much truer this is in prison, in which the person accepts the routine nature of crime, partly because *everyone* else is an offender! But this becomes even more important when the prisoner in question also identifies with the role of offender.

Familiarity in personal terms matches Bottoms's suggestion that new prisoners would be more likely than their established peers to feel fear because they are confronted by a sea of unfamiliar faces. Knowing that any of them poses an unspecifiable threat to personal safety, the new man is likely to hold a general fear of all of them. As he meets others previously known to him or introduces himself to people who do not threaten him, his sense of interpersonal safety could be expected to grow.

In territorial terms, the hypothesis would be that when someone encounters a new space – either prison or council estate – the setting evokes fears, because they are aware that they do not yet know safe from dangerous places or routes. As they settle in and the routes become familiar, they gain confidence in their knowledge of certain spaces as risky. Further, they confer safe status upon the best known spaces, in part because of a sense of greater control. We discuss fears and spatiality below. We found that prisoners tended to rate the early spaces (reception) and those least familiar (the segregation unit) as dangerous, while rating familiar spaces (own cell) as safe.

Foster pointed out that one factor governing the appreciation of spaces as safe is 'territoriality'. The strongest feelings of one's own territory are attached to one's domicile. Somewhat more broadly, one feels at home on a particular landing of a particular wing. Foster also interpreted territory in terms of informal networks. The sense amongst a group that 'we all look out for each other' increases their feeling of safety.

If people come to prison already familiar with the ways of the hidden economy, reluctant to confide in those in authority and with experience of witnessing, or participating in, fights and assaults, how might this background influence their perceptions of the risk of crime inside?

Fear and space →

Randy Atlas (1983) conducted a survey of prisoners in Florida to determine the extent to which they perceived particular areas of the prison to be dangerous. He then compared their perceptions with official reports on actual assaults. Prisoners were not accurate in identifying areas of particular risk. For example (ibid.: 68–9):

Inmates at [one prison] thought most incidents (43 per cent) occurred outside, while actually only 11 per cent occurred outside. Only 14 per cent of respondents thought dorms were the most frequent location of assaults, and none thought cells were a frequent location. Yet cells had 27 per cent of the assaults and dorms 6 per cent. The dining area . . . was perceived as a safe area, yet this was the second largest area for assault (23 per cent).

The prisons differed in the extent to which prisoners recorded that they felt fear. In two of them, 50 per cent said they felt fear, whilst in the other two, over 85 per cent said they felt fear. At the two 'less-safe' prisons, prisoners tended to feel that the corridors were unsafe.
Atlas (ibid.: 70) concluded:

Often areas low in frequency of assaults are overestimated as high risk areas. It would be expected that inmates would feel safe in their housing areas since they are most familiar and the inmates can exercise the most control over their environment. Yet 68 per cent of the inmates perceived their housing areas as being unsafe.

Most inmates in our victimization survey stated that they felt safe in most places in the institution. For both adults and young offenders the greatest number (but never more than one in four) felt unsafe in the segregation unit, in the showers, during their reception to the establishment and when travelling to and from their residential wing. Table 5.3 shows the proportion of inmates who reported feeling 'unsafe' or 'very unsafe' in a variety of locations within the prison. Locations are ranked in descending order of their perceived safety (i.e. those seen as least safe are listed first).
Overall, self-reported feelings of safety across institutions were similar. Association, during which time prisoners are unlocked and allowed to mingle, is a period of relatively high opportunity for perpetrators, but did not seem to be considered unsafe by the great majority (more than 85 per cent). This may reflect higher levels of

Table 5.3: Prisoners who reported feeling 'unsafe' or 'very unsafe' (per cent)

	Young offenders (Feltham and Huntercombe)	Adults (Bullingdon and Wellingborough)
Showers	23	23
Segregation unit	23	26
Travel to and from wing	16	21
Reception	19	16
Association	14	15
Gym	19	12
Education	12	12
Work	12	11
Hospital	13	12
Meal times	6	15
Prison shop	10	10
Visits	10	8
Chapel	7	7
Library	9	7
Own cell	5	9

supervision by staff and the greater freedom to circulate which might allow potential victims to avoid potential victimizers. Inmates also felt safe in their own cells (where much victimization actually took place), when they were attending the library, receiving visits or making purchases at the prison shop.

Certain areas were considered more dangerous at Feltham than at Huntercombe. The visiting area in Feltham was considered unsafe, perhaps because it was larger and prisoners were required to wait in a small, and often crowded, room before being escorted back to their wing. Reception was a second danger area in Feltham, which could be explained by the fact that this young offender institution had a remand centre. Thus, many more of its inmates than those at Huntercombe were likely to have had no previous experience of custody. Hence the reception process would have been new and frightening. A higher proportion of inmates at Huntercombe than Feltham reported feeling unsafe in the corridors between wings. Again this may have been influenced by the design of the institution: the corridors in Hunter-combe being long and poorly supervised.

Although inmates in Huntercombe were almost as likely to be robbed, threatened or assaulted as their counterparts in Feltham, they reported feeling much less anxious about victimization. In Hunter-combe 71 per cent felt safe from being assaulted (58 per cent in

Feltham), 73 per cent felt safe from having their things taken (59 per cent in Feltham) and 78 per cent felt safe from being insulted (64 per cent in Feltham). Amongst the young offenders, Asians were most likely to state that they felt anxious. Black young offenders felt no less at risk than whites.

No appreciable differences arose between the two adult institutions in feelings about safety. Gym and meal times were considered slightly less safe at Bullingdon than at Wellingborough. Education was seen as somewhat more dangerous at Wellingborough, perhaps because of its location. The education department formed a key corridor for all movement within the prison, and there was a marked tendency for people to loiter in groups outside the classrooms.

Adults reported feeling safe from insult, injury or theft at a slightly higher rate than the young offenders at Feltham, yet they felt less safe than those at Huntercombe.

The perception of prison as a high-risk setting

Craig Hemmens and James Marquart (1999) interviewed 775 men who had recently been released from prisons in Texas. The Texas prison system had been through tumultuous times in the 1970s and 1980s. The 'building tender' system whereby more aggressive inmates were co-opted to help staff control the institution had been dismantled by the courts. The power vacuum that followed its disappearance was filled by prison gangs. This resulted in unprecedented levels of violence, reaching a peak in 1985 when 52 prisoners were killed by other prisoners in Texas. Paradoxically, inmates had not reported feeling safer during the building tender system, when they were much less at risk, than during the violent years of the 1980s. There were interesting racial patterns in feelings of safety. Black ex-prisoners were less concerned with being attacked in prison than either whites or Hispanics. Also younger ex-prisoners were more likely to perceive prison as a dangerous place. Despite this, however, they were no more worried about being attacked than their older counterparts. They could distinguish between risk and fear.

In prison, the nature of the setting and the behaviour of others can lead to perceptions that violence is required. The 209 prisoners interviewed in the conflicts study, who had recently been involved in fights, assaults or disputes with other inmates, were asked how they would have dealt with the situation if it had occurred in the community. Eighty-six respondents (over 40 per cent) replied that the situation would not have arisen outside. In other words, in their view, the prison environment promotes violence in particular ways. Three central concerns that prisoners expressed about their environment were physical danger, intimidation and exploitation.

Danger

Prisoners accept that there is a pervasive risk of being involved in physical violence. Perceptions of prisons as risky settings were supported by the actual rates of assault, theft and threat (see Tables 3.1 and 3.2). Prisoners might not have expressed fears of being assaulted, but our evidence showed clearly that they viewed prisons as dangerous and violent places: 89 per cent of those interviewed believed that violence in prison was inevitable.

Many prisoners believed that if they failed to stand up for themselves when challenged by an inmate, they risked being victimized by others. As Toch (1992: 198) wrote: 'The man who shows fear when he is under fire from practised diagnosticians of fear is classified as unmanly.' Comments by two prisoners whom we spoke to illustrate this point:

> You got to go for it, even if you get a good hiding. It will go on and on if you don't stick up for yourself.

> I don't like anybody trying to take the piss. In here, you can't get up and walk out. If you let them do it, the whole place will.

Crucially, feelings of being at risk seem to originate in anxieties about the judgements their fellow inmates make about them. In the victimization study, one of the 31 prisoners who identified himself as being a victimizer explained his reasons for trying to dominate others: 'I didn't start out bullying but you watch. You see what happens if you don't bully. Then if you bully you don't get pressured.'

Examples of mutual intimidation – such as the power contests we will outline in Chapter 8 – cast doubt on this claim. That is, prisoners who feel intimidated may believe that an aggressive response will force the other inmate to back down, whereas it may initiate a cycle of violence.

The atmosphere of distrust and suspicion in which disputes developed often led to presuppositions about what the other person was trying to achieve. Conflict-ridden prison societies generate a perverse cycle in which seemingly rational individual responses to danger increase the risk within the prison as a whole. Individual prisoners, believing that they would be picked on unless they show themselves to be tough, assault those they fear would pick on them. In doing so, the individual victimizes the potential victimizers, with the social consequences of a rise in the risk of physical injury in the prison community. His individual judgement that force was necessary for self-protection conflicts with the collective rationality – that the use of force needs to be minimized to protect the society from violence and disorder.

Giddens (1984: 311) provided a framework within which this tendency can be explained:

> Contradictory consequences ensue when every individual in an aggregate of individuals acts in a way which, while producing the intended effect if done in isolation, creates a perverse effect if done by everyone. If all the audience in a lecture hall get to their feet to obtain a better view of the speaker, no one will in fact do so ... These are outcomes not only that no one intends but also that run counter to what everyone in the situation wants; nonetheless, they derive from conduct that is intended to satisfy wants, and could do so for individuals, were it not for the fact that the conduct in question becomes generalized.

The individual prisoner's decision to use aggressive force in an attempt to secure personal safety by deterring would-be predators precisely matches this concept of contradiction. It is obvious that contradictory consequences of the type Giddens portrays will intensify conflict, for at least three reasons: first, because the interests that motivated the individual action are still not being met; secondly, because the situation makes competition explicit – it is blatantly obvious that the reason the interests are not being met is the behaviour of other people, and thirdly (a psychological element), because having attempted to meet their needs without success, the individuals concerned are more likely to feel frustration and this may lead to further aggression.

To tie this analytical scheme to our present concern, a basic human need of the prisoner is personal safety. If he attempts to ensure his safety by non-violent means – sharing possessions when he can, discussing problems in an open and non-threatening manner, forming alliances – he runs the risk that someone will label him weak and use force to try to exploit him. So, there appears to be an incentive to use force to meet his need for personal safety. The victim–perpetrator overlap we cited in Chapter 4 suggested that fighting was not an effective method of securing personal safety. Giddens's thinking explains why this is so by describing the societal consequences of tactics that appear rational on an individual level.

From the prisoner's perspective, he is living in a social setting in which the risk of being assaulted is substantial. When he is faced with a dispute that is becoming increasingly volatile, he must be aware of his opposite number's capacity to use aggressive physical force on him. The interaction of the social setting, with its pro-violence attitudes and high incidence of assault, and the dyadic dispute, in which he perceives hostility directed towards him, lead him to define a violent response on his part as justifiable and rational. If he were alone in using force in this way, or if everyone only used force genuinely in self-defence, then perverse consequences would be minimized. In practice, the perverse cycle of the violence-prone prison is more prevalent. Individual prisoners, using force to defend their interests, build up patterns of interaction, thus collectively defining the prison as a dangerous and violent environment, though not necessarily a frightening one. Inmates' belief that their environment is dangerous coloured their reading of specific encounters with others so that violence sometimes became a self-fulfilling prophecy.

Intimidation

The fear of being intimidated led to violence in a wide range of situations. Prisoners were sensitive to the presence of an audience. They concluded that their counterparts intended to intimidate them when they were subjected to threats, glaring or other behaviour, such as:

Shouting
She carried on shouting so that everyone knew she was intimidating me.

Ridicule
This other guy was calling me a sheep-shagger, because I am from Wales. If I would have been alone with him, I would probably have laughed. But in front of everyone else I felt intimidated.

Harassment
They were . . . pushing into me, giving me bad looks, walking the walk.

When prisoners believed that their counterpart was attempting to intimidate them, an aggressive response was likely. Despite the common perception that intimidation is a problem mainly amongst young offenders, we found that all prisoners – especially adult males – were likely to express concern about being intimidated.

Exploitation

In a study of the culture in Dutch prisons, Grapendaal (1990) found evidence of three norms or attitudes:

1. opposition – to the custodians;

2. exploitation – of other inmates and staff; and

3. isolationism – an aloof attitude to staff and self-reliance vis-à-vis other prisoners.

He tested for inmate solidarity and found that such an attitude lacked sufficient acceptance amongst the prisoners to serve as a value fundamental to prisoner culture. For our purposes, though, the most important attitude was exploitation. Grapendaal found that prisoners shared a sense that exploitation of others was a way of life.

In our conflicts study, the fear of being exploited was a wide concern. Opportunities for getting the upper hand included jumping the queue for the phone, food or a game, winning a verbal sparring match, assuming the right to give orders, showing superiority in sport or play fighting or taking another person's possessions. Everyday situations in prison required inmates to judge the intentions of other prisoners with whom they interacted. In a prison context shaped by material deprivations and a lack of autonomy, the fear that someone might take advantage assumes special significance. As one young offender told us: 'He thought he could take a liberty, I just ignored him. Then he pushed it too far and I had to break him up a bit. People take kindness for weakness in jail.' Similarly an adult with long experience of prisons explained: 'When violence was offered me, it's not bravado – it's fear makes me do what I do.'

Economic exploitation – for example, fraud or dishonest dealing – was seen as unacceptable, in particular by females. In the women's prison we explored 40 disputes, 12 of which involved attempted exploitation. Eleven of the 12 ended in violence. As a young woman who punched a suspected cell thief explained: 'It sounds silly fighting over tobacco, but you can't let it go without losing your respect. You wouldn't fight about it on the out, but we are not on the out. We're in jail.'

Vulnerable prisoner units

One way that a prisoner can respond to his sense that he is in danger is to apply for protective custody (vulnerable prisoner status) and be segregated on a vulnerable prisoner unit (VPU). Two of the institutions included in the victimization study had such units (Feltham and Bullingdon). This enabled us to analyse the extent to which this kind of arrangement promoted feelings of safety.

It was something of an achievement that the 53 young offenders on the VPU in Feltham did not feel any less safe than those located on other wings. These were high-risk inmates who were targeted for victimization throughout the rest of the institution. The VPU in Bullingdon was very different. The 44 inmates located there felt far more fearful for their safety than other prisoners in the same establishment. It was clear that a small group of vulnerable prisoners in Bullingdon was living in chronic fear. For example, only about a third (39 per cent) of them felt safe from being injured compared with two-thirds (68 per cent) of other prisoners. Similarly, while 74 per cent of inmates on normal location felt safe from being insulted, this was true for only 45 per cent of those on the VPU.

As well as being much more fearful, inmates on the VPU in Bullingdon reported being insulted more than twice as frequently as other prisoners (48 per cent versus 21 per cent on at least one occasion in past month) and being assaulted, also at twice the rate for other prisoners (34 per cent versus 17 per cent). There were no major differences for cell theft (34 per cent versus 28 per cent) or being threatened (27 per cent versus 24 per cent). This VPU offered neither shelter nor a sense of personal security.

It was clear from the self-report data that black prisoners were regularly being victimized. However, the VPUs we studied held disproportionately few black inmates. Sparks *et al.* (1996) also found that the VPU population was predominantly white. Because the prison cultures are so different, comparisons to the USA are speculative. However, it is worth mentioning that Adams (1992: 288, 301) also provided useful information on race, resilience and victimization. Like us he found that black inmates were less likely to be found in protective custody. Unlike us he found that black inmates were more likely to be predatory.

It may be that the unusual racial composition of the VPUs in Feltham and Bullingdon reflected differential coping strategies, differential patterns of reporting or a selective response on the part of the institutions. Also it may be that this phenomenon was exclusive to the institutions studied, rather than a feature of prisons more generally. The racial dimension is one aspect of the response to victimization which should attract further study.

Walmsley *et al.* (1992: 53–4) also found that prisoners on a separate VPU or otherwise segregated for their own protection reported feeling unsafe more frequently than other prisoners (26 per cent versus 18 per cent) and were more regularly assaulted (14 per cent versus 9 per cent during the previous six months). The levels presented here are higher, possibly because the VPU in question was atypical, and possibly because the questions asked were more narrowly focused.

The role of environmental factors was important. At the time of the victimization study, the vulnerable adult prisoners in Bullingdon were a highly visible group, occupying one spur of a wing, separated from other prisoners only by a sheet of clear perspex (put in place to prevent prisoners on other spurs hurling missiles at them). They were tormented by other prisoners whenever they left the wing. In addition there were serious tensions on the wing between the sex offenders and the others – often debtors – who had been given protected status (under the old Prison Rule 43). Life on the unit consisted of a constant battle between these two groups. A vulnerable prisoner described the tense atmosphere to us:

> The VPU was designed to keep a particular kind of prisoner outside of normal location. Here there's two warring camps – VPs [vulnerable due to offence] and Rule 43s [vulnerable due to prison conduct]. We are in a no-win situation. VPs are bullied by 43s and VPs don't have the character to fight back. People who run from trouble on other wings come here and get a tough image by bullying the VPs. To have a gang throwing water down, spitting, etc. is frightening. This spur is at a crisis point. There will be a serious injury. One day a 43 will injure or mutilate a VP.

The problems of accommodating prisoners who are kept apart for administrative reasons (e.g. debtors) with those who are vulnerable by virtue of their offence (e.g. rapists of children) are acute. A number of vulnerable prisoners said that they had been threatened frequently by others on the VPU. Others described physical assaults which were used as constant harassment.

Perhaps the most powerful evidence of this VPU's inability to prevent victimization was an inmate who had been removed from it for his own protection. Interviewed in the segregation unit he spoke of having been assaulted on the VPU, when an inmate shoved him back into his cell: 'He was saying, "We want you off the wing. Get off the wing".' He was regularly threatened: 'Shouting through the flap, saying they were going to take my eye out. I was too scared to come out for meals.' Another vulnerable prisoner linked his sense of insecurity to a lack of staff activity: 'The spur is not properly supervised. Prison officers are always at the end of the landing in the wing office.'

The failure of some staff to confront the alleged victimizers directly may have stemmed in part from the fact that they were already on a VPU and could not easily be relocated within the prison. A second factor may have been the practical difficulty associated with charging a prisoner for using abusive language, particularly when insults were so pervasive. When Bullingdon was visited again during the conflicts study, the VPU had been moved to another part of the prison and its troubles appeared to have eased considerably.

Chapter 6

Conflicts I – interests, relationships, catalysts

> Conflict is essential to, ineradicable from, and inevitable in human life; and the source, cause and process of conflict can be turned from life-destroying to life-building ends (David Augsburger 1992: 5).

The first, and most basic, point to make in seeking an explanation for fights and assaults is that there is no one cause, no single background factor, that explains violence. Despite this, it is clear that violent interactions are structured and patterned. They are much more than random and senseless interactions. One way to integrate the diverse circumstances out of which acts of interpersonal violence arise is to explore them as conflicts. This chapter, and the two that follow, are based on the findings of the conflicts study.

What does it mean to see an interaction as a conflict? Our use of the concept encompasses six components. These are illustrated in what we call the conflict pyramid, shown as Figure 6.1. The elements of conflict shown in Figure 6.1 have been distilled from thousands of hours of interviews with prisoners and several years working with, and reflecting on, transcripts, observations and survey questionnaires. We follow Toch's method of analysis (1992: 12), which is 'to proceed from the unique to the general sequentially, by moving from a full-blooded phenomenology of inmate experiences to a description of the dimensions of environments that appear significant to large numbers of inmates'. Central to this work is the attempt 'to explore the personal connotations of prison environments for inmates, in an effort to reconstruct their "reality worlds" as faithfully as possible' (ibid.: 12).

The conflict pyramid can be applied to any dispute between two persons. Our model is abstract. It is race, age and gender neutral. We hope that it will prove useful to examinations of violent interactions in non-prison contexts. The tiers of the pyramid can be briefly defined as follows:

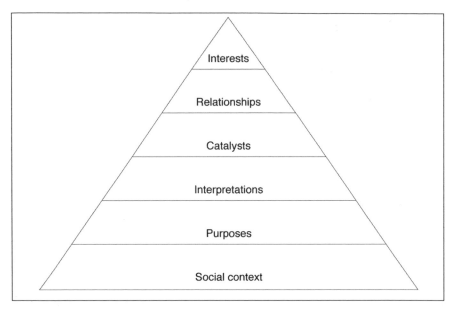

Figure 6.1   The conflict pyramid.

- *Interests*: what each person wanted out of the situation (including both material goods and non-material values such as honour, safety or revenge).

- *Relationships*: the social distance between the parties involved – whether strangers, associates or friends; and the impact of the dispute on the way they saw each other.

- *Catalysts*: the tactics each used to deal with the problem between them. These included verbal 'games' (e.g. accusations, threats, and challenges), but also body language (e.g. hostile gestures) and personal invasions.

- *Interpretations*: the inferences each made about the behaviour and intentions of the other party in the interaction.

- *Purposes*: the objectives that prisoners who used force believed it would achieve.

- *Social context*: the impact of the prison setting on interactions – the influence of peers and prison officers combined with environmental features, such as limited surveillance of shower areas or restrictions on time available for phone calls.

Looked at in this way, the interactions between prisoners that resulted in violence can be described as conflicts in that the parties pursued competing interests in uncompromising ways. Accordingly, we refer to the perspective on violence pioneered in this book as a 'conflict-centred' approach. In this chapter we analyse interests, relationships and catalysts. Interpretations, purposes and social context are discussed in Chapter 7.

Interests at stake: what conflicts were about

Conflicts between prisoners often began in a clash of interests over what each party wanted out of a situation. Disputes over material items provide clear examples of the role of interests in initiating a conflict:

> Dover lent a CD to Leominster. When it was returned, the CD case was broken. He demanded to know how this had happened. When Leominster left the wing, Dover continued to demand an explanation from Leominster's friend, Wharton. Still unsatisfied, Dover challenged Wharton to a fight. Subsequently they fought twice.

> Knighton was next in the queue to play on the computer game. When it was his turn, Pembroke came up and grabbed the joystick instead. Knighton asked Pembroke if he wanted to fight about it. Pembroke agreed and they went together to a private space in which they could hold their fight.

> Reeth had been in a cell with Fulford for a couple of weeks when he began to suspect that Fulford was reading his letters. He confronted Fulford; they argued, and grappled with each other.

Drugs were the most common possession in dispute. By our analysis, 13 per cent of the 141 incidents ($n = 19$) were about drugs. We judged two levels of drugs involvement:

1. *Primary*: disputes escalated into violence because differences over drugs could not be resolved; the ownership, distribution or use of drugs provided a sufficient explanation of why violence resulted.

2. *Secondary*: drugs played an important role in the emergence of conflict, but to understand why the disputes ended in violence other explanatory factors were needed.

There were an additional seven incidents in which one or both parties mentioned drugs, but where they played no significant role in the escalation of the conflict. At best, the presence of drugs was a peripheral factor. The ways that disagreements over drugs could lead to violence can be illustrated by a situation in which they played a secondary role:

> Chorley and Elton fought as members of two groups after they clashed over a drugs deal. Chorley supplied the drugs and Elton refused to pay him back. They agreed to hold a fight about it, and others joined in. The basis of the fight, in Chorley's words, was that 'that lot think they run the wing'. He also stated that by the time of the fight he was motivated by the principle (namely, that others should not try to take advantage of him) rather than the drugs per se. Thus, although the conflict began over a drugs deal, their influence over the development of the conflict was secondary.

Even when a participant did not believe that the fight or assault was about a material object, our analyses showed that they sometimes played a role. All together, then, goods played some part in almost half the 141 situations. The effect exerted by material goods included, disputed ownership, a disputed deal, gambling or trading debts, payment for a contract, robbery or theft, or the misuse of authority. Disputes over ownership or deals were the most common reasons prisoners argued about material goods. In contrast, debt was mentioned in only 4 per cent of incidents.

John Burton (1990: 46) distinguished between interests and the deeper sources of conflicts that are found in values and basic human needs:

> Traditional power theorists correctly hypothesized inherent human propensities, and conflicts over scarce resources. Where they may have been wrong was in assuming that human behavior was determined mainly or solely by material benefits, and that the source of conflict was over competition for scarce resources. Human behavior may be equally, and in many circumstances far more, oriented toward deeper concerns of identity and autonomy.

What the person wanted out of a situation *always* included some non-material values and needs, such as mutual respect, privacy, fairness, loyalty, personal safety or honour but these did not always clash. (Both prisoners could act on their need to maintain personal safety.) In the vast majority of the disputes, one or both prisoners felt the other person was trying to intimidate, exploit, threaten or wrong them; or that their beliefs or image were being challenged.

When asked directly whether the conflict was about intimidation, over half the respondents said it was and almost as many cited 'emotions'. Many inmates cited both: 'He was emotionally upset cos he was intimidated by what I was calling him.' This prisoner's counterpart said: 'It all happened because people started to call me that [name]. That was the intimidation. The emotion was me getting upset.'

There was some variation among the four types of prison in the extent to which particular interests were active. However, because the numbers were small, these findings should be treated with caution. The highest proportion of young offenders (about half) identified emotions as an important factor in their conflicts. The female prisoners were the group most likely to report that their conflicts were about drugs and group loyalty (both factors reported by about one-third of the women). In the dispersal prison, intimidation was cited in 63 per cent of incidents as being central to the conflict, and it was also considered central in 57 per cent of the incidents in the local prison (also adult males). Far too often, bullying and intimidation are assumed to be problems specific to the young offender estate. Yet, the long-term high-security prisoners interviewed frequently believed that intimidation had led to fights and assaults.

The distinction between material interests and non-material values and needs becomes less stark when we consider the symbolic significance of personal possessions. The deprivations inherent in prison life show why prisoners place such importance on material goods. For example, for prisoners, a phone card represents the means of maintaining contact with loved ones – not just its £2.00 value. As one prisoner commented: 'Letters and phone calls are time bombs here – if you muck about with people's letters or phone calls it is serious.'

Material deprivations tempt prisoners to stretch their budget at the expense of others. In many disputes over material goods, the prisoner's interpretation that someone else was trying to exploit them became the key factor in the escalation of a dispute towards violence. (We observed this in Chapter 5, in discussing prisoners' perception of the prison setting as a place of danger.) A conflict that began over the disputed ownership of some item could quickly be interpreted by both parties as a test of who could exploit whom.

The interests of participants changed over the course of disputes.

What they wanted at the beginning was not necessarily what they wanted by the end. Many disputes that began over a material interest escalated into conflicts about honour or fairness. Dover wanted compensation for his CD cover (see above). But by the time he and Wharton fought, as Dover acknowledged in his interview, his interests has altered: 'The fight was for satisfaction of being wronged – nothing to do with the CD cover. He should have just said, "I broke it, I'm sorry".'

The final point to make about the role of interests, values and needs in conflicts is that they interact with other dimensions of conflict. Prisoners in conflict often interpreted their counterparts' behaviour by reading their intentions from the way they handled a specific object. Relationships, catalysts and social context all played a role in the following dispute, which began over a broom:

Buckden wanted to clean his cell. When he was unlocked he went to the cupboard to get a broom. Irlam came into the cupboard behind him and tried to pull the broom away from him. Buckden described their discussion:

'He says, "I'm having the broom". I said, "No. You can have it after me". Then he says, "I'll smash your teeth in". I said, "If you think you can do that, carry on".

Buckden explained how he interpreted Irlam's intentions when the latter tried to wrestle the broom from him:

'I think he was trying to bully me for the broom. When he knew he couldn't, he changed his tune.'

Thus, when material interests led to a dispute, the significance of the object was partly determined by interpretations that each party made about the intentions of the other. Although we will discuss interpretation as a distinct theme in the next chapter, we note here that the influence of interests, catalysts, relationships and purposes is mediated by interpretation.

The starkest influence of interpretation at this level – what the conflict was about – emerged in two-person accounts in which one party's explanation of the problem differed dramatically from his counterpart's. Their lack of mutual understanding contributed to the escalation of the conflict as the dispute between Atworth and Glastonbury demonstrates (see Appendix).

Relationships: social distance between prisoners

The basic requirement of the prison, to hold people in custody, leads to pressures on prisoners who do not choose to live together. An inevitable consequence is that people who do not know each other and would not need to or wish to associate under other circumstances must negotiate encounters with unfamiliar fellows to get through the day without incident. In this section, we consider the social distance between prisoners in the conflicts leading to fights and assaults, the impact of fights and assaults on relationships and the role of relationships with third parties.[1]

Let us look first at the influences of relationships on fights and assaults. Data describing the prisoners' sense of their relationships before the conflict are presented in Table 6.1. In nine incidents each party felt the other was a stranger, while in three incidents each described the antagonist as a friend. The most significant category, in numerical terms, represents situations in which there was a difference of opinion about the nature of the relationship. We call these cases cross-descriptions.

Table 6.1: Assessment of relationships before and after violent incidents

Relationship	Before	After
Strangers	9	3
Anonymous ('just someone on the wing')	9	3
Associate	10	3
Long-term acquaintance	2	1
Friend or mate	3	3
Pejorative description	1	11
Cross-descriptions	24	28
No longer relevant (moved off wing)	—	6
Total	58	58

As a general comment, it appears that friends and long-term acquaintances were less likely to enter into the kind of conflicts that resulted in fights than people who did not know each other well (although it must be said that relationships in prison may be more impersonal and anonymous than they are on the street). The highest proportion of incidents arose out of relationships in which one person had a different understanding of their social distance than the other (cross-descriptions). The disparities were not often profound. In seven of the 24 cases of cross-descriptions, one person felt that the two had

been strangers, while the other considered them to have been anonymous ('just someone on the wing'). We will look first at stranger, then
anonymous, then cross-description conflicts.

A common element in conflicts between strangers is that they tended
to spring from tensions that arose spontaneously. For the most part, the
conflicts between strangers did not arise out of trades or playing
games, but in impersonal situations. Logically, disputes between
associates or between friends were likely to take much longer to lead
to a fight or assault than aggravation between strangers. If an argument
had persisted for several days, the two could hardly be expected to
refer to each other as 'strangers'.

A quick sketch of two conflicts between strangers suggests that they
resulted from misunderstandings or interactions exacerbated by a lack
of knowledge about the other party:

> Drayton was in the food queue and he called back to his friend,
> using his friend's nickname. Another prisoner in the queue,
> Scalby, had the same nickname. Scalby challenged Drayton about
> daring to speak to him. They exchanged threats and, later in the
> day, fought briefly. Had Drayton known Scalby, he would have
> known that he shared the same nickname as his friend.

> Hesket was talking out of his window to some friends. A prisoner
> from another wing interrupted to tell Hesket to shut up. They
> argued briefly and the other prisoner called Hesket 'the mouthy
> one'. Hesket asked the unknown prisoner how long he was
> serving. When the reply came, 'four months', Hesket called the
> other prisoner a 'baby'. The other told Hesket, 'The only baby
> you'll see is your mam's baby when I fuck her'. As a result, Hesket
> asked people from that wing who the other prisoner was, sought
> him out and assaulted him.

Misunderstandings also arose when the two parties saw each other as
anonymous and did not know each other well enough to predict how
the other would react:

> York and Chelford were co-workers. Chelford was complaining
> about work. York commented that he was always complaining.
> York did not like the way Chelford reacted, so he invited him to
> go to the showers to fight about it. In his interview, York agreed
> that the dispute had arisen out of a misunderstanding:

> 'He took it too seriously. I didn't mean exactly what he took it for.'

Even a slight difference in the parties' sense of their social distance from each other could have important implications for the conduct of the conflict:

> Bampton had been sitting with her cell mate on association when another prisoner came to pester the cell mate. After she left, Bampton turned to her cell mate and asked, 'Why didn't you just tell her to fuck off?' Bampton was new to the wing and could not have known that the other prisoner's cell mate, Stroud, was sitting in front of them. Stroud stood up for her cell mate; she argued with Bampton; and knocked her to the ground with a headbutt to the face. Bampton referred to Stroud as a stranger, while Stroud, an established prisoner, saw Bampton as 'just someone on the wing'.

The cross-description suggests that, in a long-term, settled prison community, the established prisoners tended to be aware of new inductees as they arrived, whereas for the new person, the wing was largely a sea of nameless faces. Had Bampton recognized Stroud, she might not have made the comment that sparked the dispute. (The complete escalator for this incident is presented in the Appendix.)

In another cross-description conflict, the differences in perceived social distance were central to the escalation of the dispute:

> Lincoln regarded Rugby as a friend and respected him. Rugby did not reciprocate, viewing Lincoln as more of a nuisance. He regarded Lincoln as 'an associate' and stated that he did not know him very well:

> 'I didn't like him very much. He kept making silly comments now and then.'

> Lincoln believed that they became competitive as friends:

> 'He was equal. We were friends. But after we'd been to the gym and he saw he could lift more, he got condescending.'

> Rugby was unaware of the growing rivalry, but he felt that Lincoln tended to intrude:

> 'I got fed up with him interfering.'

> Lincoln, upset at the way Rugby was treating him in what he saw as their friendship, teased Rugby by publicly insulting him. Rugby

responded angrily with a challenge to fight. By agreement, they met in a cell and fought.

The differences in the way each saw their relationship meant that Lincoln treated Rugby as an equal and a mate, an attitude that was irritating to Rugby and aggravated their conflict.

The effects of physical violence on relationships

In Chapter 3 we cited a young offender's belief that a good fight could build friendships and mutual respect. The data on relationships enable us to test this belief more rigorously. Table 6.1 also shows the prisoners' assessments of their social distance after the violent incidents. Not surprisingly, there is a strong shift away from anonymity: fights and assaults led those involved to regard the other no longer as a stranger or anonymous presence on the wing. Further, the damage to relationships is hinted at in the rise in the number of incidents in which both parties described the other in derogatory terms.

This shift is understated by these findings. In their characterizations of relationships before the incident, none of the cross-descriptions included a pejorative comment. In contrast, 15 of the 28 cross-descriptions afterwards included a pejorative comment by one of the parties. Had these been counted as pejorative descriptions, at least one participant saw the post-violence relationship in pejorative terms in 26/58 (45 per cent) of incidents, compared with 1/58 (2 per cent) before.

In only three of the 58 cases (5 per cent) did both parties describe their relationship as friendly after the event. In one of these, they had been close friends before a misunderstanding:

Following a bad visit, Romney went to work. Blyton started teasing Romney to cheer him up, but Romney was in no mood for teasing. He told Blyton to stop poking him in the leg. Blyton tested him, doubting he was serious. Romney pushed Blyton against the table. Afterwards, both regretted that it had got out of hand and believed that they remained good friends.

Blyton explained his mistake:

'I misunderstood him. Usually we like messing around. We'd have play fights. I didn't think he'd lose it.'

In hindsight, Ramsey felt that he had been wrong to shove Blyton:

'I didn't make it obviously clear. I didn't say I'd had a bad visit. I just kept on, "Be quiet! Be quiet!" Then I just went for him.'

Clearly, the level of force used by the two was low – particularly in comparison to some of the incidents we have already mentioned in which the combatants' relationships were more profoundly affected. Thus, there was very little evidence that a violent confrontation could encourage closer relationships, and strong indications that it would create antipathy.

Wider relationships

The focus thus far has been the influence of relationships between two people on the ways they conducted conflicts and on the physical violence that sometimes resulted. Relationships influenced the process of conflicts between prisoners in terms of social distance, but there was another influence of relationships, namely, each person's allegiances with third parties. Mark Cooney (1998) explored how third parties shape violence. In his words (ibid.: 133), they 'can bring peace to the most violent disputes, persuading belligerent antagonists to lay down their arms and talk out their differences. Or they can urge irresolute disputants to take offence and to fight, thereby causing the most innocuous of disagreements to flare up into prolonged feuding'. Third parties can act as both warriors and peacemakers.

The paths disputes took were often shaped and influenced by the involvement of others. At the extremes, there were disputes between two prisoners which were not witnessed by anyone else and in which no third-party influence could be discerned. These accounted for 13 of our 141 incidents (9 per cent). On the opposite pole were fights and assaults between two prisoners which were based on a conflict one of them had with a third person (13 per cent). In the middle-ground – between these extreme situations – the role of third parties varied from merely witnessing the altercation (39 per cent) to direct involvement (38 per cent). When, in the interviews with witnesses, we asked about the possibility of them intervening, three-quarters thought that it was not necessary to take any action while the incident was unfolding. Only one of them called for help.

We discuss disputes about a third person or in which third parties became directly involved. Dufton described a drawn-out argument with two others whom he suspected of exploiting a younger offender:

A young lad on the wing was being pressured to give up his goods for late repayment of phone cards. I overheard a mate and his friend discussing taking stuff off the lad. I told them to leave it out. The boy's okay, no need to treat him badly. Others who owe them aren't under pressure. They told me to stay out of it. They went to him and took the stuff off him and he told me. I went to my mate's cell and confronted him. His friend left and we had a row. He struck me on the nose and a fight followed.

This physically violent incident arose, not because of a conflict directly between two prisoners, but because one of them chose to take on responsibility for the safety of a third prisoner. The friend who told Dufton to stay out of it expressed a norm that a prisoner should not interfere in interactions between two other prisoners. Dufton explained his motivations for ignoring that norm: 'From an early age I've done that, protecting my brothers. We were brought up in care and I always protected them. I think it stems from there, basically. I don't like seeing weaker people trampled on.'

More typically, disputes that were between two prisoners were influenced by third parties, either as witnesses (peer pressure) or through their direct involvement in the conflict. The roles of prisoners who were involved directly as third parties ranged from stirring up tensions to a point at which some were physically involved in fights. The type of prison had a clear impact on the likelihood that there would be third-party involvement in the development of a conflict. For example, young offenders were the most likely group to witness fights and assaults, while female prisoners were most likely to become involved in disputes among their peers:

Wilton, Arkle and Chatham (three women prisoners) were on association. Wilton was sucking her thumb. Chatham took exception to this and poked Wilton's face. Arkle intervened to prevent Wilton from attacking Chatham. She told Wilton, 'Just leave it'. Arkle described what happened next:

'Wilton said to me, "You going to fucking start it or what?" and she grabbed my shirt. I hit her on the face. She hit me back and we fell on the floor.'

The conflict, originally between Wilton and Chatham, led Arkle to intervene. Arkle's intervention and Wilton's reaction to it led them to a fight. Arkle explained that Chatham was her friend and she was trying to protect her. All three used physical force and ownership of the conflict shifted from Wilton and Chatham to Wilton and Arkle.

Third parties also became directly involved without intervening physically:

Dawlish complained about loud music late at night. In the end, she threatened to complain to the officers if the other prisoners did not turn their music down. A few prisoners were upset that Dawlish had made the threat and she, in turn, was threatened with violence. The following morning, Dawlish asked who had been calling her names. Other prisoners identified a prisoner who denied any role. Trimdon heard the conversation, rushed to Dawlish and assaulted her. The dispute was not solely between Trimdon and Dawlish. Others wanted the music turned down; others were angry at Dawlish for her threat to inform on them. But only Dawlish and Trimdon actually exchanged blows.

Trimdon justified her behaviour by appeal to the judgement of other prisoners on the wing:

'She pissed a lot of girls off cos of her attitude.'

Dawlish confirmed that her problems were not with Trimdon alone:

'They were going against me. I would ask them for a light and they would say, "Fuck you".'

Although the influence of third parties and the social distance between disputants can help to show how conflicts escalate, further detail about the ways prisoners managed their conflicts is needed to show why some disputes resulted in physical violence while others were able to be resolved (see Chapter 9).

Catalysts: behaviours that fuelled conflicts

As we have shown in Chapter 3, prisoners routinely insult, threaten and challenge each other. The ways prisoners responded to problems with others – the tactics they used – often aggravated their disputes and increased the likelihood of a violent outcome. For this reason, we refer to these tactics as 'catalysts' of violence. Greater detail about the most widespread catalysts will illustrate how they fit into emerging conflicts. First, however, we need to emphasize that these catalysts rarely operated alone, that they interacted and were mutually reinforcing.

Table 6.2 lists catalysts in order of the frequency with which each appeared in the 141 conflict situations. The frequency of each behaviour is only half the story. Equally important is the way each catalyst

Table 6.2: Number of occasions catalysts reported present

Catalyst	Occasions
Accusations	65
Threats	65
Verbal challenges	59
Personal invasions	45
Insults	44
Commands	43
Undermining behaviours	40
Verbal abuse	38
Invitations	37
Hostile gestures	34
Harassment	27
Rumour spreading	21
Deception	20

functioned in a dispute, to escalate the tensions and move the interaction towards violence, as can be seen in examples of accusations, threats, challenges, insults, undermining behaviours and personal invasions.

Accusations

Accusations, together with threats of violence, were the most common catalyst. An accusation laid a claim that the other was totally to blame, that they had sole responsibility for resolving the conflict. Blaming closes off discussion rather than opening the conflict to creative solutions. Inmates who issued accusations generally assumed that their counterparts were guilty, without waiting for verification:

Urmston was a remand prisoner. Returning from court, she heard a rumour that in her absence a young inmate, Truro, had propositioned her girlfriend. Urmston found Truro and approached her. According to Truro's account, Urmston said to her, 'What's this I hear? You were trying to chat up my missus', and immediately head-butted her. Urmston was not interested in waiting for an explanation – the accusation was assumed to be accurate.

Whether an accusation was true or not, it damaged the relationship between the two and made violence more likely:

Trent made a deal with Coniston to sell him drugs. Trent took the drugs from Coniston but he claimed that he had received less than they had agreed.

Trent:

'He gives it to me and says he wants sorting out for it. I looked and I could see it wasn't all there, so I said, "I can see you've already sorted yourself out".'

How did this accusation affect their relations? Trent's claim that Coniston had already taken his cut alerted Coniston that there was a conflict over the transaction. The allegation suggested that Coniston was dishonest, undermining his credibility. It also implied that Trent was going to determine for himself how much he was prepared to pay. This last implication shifted the balance between trader and customer, as Trent was now suggesting that he was going to pay Coniston less than Coniston expected:

Coniston confronted Trent on the exercise yard; they argued again; and Coniston slapped Trent.

Trent explained how his accusation led Coniston to assault him: 'I think the way I put things to him, he had to. I proved he was out of order.' He suggested that when he made his allegation in public this threatened Coniston's reputation as an honest dealer. To maintain his honour Coniston had to resort to violence.

Threats

Threats were a direct spur to violence. A list of the verbal threats reported to us by the prisoners highlights the implied violence they contain:

I'm going to spark you.
You're going to get battered in the morning.
He said he'd fuck me up.
Do that again and I will knock you out.

When a prisoner brandished a pool cue, his counterpart reacted with a strongly worded threat: 'He said, "If you hit me with that pool cue, I swear on my baby's life, I'll cut you".' Here, the function of a catalyst in aggravating conflict and generating violence is unmistakable. As we discussed in earlier references to threats, they were often intended to coerce the other person into doing something they did not want to do:

> Crawley, Moulton and Whitley shared a cell. They were getting along well, but Whitley and Moulton started play fighting. Whitley wanted Crawley to join in. Crawley resisted – he didn't enjoy play fighting.
> Crawley:

> 'Whitley said to me, "Come on, lets have a bit of a spar". I said, "No. I'm not into it". He says, "Come on, come on. It's a bit of fun". Then he threatened me, "If you don't fucking get up and spar, I'm just going to punch you". The other cell mate was laughing. I got up and half-pretended that I was going to have a spar. Whitley punched me hard on the arm and said, "Come on, Crawley, come on". I said, "No, leave it out". Then he punched me again, showing me what to do. I said, "No, mate. Leave it out." He was just pumping himself up and kept hitting me. Moulton joined in at one stage. They were holding me down and he gave me a couple punches on my leg. At one stage he head-butted me.'

Crawley had been drawn into a play fight he did not want by the threat that he would be hit even if he refused to fight. Nor were his problems with Whitley resolved by giving in to the threats. The second time, Whitley used punches as symbolic threats of more serious aggression.
Crawley described the escalation of the play fighting:

> Nothing happened until Wednesday after lockup, when he said, 'You've got to toughen up, Crawley. You've got to learn to fight, mate'. So I was then forced to fight with Moulton. Whitley gave me a few punches to start with and then made me fight Moulton. We exchanged a few blows. I think Moulton was half-intimidated by Whitley and half wanted to fight. I gave him about five blows to the head and then Whitley starts to hit Moulton where I've been punching him. Then it died down after that, a few more punches. He gave me a double punch on the chest – that was where I cracked my ribs. He also burned my hand with a cigarette and put a book against my ear and punched there as well. I had internal bleeding there. He put his hands round my neck and pressed until I kissed Moulton's feet. During Thursday I had constant verbal abuse and bullying. I was thinking about it all day and I was really worried about it and I told [staff].

Whitley used a combination of verbal and physical threats to coerce Crawley into doing what he did not want to in a way that drew Crawley into incriminating behaviour.

Equally important as the intentions of the person issuing the threat was the role of the person who received it. The recipient had to interpret what his counterpart was trying to accomplish. He might have believed that the threat was an empty one, but this interpretation is risky in prison. As one participant told us: 'There is no borderline in jail. It's hard to judge. You don't know if it is serious or not, so most people put their guard up just in case.'

The context in which threats were issued was crucial, as the recipient had to decide whether the other person's intentions were genuine. However, prisoners took a risk if they decided to ignore a threat. A more cautious course was to prepare, psychologically as well as practically, for a physical confrontation:

Midgley tried to intimidate Hatton into taking the blame for something that Midgley had done. But Hatton resisted. He took Midgley's threats seriously and decided to get to him first. Hatton explains:

'I said I wasn't going to take the rap. He then started to threaten me through the pipe. He threatened to cut me up and throw hot water at me if I didn't agree. I became paranoid about it. I waited till dinner time when we were unlocked and then I hit him.'

Challenges

Challenges criticized or questioned someone's behaviour. The in-mates' accounts of conflicts provided a wide array of examples. Taken out of context, they none the less convey aggression and underlying threat:

What's your problem?
What are you looking at?
What the fuck are you doing?
Are you calling me a liar?
What are you going to do about it?

Challenges entailed an ultimatum – either spoken or implicit – and were often met with counter-challenges. Each challenge was a claim by the speaker for superiority. As such, challenges tested the recipients' determination to stand up for themselves with force if necessary. When a challenge such as 'What are you looking at?' was issued in public, it committed both parties to a test of honour.

Challenges also aggravated conflicts by limiting options. The person who was challenged often felt that if they ignored the challenge or gave in, they would show that they were afraid. At the same time, a challenge restricted the options of the person who made it. As an ultimatum, if the challenge was not respected, the challenger had to take forceful action. Hence when someone rebelled against a challenge, violence was the likely outcome:

> Boston explained what happened when a trader came to collect his debt:
>
> 'I owed someone an ounce of burn. They came in at ten o'clock in the morning, demanding it. I said to him, "Don't come in my cell acting like you're some total Yardie on the street". He said, "What are you going to do, make me get out of the cell?" I said, "If I have to, yes". He said, "You won't be able to". I kicked him in the bollocks and hit him with the jug. Pushed him out of the cell. That was it.'

Every statement in this interaction was a challenge to the other, ratcheting up the risk of violence.

An underlying theme in our discussion of catalysts is that the uses of these tactics have a reciprocal quality – one person's aggressive handling of a conflict brings out aggressive reactions from his counterpart. This is powerfully illustrated in counter-challenges of the sort described by Boston. Diego Gambetta (2002) has explained that the target of a challenge does not merely have the alternatives of fighting or submitting. Rather, the target can also choose to return the threat, forcing the challenger into the fight or flight alternatives. Gambetta (ibid: 145) added that, to make this move, the target needs to put on a convincing show:

> Threatening signals in order to work and persuade the opponent as to the seriousness of the threat have to be credible, of a kind that a mimic could not easily afford. Targets may raise their fists, advance towards the challenger, fix their gaze on and get close to him, while maybe verbally describing what they are prepared to do.

Challenges were an expression of a struggle for dominance between the two participants. When challenges were met by a counter-challenge they had failed to achieve the speaker's intention to gain submission from the recipient. A power struggle became obvious to both parties, and the contest was moved closer to violence – as the preferred means to settle the question of dominance.

Insults

As we have seen, insults are commonplace amongst prisoners. Yet insults did not always result in violence. A crucial element was the link between verbal abuse and conflict. Insults could spark a conflict, by hurting the recipient. During conflicts, insults were used to gain some advantage, for example by ridicule. Finally, there was a public function of insults, as both parties aimed to win a war of words in front of an audience.

When insults were used to ridicule an opponent, other inmates performed an important role. In verbal sparring, insults functioned like punches in a boxing match – the goal was to win the war of words with the most cutting insults. The foes tried to hurt the adversary and expose any weaknesses, forcing them to lose their temper, falter for words or exhibit distress. The following incident provides an example:

Belsay insulted Orton, who had tried to borrow some shower gel. Orton felt humiliated when Crosby – whom he did not know – joined in to ridicule him. Orton made jokes at Crosby's expense as well and insulted him. In terms of the verbal exchange he was the clear winner:

'I was talking to one of them and the other one answered. I called him an idiot and a dickhead and said, "What, you're a ventriloquist and he's the dummy?"'

Orton explicitly stated that, though he did not want to fight, he wanted to win the confrontation:

'Physically I had backed down but I couldn't let the verbal [go]. I was still trying to win the situation but I went too far – I wanted a fight without a fight.'

As we shall discuss below when we consider peer pressure, the audience plays a key role when prisoners engage in verbal sparring. A participant in another incident recalled that, when he traded insults with his foe, the audience provoked each contestant to defend his honour: 'People were laughing, saying, "Are you having this?" to me. I was saying, "No".' Although such verbal sparring was most common amongst young offenders, it occasionally featured in disputes between adults as, for example, in this encounter:

119

Portishead, who was disabled, became annoyed one night because someone was shouting out their window when he was trying to sleep. He called out, 'Get your head down, dickhead'. Crediton, who had been talking to his friend, reacted by telling Portishead to shut up and commenting on his disability. Portishead retaliated by racially abusing Crediton. He concluded by telling him, 'See you in the morning'. The following day Portishead rushed at Crediton and they grappled on the floor until staff intervened.

Undermining behaviour

Undermining behaviour featured in conflicts in two main ways: labelling or showing disrespect for the person's authority.

Labelling impugned the person's reputation or honour. Commonly used labels included accusations that someone had informed on other inmates, committed sexual assaults or harmed children. Other undermining labels included the claim that someone cheated or lied, or was a cell thief. Each of these had the potential to ruin one's reputation. They evoked a desire to defend one's name, and physical force was one means of restoring honour.

Showing disrespect for authority undermined the person in the role, whether that authority was illicit or formally recognized:

> Leeming approached the servery and demanded, 'Serve my food now!' Hornby, the servery worker, took exception and slopped the meal upside down onto the plate. Leeming threw it back in the tray and an argument ensued. At stake for Hornby, in his official role, was the lack of respect shown to him by Leeming.

The most common situation in which illicit authority was undermined was trade:

> Thorpe stated that Alderley owed him some tobacco. When Alderley delayed paying him, Thorpe went to his cell to take what he was owed. Alderley found him there and demanded to know what Thorpe was doing in his cell. Thorpe could not tolerate having his actions questioned by a debtor, so he punched Alderley:
>
> 'He comes into the cell and sees me there. "What the fuck are you doing in my cell?" I could have left it but I couldn't have a fraggle talk to me like that in front of my friends, so I smacked him.'

The foregoing catalysts are primarily verbal, but prisoners were also sensitive to the use of gestures and other non-verbal tactics. These included deception, invasions of space, physical intimidation, hostile gestures and the presence (or threat) of weapons.

Personal invasions

Personal invasions included physical contact, as when one prisoner shoved another one; invasions of privacy; and hostile gestures, such as staring at someone across the room. Personal invasions were often considered to be evidence of intimidation:

Dalton described a bump that led to a fight:

'On association we had an argument over him pushing me. I said, "Oi! What you doing? Can't you say sorry?" I probably swore at him, too. Straight away he says, "Come in the showers". No hesitation.'

In another situation, Skelton had an argument with Plumley's friend. In the classroom, Plumley thought that Skelton was staring at him in a hostile fashion. He described the quick escalation into violence:

'In education – Skelton stared at me for a long time. I said, "What are you looking at?" Skelton swore at me. I walked towards him with the intention of a fight. He took a swing at me but missed. I gave him about five blows – I can't remember if he hit me back. The alarm bell was pressed and staff came.'

Body language played an important role in many of the situations we examined. Gestures often contributed to the escalation of the dispute towards a violent outcome. The following example shows how the recipient of a gesture is free to interpret it in a variety of ways. However, we shall also use this particular conflict to summarize this section on catalysts, showing how threats, challenges, insults and physical gestures worked together to escalate conflicts to a point at which they became violent (the escalator for this case is included in the Appendix):

Sutton was arguing with an officer about the food. Whaley told Sutton to shut up. Sutton said that Whaley also threatened him. Sutton described the next step:

'He came towards me and started to take his jacket off.'

The removal of the jacket indicated Whaley's intention to fight. Sutton understood this, and he interpreted the gesture as an attempt to intimidate him:

> At that point their dispute was interrupted by a second officer, who escorted Sutton to his cell. The officer had inferred from Whaley's body language that the two would soon fight.
>
> In the afternoon, Whaley had a visit. He returned to the wing and friends told him that Sutton was making threats against him. He saw Sutton on the far side of the wing. Rather than rush up to him – which might have attracted attention – Whaley used a non-verbal signal to invite Sutton to a fight:

'He was at his end of the landing and I was near the showers. I opened my arms in a gesture which said, "Come on then, let's take it in the showers".'

Sutton understood and immediately went to the showers. They did not fight, as another officer came into the showers just before they could start. But the tension between the two was aggravated by a further non-verbal signal. Whaley recalled his anger when, in the showers before they fought, he noticed that Sutton had brought a weapon:

'We went in the showers and he put his hand in his pocket and pulled out the plastic knife – he swung a couple of times – no contact was made. I was pissed off when I saw the instrument.'

Whaley stated that the glimpse of the weapon was decisive:

'My mind was set and him pulling out a makeshift knife, that was the ultimate insult.'

By this point, the tension between them was such that both became intent on fighting. Sutton felt anxious about their dispute and believed that a fight would settle it:

'Whaley came up and was threatening me, "I'm going to kill you", etc., talking, talking.'

They met again in the evening. They argued again about whose cell they would use to stage the fight. Eventually, they went to Whaley's cell and had a fight during which both used weapons and both were injured. The dispute that had begun over diet escalated, in part due to body language and the interpretations each made of the intentions of his counterpart.

This sketch shows how threats, verbal abuse, harassment and the other catalysts exacerbated conflict. Each in its own way violated the other person – they could be seen as degrading, intimidating, humiliating and distressing. The hurtful impact of such catalysts provides good grounds for a definition of violence that is open to non-physical harm.

A common theme surfaces as we consider the effects of catalysts, such as accusations, challenges, threats and hostile gestures. These are coercive methods of responding to conflict and they have a powerful impact on the decision-making of both parties. Many prisoners who used force stated that they did not want to fight, but that they had no option. The coercive tactics prisoners used to deal with conflicts influenced the course of their disputes by reducing the options available to the parties involved. As we have described above, a threat or challenge not only forces the recipient into the stark alternatives of submission or aggression, it also commits the speaker to the use of aggressive force if the challenge or threat is dismissed.

The prisoners' use of catalysts demonstrates their lack of options in dealing with conflict. Or, perhaps a more accurate reading would be that, in the heat of the moment, when they were faced with catalysts from their counterparts, the prisoners were unaware of the non-violent options available to them. In either case, this sketch of the techniques prisoners used to manage conflict has shown how these tactics often escalated their disputes (perhaps unintentionally) to a point at which the use of injurious force seemed to be inevitable. Catalysts were a major contributor to prison violence.

Note

1 Our findings about the role of relationships in the conduct of inter-prisoner conflicts are based on a subset of the in-depth interviews: 58 incidents in which violent physical force was used (or its use was disputed) and for which we have recorded the perspectives of both parties. Because views about relationships were recorded after the fact, it is possible that some participants allowed recent events to influence their descriptions of the other party before the incident. For example, we suspect that prisoners used the adjective 'stranger' a little too freely, as if they wished to stress the social distance between them and their adversaries. In our discussions, the terms used – stranger, associate, mate – replicate the language used in the interview. However, the prisoners were free to use other terms to describe their relationships. On the basis of descriptions of the other party as 'wanker', 'tosser', 'fraggle', 'idiot', etc., we added a category of 'pejorative descriptions' to Table 6.1.

Chapter 7

Conflicts II – interpretations, purposes, social context

In social life, there is only interpretation. That is, everyday life revolves around persons interpreting and making judgments about their own and others' behaviour and experiences. Many times these interpretations and judgments are based on faulty, or incorrect, understandings (Norman Denzin 1989: 11).

Interpretations: inferring the other's plan

The ways prisoners interpreted conflict situations were crucial. At one level, recognizing that there was a problem was an act of interpretation. However, as each conflict unfolded, the prisoners were interpreting the other party's words and behaviour, inferring the other party's intentions from what they could observe. We will discuss the role of interpretation at both levels.

Most of the time, the parties to a conflict described the core issue that divided them in similar terms, whether the interests at stake were material, such as access to a telephone, or non-material, such as loyalty. When the two parties gave contradictory explanations of what the problem was about, it was clear that their lack of mutual understanding had contributed to the tension between them. Such misunderstandings were often complex:

> Atworth and Glastonbury inflicted injuries on each other as the culmination of a dispute based on mutual misunderstanding (see the Appendix for the complete escalators).
>
> Atworth had not been in prison before. He found himself on a remand wing and was fearful of being assaulted by other prisoners. He focused his suspicions on another prisoner, Glastonbury. Glastonbury felt that Atworth was acting oddly:

'He kept smiling at me and saying silly stuff. He was acting strange. So I said a couple of words to him, like, "What are you playing at?" '

When Glastonbury insulted and threatened Atworth, Atworth flicked cold water on him. Atworth explained that his intention was to deter Glastonbury:

Q. What did you hope to achieve when you flicked cold water on him?

'Because he done it. I thought I'd do it back to him. Retaliation. If you keep taking it, he'll do just it more and more.'

Q. What happened as a result?

'It is going to annoy him, which it did. He is liable to punch me, but he is going to do that anyway. It probably speeded it up.'

Atworth's fears led him to focus attention on Glastonbury as a potential danger to him. Glastonbury, however, considered Atworth strange and felt anxiety at Atworth's apparent interest in him:

'Really funny. He had a dirty smile on his face all the time – staring at people all the time; not just me.'

As Atworth's fears centred on Glastonbury, Glastonbury felt singled out by Atworth:

'I know he had something against me. He kept on at me all the time.'

Atworth's threats, intended to drive Glastonbury away from him, produced the opposite result. Glastonbury felt he had to pay particular attention to Atworth's behaviour. Their interpretations of each other's intentions put the two on a collision course.

Glastonbury confronted Atworth about his behaviour. When Atworth did not back down, Glastonbury slapped his face. Atworth reacted by throwing a cup of scalding water on Glastonbury. Their conflict had developed out of a misunderstanding, based on different interpretations of the situation.

Other examples of conflicts that arose out of misunderstandings, briefly summarized, included:

Nantwich became upset with Baldersby because he felt Baldersby kept interrupting when he was trying to talk to a mate. Baldersby had been angry at Nantwich for publicly ridiculing him the previous night. Nantwich did not know that Baldersby was angry about the name-calling. Baldersby did not know that Nantwich was annoyed about the interruptions. But minutes later, they were both in the showers. Baldersby threw down his kit bag in disgust, and Nantwich correctly interpreted this gesture as an invitation to a fight.

Halton and Slyne were friends. Slyne was teasing Halton by crowding him as Halton tried to work. Halton warned him to go away. Slyne, sensing that his teasing was having its desired effect, continued to crowd close to Halton. Halton, frustrated by Slyne's failure to take him seriously, shoved Slyne forcefully, but Slyne clung on and tore Halton's T-shirt. Halton reacted by attacking Slyne with his fists.

Misunderstandings could lead to conflicts when the parties involved defined the problem in different ways. Far more common, however, were situations in which the parties both understood what the problem was.

The specialized context of the prison forces people to mix with others whom they do not know well and whose reactions they cannot easily predict. Thus, everyday situations require prisoners to judge the intentions of others with whom they interact: 'At the time, you don't realize what's on someone's mind. They could have family problems or whatever. And when they fight they have all that anger in them coming out.'

In exploring the role of interpretation in the circumstances leading to violence, we need to consider how prisoners in conflict interpreted the behaviour of their opposite number. We have already made the point in Chapter 6 that interests, catalysts and relationships were mediated through interpretation. Prisoners who were insulted, challenged or undermined interpreted what was said and done through their understanding of the speaker's intentions.

Describing the method of symbolic interactionism, Herbert Blumer (1969: 9) explained how exchanges of meaning are essential to human interaction:

A gesture is any part or aspect of an ongoing action that signifies the larger act of which it is a part ... Such things as requests, orders, commands, cues, and declarations are gestures that convey to the person who recognizes them an idea of the intention and

plan of forthcoming action of the individual who presents them . . .
The meaning of the gesture flows out along three lines . . . It signifies
what the person to whom it is directed is to do; it signifies what the
person who is making the gesture plans to do; and it signifies the
joint action that is to arise by the articulation of the acts of both.

In conflicts, each person's interpretations of the other party's actions
and intentions shape their responses. For example, a dispute between
Milford and Shap about left-over food was exacerbated by Milford's
interpretation of a gesture:

Shap took an extra yoghurt. Milford objected. During the argument, Shap raised his arm. In the interview, Shap explained his
response to Milford's complaints:

'I said, "Shut up – I ain't interested. I don't care. Don't run your
mouth off at me". It did escalate – I turned round and lifted my
arm up as if to say, "Shut up".'

In hindsight, Shap stated that his intention in raising his arm was
dismissive, as if to say that arguing about a yoghurt was trivial.
But that was not how Milford interpreted the gesture. Milford
explained:

He raised his hand – to say go away – but it was a threatening
gesture and I said, "Don't raise your hand to me". He said, "What
you going to do about it?" so we squared up and he threw his
hand back to throw a punch, he fell over and we both went sliding
all over the floor, in the food.'

The catalyst – a hostile gesture – aggravated their dispute in part
because Milford interpreted the arm-waving as a threat.

In the dynamic interaction of a one-on-one conflict, each person adjusts
his understanding of his opposite number's overall intentions (what he
was trying to achieve) in the light of individual actions which are open
to interpretation. The influence of interpretation on the development of
a conflict can be seen if we follow a single dispute from beginning to
end. To do this, we will first set out what happened. We will then
revisit the steps to show how each party's interpretations ratcheted up
the potential for violence:

Eastleigh and Kennet were working together. Kennet complained
that Eastleigh wasn't pulling his weight and he threatened him.

Eastleigh tried to avoid Kennet, but first he warned Kennet, 'if he carried on, he'd get one. I'd thump him'. The next day, Kennet again complained and made further threats. Eastleigh went up to him and retaliated with more threats. Kennet picked up a broom to hit Eastleigh; Eastleigh punched him, and Kennet's injuries required stitches.

What role did interpretation play in the escalation of the conflict? Kennet's interpretations of Eastleigh's behaviour defined the conflict between them as an issue of fairness. He believed that Eastleigh was intentionally taking advantage of him, making him do all the work: 'I'm not his lackey. If he's going to take on a job, he should do it. If not, sit in his cell. He was expecting me to do his work for him.' Simultaneously, Eastleigh was interpreting Kennet's actions. Eastleigh explained how he viewed Kennet's threats and complaints:

Q. When he began to threaten you, what was he trying to achieve?

Eastleigh: '[He was] trying to intimidate me, cos I wouldn't rise to his threats.'

At the time, Eastleigh had assumed that Kennet's intentions were to dominate him. Further, he linked this interpretation to his own tactics of avoidance:

'I think because I backed off at the very beginning and wouldn't rise to his taunts, he thought I was a pushover.'

His interpretation that Kennet's threats were intended to gain dominance over him was selective. Kennet had originally complained about Eastleigh's work. It did not seem to occur to Eastleigh that Kennet was trying to achieve a fair distribution of the workload. Eastleigh thought that avoiding Kennet would solve the problem. In fact, his avoidance aggravated the conflict by ignoring Kennet's problems about working together.

Eastleigh also believed that Kennet saw withdrawal as evidence of weakness. This interpretation reduced his own options. From this perspective, he would have to show Kennet that he was tough. His understanding of the situation shows why he reacted to Kennet with an ultimatum, threatening to punch Kennet if he didn't back off:

Q. When you went right up to him and warned him, what were you trying to do?

'That he would shut up and give it a rest.'

Q. What was the impact on him?

'I think he thought I didn't mean it, I wouldn't back it up.'

Eastleigh's threat demonstrated his belief that violence was the only way to change Kennet's behaviour. But the threat also committed Eastleigh to a violent course of action should his ultimatum be ignored. A conflict about work had become a reciprocal stand-off about relative power. Threats and counter-threats left the participants with little room for manoeuvre.

The examples of Eastleigh versus Kennet and Milford versus Shap might seem to suggest that the key factor was whether the recipient of the gesture perceived it as aggressive. But this would be simplistic. Participants told us that they had read into the behaviour of their opposite number an array of intentions, such as to ridicule them; provoke them; demonstrate toughness; set them up for exploitation; show dominance over them; and intimidate them. Indeed, far fewer believed their counterpart's behaviour represented a direct physical threat than saw it as intimidation, or an attempt to dominate, or demonstrate toughness.

Intimidation

In introducing the influence of interpretation we made the point, following Blumer, that, within interactions, interpretation functions on two levels: understanding the meaning of specific actions and seeing the person's wider plan into which the particular action fits. The concept of intimidation straddles both levels: actions (interpreted as being coercive or threatening) and a wider plan (gaining dominance). In other words, intimidation is both a means and an end. Recalling our definition in Chapter 4 of bullying as an enduring relationship of dominance, intimidation can be seen as a tool that can establish a bullying relationship. Alternatively, however, intimidation can serve short-term goals, such as the accomplishment of a one-off robbery. And, significantly, intimidation can be used by both parties to a conflict to try to force the opponent into submission. This last function is described in depth in Chapter 8.

The perception that another prisoner was making an attempt to intimidate them played an important role in the escalation of many – if not most – of the conflicts between prisoners. Our estimate of the prevalence of intimidation in conflicts is deliberately imprecise, for two reasons. First, when a prisoner perceived intimidation, we sometimes found it difficult to determine how influential it was in escalating the conflict. Secondly, intimidation is not a behaviour which is clearly defined and measurable in the same way as assault or theft.

Among the 141 conflicts were situations in which (for example) one prisoner:

- felt frightened even though the other prisoner had not intended to frighten them;
- did not feel frightened even though they believed that the other party tried to scare them;
- felt frightened and reacted by trying to frighten the other; and
- intended to frighten someone else who, instead of being afraid, became angry and violent.

In short, like bullying, there is a subjective element to the definition of intimidation. Someone might shout at you or physically crowd you, yet you might not see it as intimidation. A word, softly spoken, might be full of menace. Judging whether your opposite number is intimidating you requires assessments of the context, the other's intentions and their capacity to harm you. Behaviour the prisoners felt had been intended to intimidate them included harassment, provocation, exploitation, challenges, commands, threats, public humiliation, public labelling, manipulation, physical harassment, tone of voice, verbal abuse, ganging up, racial abuse and exclusion.

Intimidation was perceived by at least one party in many of the incidents we have cited already. For example, Buckden thought Irlam tried to intimidate him to get the broom; Knighton saw it in Pembroke's attempt to take his turn at the computer game; and Midgley assaulted Hatton because of it. Intimidation was central to the disputes between Sutton and Whaley, Milford and Shap, and Eastleigh and Kennet.

Intimidation featured in three distinct guises: first, there was the unilateral use of assaults and threats to coerce another prisoner; secondly, intimidation was sometimes used by both parties to try to force the other to back down; and thirdly, prisoners who felt intimidated by another prisoner might use violence for what they saw as self-defence:

> Grantham said that before she entered the prison a rumour went round that she would be bringing in some heroin. After she got through reception, she was confronted by Mumby and her two

mates, who asked her if she wanted to trade. Suspicious, she asked them, 'Trade what?'

The next day, they confronted her again, this time making explicit their interest in getting her drugs.

'They said, was I frightened to show my drugs?'

The implication that she was scared of them seemed to confirm Grantham's suspicions that Mumby and her mates intended to use intimidation to get hold of her drugs:

'I looked them eye to eye and said, "Nothing frightens me. Why?"'

Grantham interpreted their behaviour – and decided on what she must do – by thinking of what the situation meant within the special atmosphere of the prison:

'It's just a prison thing – make or break. They frightened other women. They thought they could do the same with me.'

In the evening, another inmate told Grantham that Mumby and her mates were talking about assaulting her to take her drugs from her by force. Grantham described what happened in the evening when they met again:

'I prepared for confrontation. The three of them were intimidating on association. I said to the leader, "Come into the toilets"' She went in, all happy. I said, "You must think I have c-u-n-t written on my forehead". She was still smirking – tunnel-vision. Just drugs, drugs and more drugs. I punched her in the face, just once. It was an opening punch. I was giving her an opening: "Okay, Miss Big. Well, come on". She gave a look of sheer terror, shocked. I said, "Go tell your friends I'm in here". I waited, angry. No one came in. And no trouble since.'

Grantham believed that she had resorted to physical aggression in self-defence because she defined their interest in her as intimidatory:

Q. When they were threatening you, what do you think they wanted to achieve?

'They wanted power over me. They wanted to rule me.'

Q. What was the effect of their threats on you?

'Angry. The self-preservation comes in.'

131

A constant theme in situations in which prisoners perceived intimidation was that some other prisoner had tried to force them to do something they did not want to do. This helps to explain why so many prisoners stated that their conflict had been about intimidation. Intimidation, in this sense, aggravates conflict because it entails a clash of interests. Mumby apparently wanted a share of Grantham's drugs. But Grantham did not want to share or trade. Hence, Mumby resorted to intimidation in order to try to achieve her objective.

When violence was seen as appropriate

Blumer argued that, through interpretation, we infer the meaning of any particular action by setting it in the context of a plan or intention. Just as no one has sex all the time, no one is violent all the time. William Gagnon and John Simon (1973) analysed the cues in a social context that reveal when an encounter has sexual overtones. They made the point that encounters between people gradually disclose sexual overtones – some embedded in the setting, some expressed and interpreted by the people involved. Gagnon and Simon argued that social context, in the form of potentiating cues, must be taken into account in explanations of human sexuality.

In conflicts that turned to violence, prisoners' interpretations of their opposite number's intentions fell under three major headings (see Table 7.1). They perceived that the other party was attempting to:

1. wrong them, for example through exploitation;

2. pose a physical threat, putting them in imminent danger; or

3. damage their image or undermine their reputation.

We have classified their concerns as primary or secondary. The most common primary concern was the feeling that the other prisoner had wronged them. Next was the idea that they were in present danger. While few acted primarily because they felt their image was at stake, this was the secondary concern of a substantial number. These inferred intentions acted as potentiating cues. They signalled to prisoners that violence was required.

The interpretations prisoners who used force had made about the intentions of their counterparts influenced their moral judgements afterwards about whether they had been right to use force in the circumstances, and whether they had acted violently. At a glance, the

Table 7.1:   *Interpretations made by prisoners who used force (n = 132)*

Interpretation	Primary concern	Secondary concern	Not a concern
Felt wronged	58	18	56
Feared harm	30	6	96
Threat to image	15	39	78
Other	20	22	90

Table 7.2:   *Explanations given by prisoners who used force (per cent)*

Interpretation	'I was right to use force'	'I was violent to them'
Felt wronged	76	82
Feared harm	96	25
Threat to image	86	73
Other	75	90
Total	80	69

figures in Table 7.2 reveal that prisoners whose primary concern was that they had been wronged believed both that they had been right to use force and that their reaction had been violent. Prisoners who believed they were under threat of harm were even more certain that they had been right to use force, but only one in four believed that they had been violent. Prisoners who acted to protect their image felt that they had been right to use force and that they had been violent. These general observations will inform the descriptions of each type of interpretation of the situations facing the prisoners.

The implication that prisoners often justified their decision to use force by reference to the inferences they made about the intentions of their opposite number chimes with Black's (1998) insight that conflict has a moral basis. This point is also illustrated in Jack Katz's (1988) concept of 'righteous slaughter' as a prime motivation in murder. What kinds of situations led prisoners to believe that their use of force was a moral duty?

Felt wronged

The most common explanation – offered as the primary cause of their use of force by 58 prisoners – was that the other person had wronged them. Behaviour judged to be out of order included theft and fraud, betrayal, personal invasions and making noise.

Some prisoners espoused the view that if you were wronged in prison you had not only the right, but a duty, to retaliate with force: 'If someone takes the piss you do them, full stop. They've done you a wrong 'un, so you've got to do them a wrong 'un.'

But how did prisoners perceive that they had been wronged, and how did they decide that the other party had intended to wrong them?

Fleet asked Broadway if she could use a couple of units on Broadway's phone card. Broadway let her use the phone card, but warned her not to use more than two units because Broadway needed to ring home to speak to her children. Fleet returned to say that she had used all the units and would pay Broadway back when she got her canteen. Broadway told her she would see her later. That evening, she walked up to Fleet and assaulted her.

In her interview, Broadway explained that Fleet knew she needed the phone card units to speak to her children. Thus, she inferred, Fleet must have thought Broadway was weak, someone she could exploit with impunity. It was this interpretation of Fleet's behaviour that led Broadway to attack her.

Amongst the women prisoners interviewed, we observed that exploitation was virtually certain to lead to a violent incident. However, exploitation was only one way in which prisoners perceived that they had been wronged. For example, informing was widely condemned, as this story from a male prison illustrates:

A prison officer placed Dorking on report for some contraband found in Dorking's cell. Other inmates told Dorking that when he walked away from his cell another prisoner – Lydd – went straight to the officer. The implication was that Lydd had informed on Dorking. Dorking described the assault:

'In the evening I was in the TV room. A mate come in and said, "Now's your chance". I leapt up to Lydd's room. I said to Lydd, "Put that plate down". He stands up, facing me, and goes, "What's this all about?" I go, "You know what it's about". He lifts his hands up and sticks out his chest. I punched him in the face – knocked him back on to the bed. Then I was out of there, down the steps and back in the TV room.'

Dorking believed that the wrong done to him – grassing him up – was sufficient reason to launch the assault:

'He shouldn't have opened his mouth. He is taking time off me. If you grass, you expect a slap in the mouth.'

Ironically, in his interview, Lydd agreed that informers deserved to be beaten, but he vehemently denied that he had told officers about Dorking.

Feared harm

An interpretation that the other party intended to harm them influenced the prisoners' responses in two distinct ways. Some took pre-emptive action when they believed that their counterparts were laying plans to assault them. Others used force when the threat of harm was far more immediate. In the latter case, the signs were sometimes so obvious that the prisoner who used force in self-defence did not need to infer an intention to harm:

Haseley said that he had had a problem with Oldham in the queue for kit change. Later, when he was in his cell, Oldham and an accomplice came in with a piece of wood to assault Haseley. Haseley stated that he believed Oldham was attempting to bully him. Haseley did not need to interpret this situation to understand that Oldham's intentions were to harm him.

However, in other situations, the intention to harm was communicated in threats – expressed verbally or by gestures just before force was used:

Desborough said that the gym orderly, Monmouth, had been making threats. Desborough ignored them, thinking that Monmouth would not risk losing his job by assaulting Desborough in front of staff. Desborough explained how he misjudged Monmouth's intentions:

'Monmouth was giving me eye contact. I tried to ignore that. He offered me out [a fight] in the toilets – in front of the gym screws. I said no. I was walking out of the gym. I sensed his presence behind me. I heard name-calling. I carried on walking, ignored it. He lunged at me, threw a punch from behind. I turned round and threw punches back and grabbed hold of him.'

We will discuss using force for the purposes of self-defence in a subsequent section. Here, we focus on the cues that led prisoners to believe that their counterpart was planning to harm them. In a small minority of cases (6 of the 30 whose primary concern was that their counterpart intended to do them harm) one of the parties to a conflict decided to take pre-emptive action. If their interpretation had been accurate, their pre-emptive strikes constituted examples of victim precipitation in that the person who was going to be attacked was the first in the situation to use physical force. However, their interpretation could have been intended to justify their use of force; or, although they had acted on a genuine belief that they were in danger, they may have been mistaken:

Leith suggested in his interview that, in assaulting Selby with a weapon, he had acted in self-defence. The conflict had arisen in the queue for food, after Selby had called out to those ahead of him, telling them to hurry up, and Leith became angry.

Selby stated that Leith had tried to entice him into the showers for a fight, and that he, Selby, had tried to talk him out of fighting:

'He gave me a bad look. He said something, "I'm not scared of you". I said, "You don't want this". I realized it must have been connected with the comment I made in the queue. He said, "Come in the showers". I said, "I'm not going in no showers". He said, "I'll see you tomorrow". I said, "I'm not bothered".'

Leith claimed that Selby had threatened him:

'The next day [after the argument in the food queue] I came back from education and I saw him and his pal and he said, "See you when we get opened up after dinner". So I said, "Sweet". I sat in my cell and thought I might as well do him before he can get to me, so I put a jar in a sock.'

Leith attacked Selby from behind, striking him on the side of the face with the weapon. It was clearly a premeditated assault, but Leith's justification for it rests on his claim that Selby intended to assault him. There is no evidence that Selby had intended to assault Leith. Further, Leith's interview suggests that he felt provoked by Selby's comments in the queue and determined to attack him.

'I went back to my cell and decided straight away that I would carry it on.'

On balance, Leith's claim to have used force pre-emptively to protect himself from assault is unconvincing. (We also cite this incident below, in discussing the influence of racial differences on the social setting of prisons.)

Another example of inferred, future harm was Crediton and Portishead (whose argument we mentioned in Chapter 6).

Portishead objected to the noise Crediton was making late at night. He told Crediton to shut up, adding verbal abuse to strengthen his point. Portishead reacted to Crediton's verbal retorts by telling him, 'I'll see you in the morning'. Portishead argued in his interview that he had good reason to fear that Crediton would attack him the next day. Crediton, to the contrary, firmly stated in his interview that he had put the harsh words in the past and had no desire to fight Portishead.

Portishead explained that a verbal exchange on the morning after their argument drove him to make a pre-emptive assault:

'In the morning, he said, "I'll see you tonight". I thought, I can't wait, cos I felt threatened he would have his mates. I felt threatened. That's why I felt I got to use as much force as I could. Once he said, "tonight", there was no other outcome. Cunt did not want to make love to me. He wanted a fight.'

Crediton explained that he dismissed Portishead's threat as prison talk:

Q. How did you interpret his saying, 'See you in the morning?'

'I've heard that everyday. He says it now; in the morning he will probably say nothing.'

Crediton's account of the incident strongly suggests that he actively tried to avoid fighting Portishead, despite the latter's fears. After breakfast, Portishead pursued Crediton to a cell he was visiting. Crediton described the next steps:

'He had his jumper round his waist and the way he was stood it was like he wanted a fight. He saw me and gesticulated for me to come out of the cell. I turned my back and carried on talking. The door slammed open and Portishead punched me on the top of my head. I jumped up and pushed him. He fell against the door and slipped. I stepped over him and walked out of the cell. I got to the middle of the landing and looked back. I went out in the middle of the landing cos I knew the officers were [there]. I thought that would stop him. Portishead got up and was coming after me. I was trying to get on one side of the table tennis table and keep

him on the other side. He threw a punch at me. I grabbed his arms.
I did not throw a punch.'

As we mentioned earlier, in most of the 30 incidents in which a prisoner believed that the other party planned to harm him, there was obvious and immediate evidence to support the inference. Situations like the accounts from Portishead and Leith were rare. We have examined their logic in some detail, however, because – in our view – both these prisoners were mistaken in their belief that the other party was making plans to harm them. If we are correct and Crediton and Selby had not intended to assault Portishead and Leith, these violent incidents occurred mainly because of a misinterpretation of the intentions of the other party to a conflict. In Chapter 5, we examined the idea that prisoners perceived the prison environment as a place of danger and that this atmosphere of distrust and mutual suspicion is likely to inspire inferences of criminal intent by prisoners about their peers.

Threat to image

A concern for image is an integral part of the code of the street described so graphically by Elijah Anderson (1999), which can be encapsulated in the notion of death before dishonour: 'In the inner-city environment respect on the street may be viewed as a form of social capital that is very valuable, especially when other forms of capital have been denied or are unavailable' (ibid.: 66). James Gilligan's (2001) view is that the desire to injure others arises from the anger caused by feeling that one has been slighted, and is therefore justified in getting revenge. Slighting involves insulting, ridiculing, disdaining, dishonouring – any behaviour that shames people by treating them with contempt and disrespect, as if they are unimportant or insignificant. Respect becomes particularly important in prison when one has little else.

In prison, dishonour could come in the form of being undermined by the suggestion that one was weak and vulnerable, untrustworthy or had committed an intolerable offence. Force was a signal, as much for the audience as for the intended victim. That is, assailants believed that those whose reputations had been smeared could win back some credibility with a violent reaction. Image was a particular concern of young offenders, who were involved in 12 of the 15 cases where the primary concern was the perception that the other was showing disrespect.

A serious assault followed a public accusation of dishonesty:

A group was playing a game during association. One of them, Appleby, began to taunt Penrith, who was losing. Penrith retorted that Appleby had cheated. Appleby offered to start the game again. Penrith felt he had been close to winning and did not want to start a new game. He again accused Appleby of cheating and offered to fight about it. They met in another room and Appleby attacked Penrith with a blade.

Asked at what point did he believe that violence was inevitable, Appleby cited the second allegation of cheating: 'The first time, I knew it was a silly thing to say. But I would have overlooked it. I didn't verbally fight back ... But the second time, that was him done.' Appleby directly linked his decision to commit the assault to the dishonour. He explained: 'Penrith was too mouthy. He called me a cheat. You can't back down from that.' He felt that the label would have affected him had he failed to defend his honour: 'If I had backed down I would have lost face and it could have been taken he was right. If I backed down the grapevine would be, "I didn't defend myself. I must be guilty".'

Nine young offenders explained that they had had to fight because another prisoner had told them to 'suck their mum'. One prisoner explained how he interpreted the remark in a prison context: 'I don't get offended, but that's the borderline – the threshold. If you let them step over and don't punish them, then you aren't willing to defend your honour. If someone takes your pride, they can take anything.'

Prisoners who had used force sometimes explained that they felt a need to prove to others that they were not easy targets for victimization. Consider the case of Darwen and Brough:

Darwen was playing pool and winning. A number of other prisoners were watching him play. Brough challenged him to a game, and they bet on the outcome. At the end of the game, they argued about who had won. Brough reacted to Darwen's claims to the winnings by threatening him, 'I'll see you upstairs'. In response, Darwen attacked Brough with the pool cue.

Darwen explained his reasons, explicitly citing his interpretation of Brough's intentions:

He was trying to show me up in front of other people. I've had it before a few times. I'm only small and when it starts you've got to nip it in the bud. The next day, a lot of people said, not you were right, but you did what you had to do. I've been in a jail before where I thought, leave it and I didn't have a fight and I was ending up having to fight a few people who thought they could do the same.

Darwen believed that his reputation would be damaged by Brough in that other prisoners would consider him to be weak. Prisoners who believed the other person had wronged them felt that physical force was required, but for retribution. And those who inferred that the other person intended to harm them physically believed that they were defending themselves in fighting back. Thus, the interpretations prisoners made about their situation – and in particular about the plans of their opposite numbers – provided a direct link to the purposes for which they decided to use force. Prisoners who considered themselves in danger used force in self-defence. Prisoners who felt they had been wronged used force as punishment. Prisoners who felt their image had been violated used force to shore up their reputations.

Purposes: what injurious force was intended to achieve

Over half the participants interviewed (132/209, see Table 7.1) had used injurious force (in 91/141 incidents, see Table 2.1). When prisoners turned to violence, what did they hope to achieve? Exploring their purposes makes clear that the circumstances in which violence was used were diverse and that the social context influenced the prisoners' sense of what might result from violence. Blalock (1989) defined conflict as a process of mutual harm. He described four 'utilities' of using negative sanctions against another (ibid.: 52):

1. the utility attached to the goal of attaining some specific objective relating to the other party (e.g., obtaining its territory, gaining freedom from exploitation, protecting against invasion, dominating a spouse, or even winning an argument);
2. the utility attached to aggression or to injuring the other party;
3. the utility attached to avoiding injury, punishment by the other party, or other costs associated with the conflict; and
4. the utility attached to gaining status or recognition as a result of participation in the conflict.

Violence in prisons can have effects not only on the antagonist in a conflict, but also on the wider social group of inmates on the landing

Table 7.3: Prisoners' purposes in using force

Purpose	No.	%
Punishment	43	(33)
Retaliation	36	(27)
Demonstrate toughness	33	(25)
Self-defence	32	(24)
Defend honour	30	(23)
Settle differences	24	(18)

or throughout the establishment. Effects on the wider prison community – the social sphere – are largely symbolic in that witnesses and other prisoners on the wing draw inferences from each act of violence. (In Chapter 5 we considered the relationship between vicarious victimization and fear.) Our analyses of inmates' purposes are listed in Table 7.3. This table is based on all interviewed prisoners who used force. The purposes are not mutually exclusive and are teased out more fully in the following sections.

Punishment

Punishment was inflicted on individuals who had transgressed prison norms. Physical assaults as punishment performed the same functions as punishment in other areas – to deter undesirable behaviour; to set boundaries of tolerable conduct (denunciation); or to gain satisfaction for some wrong (retribution). In these circumstances one prisoner (or a group) assumed the authority to impose sanctions. By definition, we limited the behaviour that could attract punishment to identified transgressions of prison norms, such as cell theft, informing, sex offences, bullying or disruptive noise-making. The use of violence for punishment was most common in the women's prison:

> Ventnor and Plumpton learned that Morland had informed on them. Ventnor threatened Plumpton; then, later, Morland assaulted her. Ventnor explained their motives:

> 'She'd grassed people up. She broke the worst rule ever. If you let someone get away with it, it is telling others it is no problem. You got to be seen doing something. She has got to pay for it.'

Didcot's punishment of Hastings exhibited signs of deterrence, denunciation and retribution:

Didcot and Hastings did not know each other outside prison, but shortly after Hastings's arrival on the wing, the two became friends. Didcot explained how the conflict arose:

'This girl who was on the wing [Hastings] was in our cell over tea time. Our tobacco went missing.'

Didcot shared her suspicion that Hastings had stolen from her with other women on the wing and they decided that Hastings had to be punished:

'Out on exercise we were telling others. Sugar, Nivea, a few other things had gone missing. We all agreed I would have to deal with it.'

Didcot knew that she risked being caught and punished by staff if she assaulted Hastings, but she felt she had to punish her for the good of the community:

'We are 100 girls and we always leave our doors open.'

Q. Was this about revenge?

'Yes, for her stealing my tobacco and other girls' belongings.'

Acting with the support of others, Didcot lured Hastings to her cell and assaulted her, as she described:

'I planned it. I timed it right at 25 past eight. On association. I'd got it organized for two girls to stand by the door. Once they saw I was all right, they closed the door. I said, "I think you stole my tobacco". She said, "Oh, I'm not having this about the tobacco again", and went to walk out and that is when I put the first one in. I hit her in the face. She grabbed my hair. I put her on the floor. I banged her head on the floor. The two closed the cell door. She scratched my face. Loads of other inmates came to the door. Two said that officers were coming. I stopped and freshened up.'

A major drawback of inflicting physical harm in reaction to wrong-doing in prison was that the standards of proof were weak. This meant that there was a significant risk that the physical punishment could be unjust. There is a parallel here with private justice outside prisons, in circumstances where communities do not recognize the legitimacy of the official forces of law and order (for an account of the consequences of such a situation in Northern Ireland, see the report by McEvoy and Mika 2002):

Devizes agreed to a deal whereby money would be exchanged outside, and then Staines would give Devizes drugs. Devizes recounted:

'Staines had had a visit. I was expecting my gear. Staines came back and said, "Devizes, the money hadn't turned up". Staines gave me a bit anyway, but it wasn't anywhere near what I had paid for. I got vexed. If I'd have let that happen I would have lost face. So I went in there – plus I was fucking angry. I went in and started fighting. We were on the floor. Two weeks later, after the fight, the Principal Officer came and said they hadn't sent the money.'

Five men went to Griff's cell with weapons, intending to beat him up. They had been told details of Griff's offence. Griff received them into the cell then asked them first to read the depositions from the trial. One of the would-be attackers agreed. The depositions gave satisfactory proof of Griff's claim not to have done what they thought and his accusers left the cell.

In addition to these transgressions of prison norms, we also came across incidents in the four prisons that concerned imported grievances. These included assaults on prisoners who had burgled the aggressor's friend's house; allegedly given evidence against co-defendants; and had the details of an offence exposed in the press.

When asked what he was hoping to achieve, the instigator of the last-mentioned assault replied, 'Nothing, straightforward punishment'.

Retaliation

Retaliation arose when a participant reacted to injurious force in kind. Our concept of retaliatory violence was intended to provide a precisely defined situation. We did not include as retaliation the use of injurious force in response to verbal abuse or exploitation (which we referred to as punishment, see above). Rather, retaliation was used to describe conflicts in which one person had inflicted physical harm. In response, the victim of the first assault (or his allies) launched a physical attack on the original perpetrator (or his allies).

A clear example of retaliation was provided by two young offenders whose mate had been assaulted on another wing. Asked what the fight was about, one of the assailants, Haughton, stated:

Race and revenge. When Sleights fought my mate on A wing, it was racist. He got moved to this wing. First time I saw him I asked, "Are you Sleights?" He says, "Yeah". I was going to fight him on Saturday, and I got someone to call him to the shower, but he wouldn't come. His friend said, "One on one", and I said, "Yeah, in the shower". I thought it would be one on one, fists only. But he arrives with three other boys and I was with my friend in the shower waiting. Sleights came in first. My mate threw the first blow and we started fighting. His mates came in behind. We were fighting for a couple of minutes. There was blood all over. I picked up a chair and I was going to hit Sleights, who was on the floor, but someone shouted, "Screws are coming", and I put the chair down. It was finished for me then.'

Q. What were you trying to achieve?

'Telling him not to mess with my co-d [co-defendant].'

Q. What did it actually achieve?

'That he would never say anything to my co-d again. It achieved its objective.'

This was clearly retaliation and not self-defence. The time delay between the original assault and the retaliatory fight, together with Haughton's explicit intentions in setting up the fight, established that his purpose was revenge.

Retaliation exhibits tit-for-tat thinking, when insults, threats or physical force were used to react in kind to the behaviour of another. Retaliation is often expressed as an intention to hurt the other one in return for a previous harm. A particular form of retaliation occurs when someone uses excessive force resisting an attack:

Eaton described a situation in which he struck first and believed he was acting in self-defence:

'I was having a shower and he comes running in with a pool ball in a sock. He swings the ball and I ducked and threw a punch which connected and I grabbed the sock. He tried to head-butt me. He said, "There's a screw coming", but there wasn't anyone and another inmate said, "No, no. It's all right. Carry on". We both had hold of the sock and were swinging punches with one hand. We both slipped and fell over on the floor. He bit me first on the back of my neck. Another inmate took the sock from him. His arm was in front of my face so I bit it. We were still throwing blows and then we saw the officer so we stopped. He ran out of the shower and I dried myself.'

Initially, as Eaton was attacked by an inmate wielding a weapon, Eaton's own use of force was clearly to defend himself from imminent physical harm. However, Eaton continued to fight after he had an opportunity to walk away. An aggressor with a weapon who attacked an unarmed prisoner gives a strong example of self-defence when there was a genuine risk of imminent physical harm. But despite the fact that Eaton's initial use of force was defensive, he continued to play an active role after the immediate danger had passed.

The violent incident with which the book opens, between Stewkley and Warslow, is another example of disproportionate force:

Warslow complained loudly when he thought Stewkley was jumping in the queue. They argued angrily but Stewkley left before the situation escalated. Later, Stewkley went to Warslow's cell to discuss their differences. Warslow tried to remove Stewkley from his cell physically. Stewkley reacted by assaulting Warslow. His use of violence in quick response to the use of force by Warslow signified retaliation:

'He started pushing me. He threw me out like I was a rag doll, and I thought that was humiliating, so I retaliated by punching him in the face. He picked me up and steamed me into the wall. I said to myself, "he's big but he's slow". He's still trying to grapple with me – I'm still hitting him to the head and face. I was upset because I didn't want to resort to that over something so trivial. I don't remember it at all but he fell down and I carried on kicking him.'

Stewkley was explicit that he used force in retaliation. He was out of the cell and did not need force to defend himself against further attacks from Warslow. He chose to return to Warslow to hurt him as a result of feeling humiliated.

We analysed the balance between fights and assaults. Unlike the women's prison, in the YOI mutual fighting was more common than unilateral assaults. Yet, young offenders were least likely to use force in retaliation. This requires some explanation. While the young offenders were much more likely to engage in mutual exchanges of physical force (fights) than other groups, this seemed to be because they often fought as a way of trying to resolve disputes; not because they were more likely to seek physical retribution.

Toughness

Prisoners who used force to demonstrate their toughness expressed a fear that other inmates would perceive the lack of a violent response as evidence of weakness and vulnerability. Their aim was to send a message to the whole wing or prison not to try to exploit or bully them. This purpose brings together prisoners' objectives in using force and the impact on them of the social context (the subject of the next section.) The victimization data presented in Chapter 3 showed conclusively that prison settings are risky. Yet it is important to bear in mind that the majority of prisoners did not perceive that they needed to demonstrate their toughness. Was the claim that others would see a non-violent reaction and conclude that the prisoner was weak merely a rationalization for assaulting someone?

The purpose of demonstrating toughness was confined to about a quarter of the prisoners who had used force (see Table 7.2). One of the factors that led to their decision was inferred peer pressure.

We asked all 209 prisoners interviewed for the conflicts study if they believed that other prisoners would think less of them if they had not used force, and obtained 153 responses. The three different replies were 'yes', 'no' and 'I don't care'. Opinions were evenly divided between prisoners who believed that others would think less of them (43 per cent of those responding) and those who felt that others would not (41 per cent.) Fewer prisoners (16 per cent) said they did not care. Clearly there was a balance of views on the possibility that other inmates would perceive a reluctance to use force as a weakness.

Prisoners who used force were only slightly more likely to believe that the presence of other inmates made violence more likely. Around half (53 per cent of those responding) said that the presence of others made violence more likely, while 39 per cent said it made no difference, and 8 per cent said others made violence less likely. Thus, not all the prisoners who used force were motivated by concerns about the wider audience.

One inmate's reflections on a fight illustrate wider concerns about appearing vulnerable to other inmates: 'I wasn't really feeling aggressive. It was just something that had to be done in order to protect myself. If you don't do something against the first one in prison, you will have to do it with two. I wouldn't react the same way outside.'

Gambetta (2002: 130) made the point that prisoners place a high premium on information about their fellow inmates. They need to know who is a threat, who is a potential victim, who might be an ally, because their survival depends on this information:

In the natural course of their interactions prisoners observe each other with a keen eye, and the acquisition of mutual knowledge seems indeed a motivation for much of what they do and say to each other . . . They display and observe signs about each other, especially signs that convey information about their fighting prowess.

Gambetta suggested that prison violence can be seen as a form of communication. The prisoner uses violence – and, more important, signals of his fighting prowess – to communicate to other prisoners that they should not try to victimize him.

An abstract distinction about the intended audience might further clarify what we mean by demonstrations of toughness. The key is whether the violence was aimed primarily at an individual foe or was undertaken for the symbolic purpose of conveying toughness to a wider audience. The purpose of demonstrations of toughness was to show the other inmates on the wing – the sea of unfamiliar faces – that one could not be victimized with impunity (a kind of general deterrence): 'If it wasn't for the other inmates, we wouldn't have fought. Most prison fights aren't about being angry. They're about what other inmates will think of you if you don't fight.'

Two indicators that violence was used to demonstrate toughness were that it was intended to be public and that the inmate who used violence in this way believed that prisoners who don't show a willingness to use violence are weak.

In contrast, other prisoners felt intimidated by a particular foe, and decided to assault them (a case of special deterrence). Their primary objective was to make their opponent give them respect. These prisoners were narrowly focused on one other prisoner. These were dyadic shows of force, and they appeared in power contests (see further, Chapter 8).

It is important to qualify the distinction between shows of force for the wider audience and for the individual opponent. In practice, of course, the two overlap to varying degrees, depending on the aims of the individual prisoner and the circumstances in which the conflicts were staged. Confrontations that were conducted in public view – during times of association, in queues for the phone or food, in the gym – increased the importance of the opinions of the wider audience.

Other concerns could inspire prisoners to use violence to demonstrate toughness. When debtors refused to pay back, good business sense sometimes suggested that a public assault was required. Earlier, we cited an incident in which Thorpe felt undermined when he was insulted by a debtor. Thorpe explained that part of his motivation in assaulting Alderley was to protect his wider business interests:

Q. Can you think of any other way you could have got the tobacco instead of fighting?

'You mean that cog skills shit? Should I be persuasive/aggressive/ assertive? No! If I had tried another way he'll think I'm soft hearted and others would do it, too. Can't afford to do that. Business is business. I wanted it back, fast. I didn't want to wait around for a month for him to pay the debt.'

Thorpe's concern for his reputation in the eyes of the general audience on the wing demonstrates the inferred peer pressure which we explore as a motivation to violence.

Violence was most likely to be used for the purpose of demonstrating toughness in the young offender institution:

Hapton assaulted Leyland, in front of others to show, contrary to expectations, he was not afraid of fighting someone who had insulted him (see the Appendix). Leyland, a big, strong inmate, had been insulting and teasing Hapton for some time. Other inmates had also started insulting him. Hapton stated:

'They started dissing me and everyone did it because I didn't want to fight.'

He decided to fight with Leyland to show that he was not afraid to stand up for himself. He knew he wouldn't win the fight, Leyland was physically superior, but he stated he did it 'So that people would stop taking me for a fool'.

Hapton carried out the assault when there were others around to pass the word on, and an officer close by to step in and stop it. Hapton punched Leyland in the face and a fight ensued. According to witnesses, Leyland landed far more blows and Hapton came off worse. Notwithstanding the fact that Hapton lost the fight, he believed he achieved his objective. He stated:

'They know now I'm not having it no more. I'm showing them that I can stand up for myself and however big you are I'm not taking it no more. It has stopped people from dissing me.'

We were unable to follow up Hapton's prison career to learn if he was subject to further victimization. Hapton's behaviour presents a possible ulterior motive for attacking a stronger prisoner in public. If the stronger inmate fought back, there was a good chance that he would be punished by the prison authorities. By using the system, the weaker prisoner can thereby punish his tormentor.

There is an important distinction between being tough and putting on the appearance of toughness. Most of the prisoners who used force did not express a need to convince others that they were tough. Prisoners who used force because they feared future victimization may have been – like Hapton – targeted by others who perceived weaknesses that would make them easy prey.

Gambetta (ibid: 133) stated that, despite prisoners' best efforts to mimic the evidence of toughness, other prisoners will eventually catch them out: 'Attempts to mimic the signs of toughness are . . . short lived in prison . . . One may fool some prisoners some of the time, but a long sequence of forced encounters with a variety of inmates makes it unlikely that false displays of toughness will succeed for long.' This suggests that the prisoner who is not tough faces a dilemma: he does not want to be victimized routinely, but he knows he does not want to fight and that other prisoners will soon discover his lack of toughness. There is a way out of the predicament and that, according to Gambetta, is for the prisoner to develop genuine toughness.

Richard McCorkle (1992) analysed the defensive postures assumed by prisoners in Tennessee. He described demonstrations of toughness in these terms (ibid.: 161): 'Unless an inmate can convincingly project an image that conveys the potential for violence, he is likely to be dominated and exploited.'

He concluded that prisoners responded to the risk of being victimized in one of two ways: either they became withdrawn from prison culture, keeping themselves to themselves; or they adopted an aggressive stance towards others. McCorkle analysed the extent to which the two strategies were effective. In Chapter 4, we showed that there was a significant overlap between victims and perpetrators of assault, but not of robbery. McCorkle's findings provide a parallel. He found that prisoners who adopted an aggressive stance tended to be protected from robbery, but not from assault. Prisoners who withdrew from inmate society tended to be less likely to be assaulted, but more likely to be robbed. Although the results are bleak, their relevance here is to suggest that the explicit aim of demonstrations of toughness – to deter potential predators – is likely to have mixed effects. Such shows of fighting prowess might reduce the likelihood of being robbed while increasing the likelihood of being assaulted.

The need to demonstrate toughness is a common theme in the ethnographic and anthropological literature. In his examination of an American ghetto, Anderson (1999: 27) argued that 'the general level of violence tends to keep irritation in check – except among those who are "crazy". In this way, the code of the street provides an element of social organization and actually lessens the probability of random violence'. Furthermore (ibid.: 72):

> The code revolves around the presentation of self. Its basic requirement is the display of a certain predisposition to violence. A person's public bearing must send the unmistakable, if sometimes subtle, message that one is capable of violence, and possibly mayhem, when the situation requires it, that one can take care of oneself.

Here, there are clear continuities between the prison and the street.

Self-defence

To protect oneself against a direct threat of harm with a reasonable degree of force is by definition self-defence. This purpose figured as an immediate reaction to having been attacked or, less often, as a pre-emptive assault in response to threats or behaviour interpreted as intimidatory.

Claims of self-defence were easy for the respondents to make in retrospect. To determine whether there was any basis for the claim, we had to judge whether:

- there was a genuine risk of physical harm;

- force was necessary to avoid being harmed; and

- the amount of force used was proportionate to the demands of the situation.

This last criterion was the most delicate, as the amount of force needed to escape depended on the particular circumstances of the assault. In some cases, where the victim of an assault used injurious physical force, their intentions were clearly not to harm the opponent, but merely to escape the danger:

> We have already discussed the incident that arose between Selby and Leith. Selby was unexpectedly assaulted whilst in the food queue by Leith, who used a weapon. Selby described the assault and his response:
>
> 'We were in the queue and suddenly I heard, "Selby look out!" and I felt the blow to the side of my head. I looked up and saw

him swinging a sock with a glass jar in it. I tried to get away but there were too many people in the way. He kept hitting me with the jar. I tried to keep him away with kicks whilst he's still hitting me. I managed to get my head through the doorway and as he tried to swing it again it caught the bars and the jar broke and cut my hand. Normally there are officers but I couldn't see any at all when I was being attacked. Once I got through the gate I saw officers who accused me of fighting and said they didn't see the attack. They pushed me against the wall and said I had been kicking him. Blood was dripping from my hand. I tried to tell them what happened, and they kept saying, "But you were kicking him".'

Selby's kicks – which might otherwise have appeared to be aggressive – seemed to be required by the situation in which he found himself. Although a kick could deliver injurious force, in this case it was used in self-defence.

The distinction between sufficient and reasonable force (self-defence), and excessive, aggressive force (gratuitous violence) is analytically clear. But it is hardly surprising that the fine balance was not so easy to determine by prisoners when they were being assaulted. In the interviews, using hindsight, participants placed great weight on their interpretation of the opposite number's intentions in judging whether force had been appropriate. Prisoners who claimed to have acted in self-defence believed they had been right to use injurious force and did not characterize their actions as violence (as shown in Table 7.2).

In our judgement, approximately one-quarter of the prisoners who used force were trying to defend themselves. However, not all these prisoners used force only whilst they were at risk of imminent harm. Furthermore, in two situations *both* the parties claimed that they had been acting in self-defence. Three others who said they had been acting in self-defence conceded in their interview that they had struck the first blow.

We have already cited the game of pool between Darwen and Brough. After arguing about who had won, Brough told Darwen, 'I'll see you upstairs'. Darwen's interpretation of that remark suggests that, in front of other prisoners, he felt physically at risk. His response was to attack Brough with the pool cue.

Darwen explained his interpretation: 'I'm thinking in these jails "upstairs" means serious – bottles or stuff. I'd have got whispers saying he's going to stab you, so I needed to do something there, not later.' Each of the purposes claimed by prisoners who used force –

most obviously self-defence – was subject to the possibility that the respondent would present an account that minimized their culpability for the use of force, recalling Sykes and Matza's (1957: 209–11) five techniques of neutralization (denial of responsibility, denial of injury, denial of victim, condemnation of condemners and appeal to higher loyalties).

Defend honour

One in four prisoners who used force did so to defend their honour. We have already seen (Table 7.1) that prisoners often interpreted the actions of the other party as a threat to their image and when this was the case, the great majority of them felt they had been right to use force. Two incidents will serve to give a flavour of the characteristic circumstances in which the defence of honour led to violence.

Marston and Cleator fought each other after a month of reciprocated insults and threats. Cleator explained that their dispute started when, one night, Marston shouted out that Cleator had been jailed for rape. Cleator retaliated by claiming that Marston was a rapist. Cleator described the effect Marston's original insult had had on him, knowing that other prisoners had heard: 'If I could have got him through the wall I would have done some damage there and then. It would have been swingers [a fist fight] straight off, or worse. Everybody hears. It is all about air time.' Cleator was a strong, confident prisoner, who had no reason to fear that other inmates would consider him soft or weak. Yet he believed that the stain on his honour required an aggressive response.

In the second incident, Cautley was approached by a friend who complained that a third inmate, Aston, was intimidating him. Cautley agreed to intercede with Aston. He explained that his intentions were not to fight, but to stand up for his friend:

> I went to talk to Aston on association. I told him he couldn't talk to my friend and disrespect him. He didn't apologize. I wanted to sort it out, but I got angry with his attitude. He gee'd me up. He was making me look like a fool in front of people. Because he wouldn't apologize, before I could even think, I said, 'If you don't like it, you can take it to the showers'. We went into the showers and had a fight. Sometimes I sit on my bed and think, 'Why did I say that?'

In a sense, Cautley was acting on behalf of his friend's honour in confronting Aston. But when Aston became indignant, Cautley felt his own honour was at stake.

Settling differences

Fighting was commonly seen by young offenders as the best method of resolving a dispute, of settling differences. This was very rarely the case for women or adult males. Only one of over 40 incidents in the women's prison featured the use of force for this purpose.

The use of violence to settle disputes was often signalled by fights taking place by prior agreement. It is possible that inmates felt that the outcome of a fight would be indisputable, whereas a verbal exchange could always lead to arguments about who got the better of whom. For many young prisoners, fighting was the only way they could think of to deal with the problem, even if they knew a fight would not produce a clear winner.

Amongst young offenders, invitations to fight were frequent, as both parties often looked to fighting as a means of conflict resolution:

> York and Chelford were co-workers. York told how he and Chelford got into a fight. In passing, it is worth noting that the timespan between the beginning of the dispute and the recourse to violence as a means of settling the conflict was very short:

> 'He started complaining about work. I said, "You're always complaining". He took offence and responded badly. I took offence with the way he responded to me. Other inmates were present who all heard the argument. I said to him, "Do you want to sort this out in the showers?" He said, "Okay". We went into the showers and had a fight.'

A particular set of circumstances indicated an inmate's belief that fighting would sort the problem out – like York, the young prisoners invited their opponent to a fight:

> As described earlier, Nantwich insulted Baldersby, and Baldersby took offence. Baldersby described the difficulties they had in settling the issue:

> 'Next morning, going to the gym, we was supposed to fight. But then he was with his people. I was with mine. So he went, "Fuck it. Leave it till there's no officers, Saturday morning". Then he came up to me Saturday and says, "Let's not fight now. Make it the afternoon". So we went down the showers and we fought.'

Why were young offenders so much more likely to believe that fights could be used to settle their differences? Gambetta (2002) offered one clue: his analyses of violence as communication suggest that young offenders lack information about their peers, in part because few of them will have established a history of fighting in the institution. Perhaps more important, young offenders might not have developed the skills they needed to read the signals given off by others.

But the young offenders' accounts of their disputes imply a broader influence of their perspective on fighting. They seemed genuinely to believe that violence could provide a solution to their differences, in contrast to the sense of resigned necessity we found in adults who fought. The young offenders did not fully appreciate the damage that fighting did to their relationships – indeed, it was among young offenders that we encountered the notion that fighting created bonds of friendship and mutual respect. Finally, it might be that young offenders were slower to recognize conflicts as they developed, and then more impatient to bring the conflict to an end. As Sutton said after two attempts to fight Wharton had been interrupted by staff: 'Talking, talking – I was getting tired of this. We had to settle this, we had to have a fight.'

Social context: the setting for conflict

Chapter 3 described the social setting of prisons in terms of victimization rates. Chapter 5 set out the social context in terms of prisoners' understandings of the dangers they faced – their perception of the prison as a risk environment. Thus, we do not need to repeat those aspects of the social setting here. Instead, our focus is on the impact of the special characteristics of prisons on the development and escalation of conflicts between prisoners.

Anderson (1999: 76) described cycles of violence and the viciousness of revenge attacks: 'People often feel constrained not only to stand up and at least attempt to resist during an assault but also to "pay back" – to seek revenge – after a successful assault on their person . . . a credible reputation for . . . vengeance . . . is strongly believed to deter future assaults.' With regard to prison sociology, the potentially cyclical nature of violence is well understood. Looking at the early 1930s, Clemmer (1940: 86) put it thus: '. . . when one prisoner overcomes the other so that he can fight no more, accommodation has occurred . . . However, the beaten prisoner may plan for a month to harm his foe . . . Thus accommodation may lead to further conflict, or a stable adjustment.'

Conflicts necessarily entail both interpersonal and social-structural dimensions. This section explains how prisoners' choices are constrained by the prison setting. Some of the limitations on prisoners' options reflect how prison authorities regulate the conduct of inmates and some of them are products of prisoner culture. We conclude the chapter by examining two areas in particular: peer pressure and racial and ethnic tensions.

The prison regime limits options (restricts autonomy) in that it imposes material deprivations, inevitably generating competition for scarce resources: 'There's too many people. There's only four phones for three wings and one phone is broken at the moment. I waited 45 minutes for a call the other night.' Prisoners' freedom of movement is controlled: they have little chance to avoid situations in which they feel at risk: 'You have to react to situations in prison that you could ignore outside.' Inmates must interact with others whom they do not know and may have good reason to distrust or fear: 'You're bunched up together. You can't put that many men together without some sort of friction.'

Another factor is the diversity of the population: 'Being in prison, all these people, it's a place for trouble. It's more likely to be a place for fights.' The emotional stress of prison life plays a role also: 'In prison there is a lot of anger and a lot of fights for stupid reasons.' The loss of privacy increases the potential for conflicts to arise: 'It's the constant in your face all the time. The way of the prison is everyone knows everyone's business. It's conflict straight away – there's tension all the time.'

Prisoner culture also shapes conflict, in a variety of ways. Trading and the risk of exploitation are widespread (see Chapters 3 and 4): 'If they can take what's yours without you knowing, they'll take it.' Prisoners are conscious of the danger of being physically harmed (see Chapter 5): 'Last time I was here one person was stabbed for switching TV channels.' The conventional response to being wronged by another inmate is to react with violence: 'I've been brought up in these environments since I was nine. I know not to let other people take the piss.' Prison norms dictate that conflicts must be resolved without turning to staff – informing officers is almost universally condemned (as we will discuss in Chapter 9): 'Probably grasses are just as low as sex offenders in my eyes.'

Peer pressures in the social context

As we have seen, few violent incidents went unobserved by other inmates. In exploring the use of force to demonstrate toughness we introduced a distinction between direct and inferred peer pressure.

Direct peer pressure was involved when one or both participants were explicitly encouraged to fight by other inmates. This factor was cited by at least one participant in a quarter of the incidents.

The most direct forms of peer pressure arose out of specific situations, in response to which others (usually inmates) advised the respondent to use force:

Corfe exchanged insults with Haydock while both were locked in their cells. The next day, Corfe sneaked up behind Haydock during association and struck him in the back with a chair. Corfe referred to the influence of the other inmates, the audience:

'I'm in one cell. There's two between us. When I shout, the one next to him is going, "Are you having that?" And then when he says something, the one next to me goes, "Are you having that?"'

In another incident, the role of a third inmate was to promote the fight to the extent that he cleared out his cell so that it could be used as a boxing ring. Two other young offenders described a conflict that was exacerbated by other inmates' provocation of both participants.

Cleator
'Everyone is going, "It's a shower thing". It wasn't an argument between us – it was other people. They wanted to see me fight.'

Marston
'People were starting an argument out the window, wanting me and him to fight.'

Dudley and Barnton fell into an argument as they and other inmates were going off to education. Barnton made a threat and Dudley agreed to fight when they returned to the wing. Dudley, who was interviewed about the incident, cites the influence of the other inmates who were present:

'They kind of played a big part really. If there had been just the two of us it would have blown over.'

Also:

'After he said he was going to hit me, they were all encouraging me to sort it out. They'd all say, "Oh, no! Are you going to take that?" – all that stuff. A lot of people in prison like to see fights, but not get in fights.'

Much of the evidence available to us about the role of peer pressure was based on suppositions by the participants about the judgements or behaviour of third parties. In most cases, we lacked the perspective of these peers. When participants told us that their peers wanted to see a fight, this belief reflected, to some extent, a desire to justify their involvement in violence. This is less true of disputes in which the respondent reported on the advice he received from others to assault his counterpart. When third-party inmates tell the participant, 'you've got to punch him', the evidence of an attempt to provoke violence is obvious.

Racial and ethnic tensions

Racial and ethnic differences were significant in exacerbating disputes. Violence inspired by racial hatred was rare – or at least not made explicit by those we interviewed. However, misunderstandings were fuelled by cultural diversity. When inmates were asked what the conflict was about, 15 participants (in 13 incidents) identified race as a factor. However, they were not always unanimous about this, and some inmates revealed during the interview that they thought there was some racial motivation even when they did not indicate this as a response to the question. Upon closer scrutiny, we identified a total of 21 incidents where at least one participant said that race had played some role in the incident.

Returning to two incidents discussed already we will describe the particular influence of racial differences in an escalating dispute. The first conflict arose between two strangers, Selby and Leith, in the dinner queue. Selby called out to those in front of him to hurry up and – according to Leith – Selby 'kissed his teeth', which Leith interpreted as a sign of disdain. Later, Leith assaulted Selby with a weapon. In his interview, Selby identified a racial motive for the assault by Leith: 'I've heard he's a racist – bad attitude.' Leith initially denied that race was a factor. He explained: 'Selby said something like, "Hurry up", then he kissed his teeth. I didn't like that and I said, "What's your problem?"' Nevertheless, later in the interview Leith conceded: 'I could say it's because he's black. It's the way he was talking. I don't let no one talk to me like that.'

Even when both parties suggested that the dispute had been about race, interpretations of intentions and the power balance between the parties could exacerbate or ease conflicts.

We have also mentioned the incident in which Ripon assaulted Checkley and Checkley reacted with excessive force. Racial differences were a key factor in the escalation of the conflict, but perhaps not in an expected way. Because the racial dimension of their conflict revolved round interpretations and cross-cultural misunderstandings, it is worth considering it in more detail:

Checkley was standing outside her cell, talking in Punjabi to her friend. Ripon walked past them. At that moment, Ripon was making a joke about her friend's smoking. They laughed. Ripon, who was already past them, heard their laughter and stopped. She convinced herself that she had been the butt of their humour. Angry that they would ridicule her, she went back to them and assaulted Checkley, grabbing her throat and forcing her back into her cell.

Ripon explained her thinking:

'Coming back from tea they started chatting in their own language and started laughing at me, so I knew it was about me.'

From Checkley's perspective, Ripon came from nowhere when she was having a joke with her friend. Checkley interpreted the assault as racially motivated in part because she knew there was no valid reason for it:

'Because it was unprovoked and I've never spoken to her before so we had no differences. It can only have been racist.'

It was only after the assault had begun that Ripon revealed the reason she attacked Checkley, as Checkley recalled:

'She came up to me and grabbed my throat and said, "Don't talk about me", and pushed me in my cell. She started to punch me and she said, "Fucking Paki!" a couple of times.'

From Checkley's perspective, it was certainly perverse of Ripon to react to the use of Punjabi in this way. Ripon confirmed that her anger was provoked by her inability to understand what they were saying:

'Before I went past they weren't laughing. When I walked past, they spoke in their language and burst out laughing. Why not speak in English? It was something they didn't want me to hear.'

Ripon came to this conclusion because she set Checkley's humour in the context of a dispute that had begun the previous day, and of which Checkley was unaware. Ripon explained:

'My mate and I barged in the [food] queue. I do it all the time. Two girls [Checkley and her mate] were arguing with my mate about it. I was waiting for them to start and I would wade in.'

Thus, Ripon inferred that Checkley was ridiculing her because Ripon had earlier exploited Checkley and her friend. Her motivation for launching the assault was clearly driven by racial intolerance: 'Why not speak in English?' The misunderstanding which led to the assault was 'about race', but it could easily have been prevented. As Checkley stated in her interview when asked what could have been done to prevent it:

'She could have asked me, calmly, what I had said in Punjabi, and I'd have told her.'

Crucially, when race was a factor in violent incidents, racial differences and racist motivations formed only part of the picture. Styles of responding to conflict, body language and peer pressure could exacerbate or ease conflicts, whether the initial spark involved racial differences or not.

Chapter 8

Power contests

Violence is nothing more than the most flagrant manifestation of power (Hannah Arendt 1970: 35).

Thus far, we have sought to explain prison violence in the context of the six layers of the conflict pyramid:

1. Interests (goods such as drugs, games or phone cards; and values such as self-respect, honour, fairness or loyalty).

2. Relationships (the degree of intimacy between the parties).

3. Catalysts (behaviours that tended to drive the conflict towards a violent outcome).

4. Interpretations (both of the demands specific to the prison setting and of the intentions of other parties to the disputes).

5. Purposes (punishment, retaliation, to demonstrate toughness or protect one's honour).

6. Social context (how prisoners' choices are constrained by the prison setting).

Power relations between prisoners were a central factor throughout. Power can be tentatively defined as the capacity each party held to determine the outcome of a conflict. Disputes can be conducted either through reasoned negotiations in which both parties have a say, or by a decision imposed by one on the other. If one person has total control of a decision affecting both him and his counterpart, then that person has power over the other.

Mary Bosworth and Eamonn Carrabine (2001: 501) have pointed out that 'prison life is characterized by ongoing negotiations of power'. Focusing on the power relations between staff and prisoners, they understood everyday, routine interactions as strategies of resistance by the latter. Goffman (1961: 42) wrote that prisoners occupy the lowest rung in an 'echelon' society. He illustrated their lack of power by pointing out that any prison officer, at any time, can decide to place any prisoner on report. As inferiors in the echelon society, prisoners are highly attuned to nuances of power in their relations with each other. Every conflict we examined was influenced by calculations each party made about the balance of power between them. In some conflicts there was already a marked imbalance of power (or pre-existing hierarchy); in others the balance of power was yet to be established.

Blalock (1989) suggested that even in situations of seemingly massive power disparities, there are likely to be mutual dependencies. He cited a slave and slave–owner relationship as an example. The owner appears to hold all the power in the relationship, until we recognize the extent to which the owner's economic viability is dependent on the slave. Blalock also drew an insightful link between interests and power. A dispute over some material interest may be transformed into a conflict about dominance, if one party perceives that the other one constitutes an obstacle to attaining the end in question. The first party may then come to believe that the best way to obtain the desired outcome (the interest) is to establish power over the other (dominance). Hence, he argued (ibid.: 29, emphasis in original):

> Many of the goals desired by both parties to the conflict will be focused on the conflict itself, with the primary resistances to be overcome being those presented by the opposing party ... We shall assume that the *primary* objectives and resistances involved will center on a single opposing party, the control or defeat of which is of central importance.

The primary focus of this chapter is the effect of power balances between prisoners on the way their conflicts were played out. In a substantial number of incidents (42/141), contests for power became the major factor driving the disputes towards a violent outcome. Participants in these incidents began to see winning the battle with the other person as their main concern; their original interests in the situation, the role of peers and the setting becoming less important.

The influence of power was present in each of the different layers of the conflict pyramid. For example, power was one of the important non-material interests that prisoners defended. Achieving or maintaining power was an underlying purpose in the use of force. Negotiating power balances was one of the determining features of relationships between prisoners.

In any conflict, determining the outcome is only one expression of power. For the purposes of understanding conflicts between prisoners, we can distinguish four ways that power can be exercised:

1. *Will-power* – variously described as 'nerve' or 'bottle'.

2. *Political power* – the advantages of networks, jail wisdom.

3. *Economic power* – relative wealth as trader or debtor.

4. *Official power* – prison job, earned privileges, relative freedom of movement.

When we speak of power as determining how a situation turns out, we need to bear in mind that control over outcomes can be established by employing any combination of these different types. Size and strength are also relevant although, as we see later, their influence can be overstated.

In whatever way power is exercised, it can be drawn from many sources. Figure 8.1 begins the task of marking the roots of power in prison. Unlike a starkly hierarchical model of prison status, with a few kingpins at the top, the chart suggests that prison power must be understood in a much more contextualized and conditional way. All the dimensions shown in Figure 8.1 influence the positions a prisoner can take up, relative to others. These positions are also shaped by wider circumstances. From a practical perspective, in a busy remand prison with a large turnover of inmates, it would be virtually impossible for any one prisoner to keep track of the activities of everyone else and the shifting sources of power.

A prisoner with substantial economic resources may wield power over better-connected and jail-wise peers who require credit to trade for drugs. An isolated, volatile, unpopular drug user may wield power over a new arrival on the wing if he alone knows the newcomer has been convicted of child sex abuse. Although there are prisoners who clearly wield more power than others, the pattern of power is distributed into small circles of influence depending on the circumstances and the kinds of power required.

John McVicar (1972: 224) argued that the power of an individual prisoner was determined by his capacity to hurt others:

> What mattered in prison, as far as respect and influence were concerned, was how violent a con was or could be. I knew that his potential for violence was the most influential power resource a

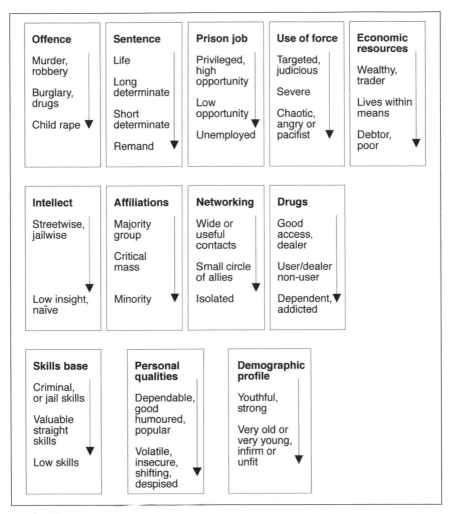

Figure 8.1 Sources of prison power.

con could wield in interaction with both other cons and warders. How 'heavy' or 'tasty' a guy was was what mattered when the rules went out of the window.

The wider understanding of power used here, including political, economic and official components, suggests that McVicar's violence-based definition is too restrictive. A prisoner who lacks networks of social support and is economically dependent on others will find himself even more ostracized if he habitually assaults others. For many prisoners, dishonour, their relationships with others or their economic viability were far more important than their reputation for toughness. Indeed, McVicar's views ignore the wider question of legitimacy and the use of force. The norms of inmate society were not uncritically approving about the exercise of power. As the victimization study found, most prisoners disapproved of bullying. The moral judgements of one's peers defined, to some extent, thresholds of conduct, and abuses of power advantages were condemned.

Finally, the power to hurt is much broader than the ability to inflict physical injury. This point can be illustrated by looking further at the relationship between size and strength and our conceptualization of power.

Power and strength

Size was not completely irrelevant to calculations about power but, as ever, it was subject to the interpretations of the parties involved. In some circumstances – particularly when it became obvious that a fight was imminent – the participants were more likely to weigh up the balance of physical strength between them. For example, asked what she was thinking just before she committed an assault, one woman replied: 'I was thinking, "It's physical – she is confronting me. And she is not big enough".'

Size and strength more often played a symbolic role in power relations. One participant, Lincoln, made explicit the differences and links between physical strength and personal power. He fought Rugby because he felt that Rugby underestimated him. We have already looked at this incident in Chapter 6 when discussing social distance:

> Lincoln and Rugby were well-built young offenders who both enjoyed working out at the gym. Lincoln made a joke about an exercise Rugby was doing, suggesting that Rugby was 'fucking the floor'. Rugby became angry and, in the changing rooms, he challenged Lincoln to a fight. Lincoln agreed to fight Rugby when they got back to the wing. At dinner, Rugby threatened Lincoln. During association, they met in a third inmate's cell. Lincoln produced a weapon and they fought.

Physical strength played a role in starting the conflict, and may have been influential in Lincoln's decision to arm himself. But will-power and the requirements of mutual respect were the key factors that led these two to fight each other:

Rugby did not mention physical strength in his interview. He said he had agreed to a fight because they had exchanged insults in the changing rooms, he felt Lincoln was trying to intimidate him and he saw fighting as a way to defend himself:

'I called him a couple of names and other people heard. He wanted a fight and it achieved a fight.'

Rugby interpreted the problem as a matter of respect. In the interview he explained that during the argument in the changing rooms, Lincoln felt that Rugby made him feel inferior:

'He thought I was taking him for a dickhead. I told him he was. He offered me out.'

Rugby called Lincoln a 'dickhead' – that is, an inferior, incapable of defending his interests – and Lincoln's reaction was to propose a fight, an outcome by which Lincoln could prove his worth.

The altercation in the gym built on a conflict that had been growing gradually. Lincoln commented that their relationship had changed after it emerged that Rugby was physically stronger:

'He was equal. We were friends. But after we'd been to the gym and he saw he could lift more, he got condescending.'

Lincoln felt aggrieved, not because of the difference in physical power, but because he sensed that Rugby underestimated him:

'He's a strong guy. I'm laid back. A lot of people, when they don't feel you're a threat, then they want to threaten you. My laid-back attitude meant he was starting to take me lightly and I resented that.'

Lincoln responded to his feeling that Rugby was condescending by pursuing a campaign of verbal harassment intended to force Rugby to treat him with more respect:

'When someone has a physical advantage, you try and psych them up by running off at the mouth.'

Lincoln's judgement that Rugby believed himself to be superior led him to deliver the insult that triggered their fight. Their conflict illustrates the complex relationships between personal power – in the sense of will-power, nerve or 'bottle' – and physical strength.

Conflict in pairs

Much sociological literature reflects one of two levels of analysis: either micro-social (focusing on patterns in the individual's decision-making) or macro-social (focusing on the social structure within which behaviour is defined). It is more unusual to consider the nature of interactions that occur in pairs ('dyads').

Berger and Luckmann (1967: 28) described the importance of the dyad for sociological inquiry: 'The most important experience of others takes place in the face-to-face situation, which is the prototypical case of social interaction. All other cases are derivatives of it.'

They add that dyadic interactions are immediate (direct sensual experiences) and unstable, in that they are moved along by a high degree of reciprocity between the two persons (ibid.: 29):

> My and his 'here and now' continuously impinge on each other as long as the face-to-face situation continues. As a result, there is a continuous interchange of my expressivity and his. I see him smile, then react to my frown by stopping the smile, then smiling again as I smile, and so on. Every expression of mine is oriented toward him, and vice versa, and this continuous reciprocity of expressive acts is simultaneously available to both of us.

They are not saying – and we are not trying to suggest – that paired interactions take place in a social vacuum, free from the influences of social structure or context. However, we propose to approach the influence of power on interpersonal conflicts by concentrating attention on how pairs of prisoners interacted. We believe that, at the level of interpersonal conflict, power was sometimes exercised in mutually confrontative and aggressive ways to reciprocally damaging effect.

The influence of aggression on interactions has been investigated by Kenneth Dodge, Joseph Price, John Coie and Christina Christopoulos (1990) in a series of studies, under controlled conditions, of playgroups of boys aged 6 and 8 years. Their theory was that (ibid.: 262): '. . . much, if not most, aggressive behavior occurs within the context of ongoing dyadic relationships. Aggression is a functional part of these interactions and is a defining characteristic of the relationship.'

Their research monitored interactions in play for the use of aggression. The boys targeted aggression to specific pairings within their playgroups. Half the aggressive behaviours were present in one-fifth of the pairings. Hence, Dodge *et al.* defined five types of dyad: 'asymmetric', 'high-conflict', 'low-conflict', 'unstable' and 'low interaction'. The last two comprised over two-thirds of the dyads they observed; asymmetric (or bullying) dyads accounted for 12 per cent; and high-conflict pairs for 6 per cent. In the asymmetric dyads, 82 per cent of the aggression was bullying (or 'proactive') by the coercive member. The high-conflict dyads were mutually aggressive, with proactive slightly more frequent than reactive aggression.

These findings are another reminder that the victim–perpetrator 'overlap' varies by type of victimization. Our findings about the unilateral quality of robbery as opposed to the mutuality of assault match these results. Although Dodge *et al.* were working with young boys in strictly controlled conditions, they too found that asymmetrical relationships featured one-sided victimization, whereas for their 'high-conflict' pairs, the victimization was mutual. The notion of a dominance hierarchy offers little to explain the latter case. Although the aggressor role was constant in each bullying pair, they also found that one boy could be a bully in one dyad and victim in another, suggesting that even at an early age there is some overlap of roles, though not complete mutuality, in bullying relationships.

The types of dyad of greatest interest to us in exploring power contests are the high-conflict and asymmetric pairs. A methodological difference between the Dodge *et al.* experiment and our study raises an interesting suggestion about the impact of high-conflict interactions on relationships. Our study did not allow us to follow up the prisoners after a fight or other violent incident. In contrast, Dodge *et al.* monitored their dyads through five sessions of play. This revealed an odd trait of the high-conflict pairs (ibid.: 266–7):

> The high-conflict dyads . . . had a high probability of disliking each other and a low probability of liking each other . . . [The] evidence points toward the mutually aggressive, high-conflict dyad as a problematic relationship. Once established, such relationships remain stable. The participants come to dislike each other, but they continue to interact and to engage in conflict that is characterized by both reactive anger and proactive coercion.

On face value, it is difficult to understand why boys who disliked each other and were frequently aggressive to each other apparently chose to play together. It is possible that each member of a high-conflict pair was trying to steer the relationship towards an asymmetric outcome. This is hinted at in the types of aggression displayed in these dyads, of which the majority observed were 'proactive' bullying. The research is illuminating because it suggests that aggression is targeted in pairs; that some pairs display higher degrees of conflict than others; and that in these high-conflict pairs aggression is used for mutually intimidatory purposes.

Imbalances of power

Dodge *et al.* (1990) demonstrated that some pairs settled into a stark imbalance of power; in some, power was continually contested; and in still others, power was shared more or less equitably. In our work, the influence of hierarchical power was marked where the purpose of force was to punish or bully.

Punishment beatings

We judged that 27/141 incidents were punishment beatings. In Chapter 7, we discussed punishment as a purpose of the use of force. In that context, we cited the beating of a debtor, Alderley, by the trader, Thorpe, after Alderley tried to evade repayment. Thorpe was motivated by a perceived need to set a boundary – both for Alderley and other customers. Similarly, Clapham described how he and another prisoner had punished a third inmate who had drunk their hooch [illicitly brewed alcohol]. Clapham's punishment was intended as a deterrent:

Q. What were you hoping to achieve?

'Just to show him don't fuck with us again or you will get it harder next time.'

A common element in these situations was the assumption, by Clapham and Thorpe, that they were superior to the extent to which they could judge, and punish, the offender. Clapham interpreted the offence of drinking the hooch in starkly power-based terms: 'I wasn't bothered what he was trying to do. I can't put myself in his position. I could drink it up, but no one on here would fuck with me. Whereas, he knew he was going to get a beating. He must have understood the price for it.'

Black (1998: 79) viewed the use of violence as punishment as an expression of social power: 'Most discipline is applied to individuals who belong to a homogeneous class in a larger hierarchy of social relations.' His understanding is supported by the majority of punishment beatings in our work, which were carried out against prisoners of a lower status. Although punishment, in this sense, implies a superior position, we heard of other situations in which the balance of power was even or unstable. Punishment was not always inflicted by a party who was clearly more powerful.

Punishment beatings also reflected the official power structure of prisons. The actions of individual prisoners reinforced the coercive power of the institution. Leaving surveillance by staff to one side, prisoners cannot escape the disciplinary gaze of their peers. A newcomer can be forced to submit to an unfamiliar order in which exclusion, verbal abuse and corporal punishment by other prisoners regulate their behaviour.

Bullying

Intimidation was a widespread concern of prisoners and clearly a major contributor to conflicts. Bullying, in the sense of an enduring relationship as we have defined it in Chapter 4, was far less common. Although the conflicts study was not intended to gauge the prevalence of assaultative behaviour (and was not, therefore, a random sample of assaults), violent incidents within bullying relationships represented a small minority of the total (18/141 incidents). This reinforces the finding of the victimization study that few prisoners were 'predators'.

Blythe and Consett were cell mates. Consett assaulted Blythe after Blythe obtained some drugs which she refused to share. However, Blythe said that the conflict had been growing for some time previously. Their relationship had clearly involved intimidation:

'I was a bit fed up of being in a cell with her. She was bossy towards me.'

Indeed, from Blythe's account, it is evident that their relationship was stable, that Consett was dominant and exploited her dominant position – in short, Blythe was being bullied:

'I was being made to make the beds and get the water like a little Joey.'

The spark that drove Consett to assault Blythe came when Blythe told Consett:

'I'm going to move out of this room, anyway.'

As Blythe explained:

'She didn't want me to move out because she was intimidating me whilst I was there and she was having it easy.'

In Blythe's view, the conflict turned to violence when she reasserted her independence from Consett, taking back control over her own life.

Binegar also claimed to have been assaulted by someone trying to bully him. He recalled that the next-door neighbour, Nailsea, had harassed him for his phone card, tried to involve him in 'stringing a line' [to pass contraband from one cell to another], verbally abused and physically threatened him. After Binegar refused to yield to Nailsea's demands, Nailsea punched him in the face:

'He thinks by using threatening behaviour and violence he can get what he wants. But he also thinks he is right in doing that so he justifies his actions to himself by seeing me as the one doing wrong by not doing as he wished. You have to decide which one to take as a point of reference. He thinks I'm wrong because I didn't bend to his threat. I think he's wrong for simply thinking that I would bend.'

In both these examples, the use of aggression was – reportedly – very one-sided. From the perspective of Blythe and Binegar, neither of them was aggressive towards their counterpart; neither attempted to control the other person.

Having considered dyads which displayed an imbalance of power, we can now turn to explore, in depth, fights and assaults that arose within pairs for whom the balance of power was undetermined or unstable.

From conflict to contest

Collecting his meal, Auckland noticed a dent in his ice lolly. He asked for a replacement. The servery worker, Sowerby, told him no. Auckland replied, 'I ain't no dickhead'. He said to another servery worker that Sowerby should do as he was told and give him a replacement. Sowerby again refused, and Auckland returned to his cell.

The following morning, Sowerby was standing in front of the servery when Auckland came for his breakfast. Sowerby glared at him and asked him why he was running off his mouth. Auckland returned the stare and laughed. Sowerby went to walk away, but then changed his mind. He came back to Auckland and began punching him. An officer intervened and was injured trying to separate the two inmates.

The episode contains the full range of power types we cited in the opening pages of this chapter. Sowerby had official power – as a servery worker, he had authority over the distribution of food. His position enabled him to exercise economic power in the dispute, denying Auckland a different sweet. Their verbal exchanges constituted mutual tests of nerves. Finally, Sowerby was an established prisoner with networks of support; Auckland was new to the prison and sensitive to the risk he might be identified as an easy target.

However, there is a deeper process at work in this situation. This development is revealed in Auckland's reply when denied a replacement – 'I ain't no dickhead' – and in Sowerby's challenge to Auckland to stop running off his mouth. Over the course of the dispute, the two inmates changed the meaning of power from control over the outcome to control over each other. The *conflict* had become a *contest*.

Auckland felt Sowerby was trying to intimidate him by giving him an inferior ice lolly, staring at him and standing in front of the servery in a threatening way. Auckland explains that he laughed at Sowerby in the morning to show him 'that his looks do not scare me at all'. Sowerby felt humiliated when Auckland turned to the other worker to over-rule his judgement about the dessert. Asked what effect that had on him, he said it 'made me feel small. He was trying to intimidate me'. They both interpreted the other's behaviour as an attempt to establish superiority:

Auckland: He was trying to take me for a fool.
Sowerby: He was trying to put me down, like he was higher than me.

Auckland and Sowerby's mutual suspicion of an intention to intimidate had a profound impact on the conflict. Each thought that the other was hostile and trying to establish his superiority. In reaction to their reading of the other's behaviour, each resorted to increasingly aggressive stances. Both participants explained that they acted the way they did to show the other person that they could not be exploited or dominated. Each set himself an objective to demonstrate his strength to the opponent. Their strategy was to use hostility to protect themselves, presumably in the hope that the other person would back down. Each judged the behaviour of the other to be aggressive. Each tried to resolve the tension between them by putting on a tough front. The decisions each made in response to the other put them on a collision course towards violence.

Forty-two of the 141 incidents showed a similar path from a dispute over an outcome to a question of who would dominate the other. Contests of power arose when one or both parties defined their situation as a win or lose struggle. They were anxious about being dominated by their opponent and tested them to gauge their personal power. They espoused values that viewed a willingness to compromise as a weakness. Although some of these participants were conscious of the possible implications of the contests for their reputation, their more immediate concern was the extent to which the opponent respected their power. When the balance of power between two prisoners in conflict was uncertain, each party attempted to dominate the other. The problems which had led to the dispute became peripheral as each party redefined the conflict in terms of a need to win the battle between them. This was a crucial shift in the process.

Each party to a power contest believed that they must resort to force and the threat of force. They judged that their counterpart had left them no choice. Mutual intimidation was widespread. Hence these contests often featured catalysts like challenges and counter-challenges, threats and hostile gestures. Interpretation was crucial, as both parties view their counterparts' behaviour as aggressive and their own responses as defensive.

There is a paradox in situations in which both parties become aggressive out of a sense that it is the only way they can defend themselves against the aggression of their opposite number. The logic of violence in such situations has been summarized neatly by Girard (1977: 71):

> Each sees in the other the usurper of a legitimacy that he thinks he is defending but that he is in fact undermining. Anything one may affirm or deny about either of the adversaries seems instantly applicable to the other. Reciprocity is busy aiding each party in his own destruction.

Others have written about the ramifications of conflicts over power, in particular the emotional consequences for each actor. Theodore Kemper and Randall Collins (1990) provided one such analysis. They argued that '... social structure is enacted in repetitive microinteractions and . . . the stable or shifting relationships of individuals provide both the glue and the dynamics of that structure' (ibid.: 33). At the heart of their argument are two dimensions through which interactions can sculpt relationships: power, which they define as 'conduct by which actors compel other actors to do what they do not wish to do' (ibid.) and status, by which they mean, 'conduct that conveys voluntary compliance, deference and acceptance' (ibid.: 32). Kemper and Collins's model sheds light on the emotional consequences of face-to-face interactions and the circumstances under which the outcomes of those encounters lead to fear, surprise or joy. In their view, power and status interact in social relations in ways that lead to predictable emotions. This allows a nuanced understanding of post-conflict outcomes. There are 12 possible outcomes for any interaction (two actors times two dimensions times three outcomes). Table 8.1 sets out the range of potential consequences for one of the actors.

Table 8.1:   Emotions and interaction

Dimension	Outcome	Emotional consequences
Power (compulsion)	Increase	Gratification/enhanced sense of security
	Decrease	Fear/anxiety
	No change	Depends on expectations
Status (compliance)	Increase	Satisfaction
	Decrease	Self responsible→shame/depression
		Other responsible→anger/dislike/distrust
	No change	Depends on expectations

Source: Based on Kemper and Collins (1990).

For example, if an actor's power increases, this signifies the ability to enforce his or her will despite resistance. The resulting feelings are of immediate gratification and confidence of similar success on future occasions. For the opposite reason, a decrease in power results in self-doubt and anxiety. The emotional consequences of no change in power relations depend on what was anticipated: if an actor expected an increase in power, then no change is tantamount to a loss and should result in some anxiety.

As for status relations, an increase in voluntary compliance ordinarily produces feelings of satisfaction and well-being, and liking for the other party will increase. Thus there is a mutual payoff and an increase in solidarity. If on the other hand there is a decrease in status, and the actor judges that it was his or her own fault, the main emotion is likely to be embarrassment. If the loss of status is deemed irretrievable, depression may follow. If blame is attributed to the other party, dislike and distrust may follow. Mutual status withdrawal turns actors into enemies. The emotional consequences of an interaction will shape future interactions. This model provides hypotheses about the conditions under which interactions raise anxiety.

In a similar vein, Katz (1988) illuminated how feelings of humiliation and rage emerge from battles over power, with potentially violent consequences. He observed that the initial effect of being humiliated is to experience oneself as an object: 'his control of his identity is lost when he is humiliated' (ibid.: 24). Cast as a mere object to one's opponent, the humiliated person thinks he is trapped; the tormentor controls him; his position is unbearable: 'Humiliation drives you down; in humiliation you feel suddenly made small, so small that everyone seems to look down on you' (ibid.: 27).

Katz argued that someone who has been humiliated becomes convinced that hurting the opponent is justified, a state of mind that he labels 'righteous slaughter' (ibid.: 12). He wrote: 'Humiliation becomes rage when a person senses that the way to resolve the problem of humiliation is to turn the structure of his humiliation on its head' (ibid.: 27). The person who was humiliated turns the tormentor into an object, thus providing the moral impulse to hurt him. While humiliation is a social experience, in that one feels stigmatized and isolated from one's peer community, rage is targeted at the tormentor.

The work of Dodge *et al.*, Kemper and Collins, Girard, and Katz identifies key themes in the ways power is manifested. The 42 power contests we identified in the conflicts study can be further understood by looking at their characteristic features in more detail. These situations shared six dimensions – sizing up, narrow focus, respect, win–lose outcomes, power values and precedent.

Sizing up

When a conflict begins, each person involved attempts to gauge the power of their adversary. Two types of situation in which assessments of the other's power become crucial are when one person is new to a wing; and when one person thinks the other is underestimating them. In the former situation, a new inmate is subjected to a process of 'testing out' through insults, threats or exploitation:

> Corfe was an established prisoner on the wing when Haydock arrived. One evening he targeted him for verbal abuse, insulting

his child. Other inmates encouraged Haydock to retaliate. Haydock told Corfe to 'suck his dead, stinking, gangrene of a mother', and Corfe responded with an invitation to fight. From the first insult, Corfe and Haydock were testing each other's strength.

Haydock inferred that Corfe insulted him to test his resistance:

'I think he was trying to weigh me out – see how much I'd take. He found the wrong person.'

Corfe confirmed this interpretation of his conduct:

'I only say those things to someone I know I can get away with it. I wouldn't do it to just any old person, if I want to live.'

Following the verbal sparring, the two inmates became locked in a long-running battle, leading to two fights separated by a week. Their feud ended when one was removed from the wing.

When both parties knew each other, sizing up came into play because one thought the other was underestimating them – or failing to give the respect they deserved.

The dimensions of conflict discussed in Chapters 6 and 7 each have a role in sizing up an opponent. For example, catalysts of violence, such as insults, challenges and invasions of personal space, test the other person's reserves as much as they demonstrate one's own power. Attempts to prevent violence can be seen as a sign of weakness. Interpretation played an important part in sizing up, as each party to the conflict made assessments of the other's power through their behaviour.

Narrow focus

As a conflict develops, the participants can sometimes be drawn into a tunnel-vision perspective of the interaction. Each participant defines the situation as one in which the most important outcome is victory over the (individual) foe. They also have a narrow focus in the sense of failing to see non-violent options, and in becoming less conscious of the ramifications of their dispute external to their particular battle. The presence of peers, the risk of detection, the potential embarrassment of resorting to fighting – all are forgotten by the participants as they become increasingly obsessed with their opponents. Their priority to prove their superiority to the one foe determined their narrow focus. Power contests were not (predominantly) issues of status in the sense of a general wing hierarchy, but centred on the paired relationship with one other person.

Young offenders were perhaps most likely of all to ignore possibilities for resolution apart from fighting. The following exchange over a game of pool shows how quickly young male prisoners can turn to fighting as a means of settling disputes: 'Eldroth comes up and takes the cue. I said, "It's my go". "Are you arguing with me?" "Yeah". "Let's take it in the showers". "Yeah".'

The question of who would play next was swiftly eclipsed by the deeper question of who could order whom about:

Lechlade was irritated by Sunderland's noise late at night and told him to keep it quiet. Sunderland told him to shut up. When Lechlade responded with verbal abuse, 'Fuck you!', Sunderland threatened him, 'I'm gonna break your nose in the morning'. Lechlade accepted the threat as an invitation to fight. In the morning, he went to Sunderland's cell and assaulted him. Sunderland did not fight back.

Lechlade interpreted the argument over the noise as a test of power:

'He thought he could take a liberty.'

Q. When he told you to shut up, what did you think he wanted to achieve?

'He is trying to say I am a dickhead.'

Q. What were you hoping to achieve when you told him, 'Fuck you!'

'Trying to make him look like a dickhead.'

Q. What were you hoping to achieve when you assaulted him?

'Victory.'

When he was subjected to a threat, Lechlade redefined the problem of noise late at night as a personal issue between him and Sunderland which he was determined to win.

Part of the narrow focus in power contests was a failure of perspective:

Poynton and Drebly argued about whether Poynton could have an extra towel. When it was refused, Poynton forgot about the towel and concentrated on the way he was being treated by Drebly. He began to fear that Drebly would say something insulting, and ridicule him. He slapped Drebly, not because of the towel, but because of his reading of the expression on Drebly's face. When he was asked if he had been trying to stop Poynton from doing something, Drebly told us:

'Yes, being a big man and embarrassing me. I didn't want him to put me down. I don't like that. You can't allow it in here – you really can't. It causes bullying and everything.'

Poynton knew there was an officer present – he had appealed to the officer for the extra towel – yet he still carried out the assault and was punished for it.

Respect

Contests of power arose when prisoners believed the other person was trying to dominate or control them. The catalysts that were common in contests – challenges, threats, commands and hostile gestures – are methods of asserting one's power. Recalling Katz's understanding of the potential for violence in situations in which one feels humiliated, conflicts often turned to contests when either party sensed they had been disrespected.

In Chapter 7 we referred to the conflict between Milford and Shap, in which Milford interpreted Shap's gesture as a threat and they fought. Central to their dispute was Milford's perception that Shap had no respect for his authority:

They worked in the kitchens, where Milford had responsibility for ensuring that the kitchen workers distributed the left-overs fairly. He said that Shap had a habit of taking more than his share. Milford confronted Shap:

'He'd just taken way too much and there wasn't enough to go round the servers. I pulled him and said, "Look, you're taking the piss. The rest of us have got to eat". He started mouthing off and then making stupid noises. Then he said, "Get lost or you'll get a slap". And that put my back up. I said, "Don't be so bloody stupid. We're only talking about food here". He raised his hand to say go away, but it was a threatening gesture and I said, "Don't raise your hand at me like that". He said, " What are you going to do about it?" So we squared up.'

In quick sequence, Milford made an accusation from his position of power; Shap responded with a threat; Milford interpreted a dismissive gesture as a hostile gesture; Shap countered with a challenge; and

Milford took the final step of offering to fight about the dispute. Each step displays assumptions about the speaker's superiority over his counterpart.

Milford viewed Shap's behaviour as demonstrating a lack of respect in part because of their recent history:

Q. Did you disapprove of his behaviour?

'Yes, bullying, picking on me, I kind of snapped because it had been going on for too long.'

Milford believed that Shap saw him as inferior:

Q. What was his attitude to you?

'He saw me as the weaker one so if he was being picked on he'd do it to me.'

Milford was asked, 'What was Shap trying to achieve?'

'He was trying to show he was over me.'

Win–lose outcomes

Over the course of any conflict, moves are made by one or both parties to wrest control of the situation and dictate the outcome. In power contests, as the participants redefine the outcome from a material change in circumstances to a new balance of power between them, they view their situation as win or lose. Each believes that they must be able to decide the outcome of the dispute. To compromise is considered weakness; the contest becomes a zero-sum affair.

Any conflict involves competing interests. When both people stay focused on achieving their objectives, and when both remain open to negotiation, it is usually possible to find solutions that meet some of the needs of both sides, that is, a 'win–win outcome'. If the objective becomes defeating the other side, any compromise is viewed as giving the enemy an advantage, and solutions become much harder to find.

Prisoners shaped conflicts into win or lose contests when either or both of them judged their interactions by keeping score of who was in the superior position. In these cases, a common response was retaliation:

As discussed earlier in this chapter, Corfe and Haydock became locked in a duel after verbal sparring that defined their relationship in competitive terms. Haydock was intent on getting the better of Corfe. Retaliation in kind was intended to gain victory.

Q. When you told him to suck his mum, what did you hope that would achieve?

'To get back at what he said about me.'

The following afternoon, Corfe attacked Haydock, striking him from behind with a chair. He explained his motivations in these terms:

'He looks a fool. He was trying to make himself look good. But I evened it back.'

Corfe was removed from the wing. When he returned, a week later, Haydock claimed retaliation as he assaulted Corfe with scalding water. Haydock's account suggests that he, too, kept score of the points they won over each other:

'Hot water definitely was revenge. One, for making a remark about my child. Two, for giving me the lip he did, and three for the chair across the back.'

Cycles of retaliation escalate violence when each party tries to inflict more harm than his foe. Interactions based in trade often raised questions about the relative power of the parties involved. Hence wherever there was a potential for one inmate to exploit the other through economic power, the interactions could be seen as win or lose situations. Prisoners felt susceptible to being exploited by others, and being exploited was defined by them as though they had lost to the other prisoner.

Consider the next dispute, in which Skipton and Hawick argued over one unit on a phone card. Hawick described what happened:

'I walked into association, went straight to the phone and Skipton kept coming up to me asking me to lend her one unit and offered me tobacco. I said, "I don't want tobacco, you can have the unit". When I finished my phone calls I gave her the card and went to sit down to write out my phone numbers. She came over and dropped it on my lap and told me she'd used two units. I said, "Go away from here, you cheeky twat". Then she said, "What did you say?" I said, "Fuck off". So she started saying, "Suck your mother". So I stood up in front of her, and I said, "I'm going to take my hat off now. Don't call my mother that and don't call me a cunt". And she said it again, so I battered her on the nose with a head butt.'

On face value, it would seem that Hawick assaulted Skipton over a single unit on a phone card. But their interaction is instructive because it illustrates how a power balance shifts through trade. When Skipton asked Hawick to borrow the phone card, she put herself in a dependent position. Whether she was able to phone home or not was in Hawick's power to decide. Hawick did not immediately agree, underlining her control over the situation. Skipton offered to pay for the card with some tobacco.

The offer of a trade altered the power balance, because it suggested greater equality between the two than a request for a gift of a phone card unit. Hawick used the offer to reassert her sense of superiority, ironically by spurning the offer and giving Skipton the card to use one unit. Although this meant that no trade would be involved, it also set up a relationship in which Skipton would be symbolically in Hawick's debt. The power to lend the card still rested entirely with Hawick. When she decided to lend the card, after keeping Skipton waiting, Hawick was clearly in a more powerful position.

But when Skipton held the card, she could determine not just how many units she would use, but how much she respected Hawick's power to dictate the terms of the agreement. Hawick was conscious of this wider significance to their disagreement. From the moment that Skipton confessed to using more units than agreed, Hawick defined their interaction as one in which Skipton had got the upper hand. She turned a problem about a phone card into a win–lose contest.

Asked what she thought Skipton was trying to achieve, Hawick replied:

'I don't know – that she was better than me.'

For her part, Skipton also perceived that the conflict had become a win or lose situation. She described her purposes in verbally abusing Hawick just prior to the assault:

'It was just to let her know she can't talk to me like that and I'm not a cunt.'

Q. What did it actually achieve?

'Nothing much except she knows I'm not an idiot.'

The main effect of defining a conflict as a win–lose situation is that it restricts the options of both parties, preventing them from finding mutually acceptable solutions. In power contests, each small victory was a spur to the opponent to raise the stakes, inevitably escalating the dispute towards a violent outcome.

Power values

What we mean by power values can be encapsulated in the phrase 'might makes right'. The norms that suggest brute force determines outcomes contrast sharply with the concept of personal responsibility. Interactions that are not determined solely by power exhibit values such as mutual respect, a reciprocal recognition of individual autonomy and a shared willingness to find win–win solutions through reasoned dialogue.

In contrast, coercive reactions – threats, intimidation, controlling behaviours – engender a sense that superior force determines what is right, and that dialogue is ruled out as a path to joint action. In a one-sided interaction, such as a robbery, the two 'co-operate' in reaching an objective, but the victim succumbs to an outcome imposed upon them by force. When outcomes are based on superior power rather than on reciprocal respect for each other's needs and interests – and power is applied arbitrarily, according to the whims of the superior party – right and wrong become arbitrary for the controlled person.

When respondents were asked what they were trying to achieve by using force, the extent to which some of them espoused power values became clear. Although the following are taken out of context, they illustrate the belief that force is a necessary method of dealing with conflict:

I wanted to show him he can't come up with that behaviour or we will start rucking.

Some people you can tell in different ways. Some you have to tell with violence.

If someone starts on me, then I will hit them.

I had just taken it for too long and he just carried on and carried on. If no one stopped him he would have just carried on with everyone. Some people don't know when to stop. They have to be shown to stop.

And, most chillingly: 'I wanted to cut his throat. He'd be dead. No more problem.'

A power contest at the women's prison illustrates the influence of power values on the evolution of this type of conflict. It is described in the words of the two prisoners, Ashby and Cerne:

Ashby: She'd been bossing me about all day. I went to do my washing and there was stuff in the machine. I thought it was finished so I took it out and put it in a bag on the floor.

Cerne: I'd gone to check on my washing in the laundry room. She's in the room and my soaking wet white jeans were in a pile on the floor. I said, 'Who the fuck's stuff's in the washing machine and who put my clothes on the floor?'

Ashby: Me. Aren't your clothes washed?

Cerne: I go, 'Even if they are, why are they on the floor? Take your clothes out and put mine back, you fucking muppet', or words to that effect.

Ashby: I said, 'It's all right, Cerne. I'll take mine out and put yours in. Calm down'.

Cerne: I turned and walked away. It was up to her to sort it out.

Ashby: She walked out of the laundry and turned and said . . .

Cerne: 'If you don't fucking do it . . .'

Ashby: . . . and pointed at me. I said, 'We'd best sort it out now'. She sucked her teeth and turned on her heel and came back.

Cerne: I closed the door. I hit first and she got one punch in. I had her head on the ironing board and I picked up the iron at one stage, but it wasn't plugged in. I had really lost my temper.

Ashby: We heard staff coming up the stairs and we stopped. An officer came in and asked if we'd been fighting and we said no.

Cerne: We both admitted to each other that it was the best rush we'd had.

Ashby felt that Cerne had previously been pushy. She judged Cerne's behaviour in the laundry by her belief that Cerne was looking for an opportunity to dominate her. She states that Cerne was trying to intimidate her by shouting at her so that the whole wing could hear. Both prisoners used force, but Ashby in particular felt justified in fighting. She argued that when she told Cerne to calm down, she was willing to back down in order to appease her. When Cerne pushed her again, she decided it was time to stand up to her by offering a fight.

Precedent

In power contests, both parties tended to believe that the confrontation they were in would fix them in an inferior position to their opponent if they gave way. Trading provides a stark example of the risk that a conflict will determine the nature of the parties' future relationship. A prisoner who lends something at a rate of interest has reason to fear that if the borrower reneges on the deal they will treat the trader as someone they can always exploit:

> Hixon agreed to sell his mate, Rochdale, some drugs. When Rochdale repeatedly failed to repay what he owed, Hixon went to his cell and assaulted him. Hixon explains:

> 'I couldn't allow people – whether friends or not – to buy drugs off me and not pay. I had to show he couldn't expect to have drugs off me and not pay.'

More generally, prisoners often regarded conflicts as a proving ground, in which they had to establish their dominance or endure permanent submission to a stronger inmate who saw them as weak. Recalling an incident we mentioned in Chapter 6 in the context of insulting behaviour:

> Orton and Crosby had an argument in the showers. Orton became angry when Crosby intervened in banter he was having with another inmate. Orton called him an idiot. Crosby asked Orton if he wanted to come over and prove that he was an idiot. Then Crosby accused him of staring. They approached each other and began to fight. Crosby says he was reluctant to fight Orton. However, he felt that both of them were motivated by a fear of what the other might conclude if they walked away from the challenge:

> 'I'd already offered him a way out, but he kept on and on. If you back down it's taken as a sign of weakness. That's why everyone has a fight now and again – either that or they're a bully victim.'

Power contests explain why prisoners place such importance on the outcome of their disputes. Despite the tendency to trivialize such encounters by characterizing them as fighting over a towel, a yoghurt, one unit on a phone card or a game of pool, our analysis shows that prisoners are often fighting for their self-respect. Hence they take perceived slights, and what they symbolize, seriously. The violence that results from power contests in prisons alerts us to the need to take seriously conflicts marked by intimidation, coercion and dominance and to look for better ways of handling such feuds when they arise.

Catalysts like challenges and counter-challenges, threats and hostile gestures often appear in power contests because they are about dominance. Defining a problem as a power contest alters the outcome from a potentially resolvable clash of interests to a battle about power over the other individual. In power contests, both parties interpret their opponent's behaviour to mean that they intend to gain control over them.

Contests became more volatile as both parties saw the problem between them as a win or lose competition. When a conflict became a contest, the people involved felt that they could only defend their interests by presenting a tough stance, and attempted to settle the conflict first through coercion and then through physical violence. Prisoners also believed that losing a contest for power to another inmate meant that an enduring relationship of dominance and submission would be established.

Chapter 9

Pathways to safety

> The causes or sources of conflict between individuals and groups cannot be separated from the totality of relationships, and the environmental conditions that promote relationships (John Burton 1990: 47).

We have seen that violence and victimization are commonplace. Assaults and fights are tightly woven into the fabric of prison life. Prison violence occurs against the backdrop of a social context in which the risk of exploitation by others is endemic. The rates of verbal abuse, threats and assault are high, while prisoners must also guard against the risks of cell theft, exclusion and robbery. Prisoners perceive their environment, rightly, as a place of danger, although they do not necessarily feel fearful. The prison's failure to meet basic human needs makes it a potentially high-conflict environment.

Returning to the four possible relationships between violence and social order presented in Chapter 1 – violence as disruption, regulator, convention and rebellion – we have shown that the functions of violence differ according to the type of prison. For example, in the YOIs violence was more likely to be used as a convention, as evidenced by a high level of routine assaults and threats. Older, settled prisoners in the adult institutions saw violence as a disruption to their routine. In the women's prison, violence was a regulator. On the occasions when women used it, violence served to punish those who had offended against the prisoner community. For a limited number of prisoners in each institution, violence was a method of resisting the imposed order.

Conflicts underlie interpersonal violence. They arise between prisoners over material interests such as phone cards, tobacco or drugs, and over values, including honour, loyalty and fairness. When prisoners respond to conflicts, their tactics of blaming, threatening, hostile gestures and challenges reduce the options for peaceful resolution. Problem situations between prisoners are also profoundly influenced by their concerns about domination. Power contests are common. In these conflicts each side is determined to win, sees negotiation as a weakness the foe can exploit, and subscribes to values that espouse violence as a solution.

It is from this background that we draw our ideas about prevention. We first describe ways in which prisoners were able to resolve conflicts without the use of injurious force. We then spell out some structural barriers to preventing violence in prison. Finally, we return to theories about conflict management and apply them to the prison context.

Prisoners resolving conflicts

What were the conditions that enabled prisoners to resolve their conflicts without resorting to violence? Looking again at the situations described to us, we identified factors that delayed, prevented or minimized physical violence. Some of these were material, such as privileges that the prisoners were unwilling to risk losing. Attitudes played a part, including the ability some prisoners demonstrated to take a wider perspective, awareness of long-term consequences and thinking before reacting. In addition, some prisoners displayed specific skills, including early recognition of potential trouble, deliberately non-threatening body language and appealing to their opponents to be reasonable.

Prisoners managed to prevent violence when the situation allowed them to negotiate their interests, when they were personally committed to finding non-violent means of solving problems and when they had the skills to de-escalate confrontations. The situations prisoners resolved – involving noise, arguments over access to the telephone, intimidation and even questions of power – closely resembled those that ended in fights and physical injuries.

We analysed 41 situations in which a dispute was resolved without the use of injurious force. The factors that enabled the prisoners involved to settle their differences can be discussed under three headings: the social context in which the problem arose; the norms and attitudes guiding each party to the dispute; and peacemaking techniques.

Social context

Social factors ranged from the interpersonal (such as the prior relationship between the parties) to the influence of the entire prison community. Prisoners who regarded each other as good friends seemed more likely to know how to negotiate than those who felt that the other was a total stranger. Also, good friends sometimes said that their friendship was worth too much to them to slip into violence. Having said this, a small minority of the fights we studied took place between close friends, suggesting that no single factor can prevent all disputes from escalating into violence. Indeed, when friends fought, friendships suffered (see Table 6.1).

In some cases, a third prisoner intervened, mediating between the opponents and contributing to a non-violent outcome. In all the prisons, there were particular settings where the atmosphere explicitly favoured and supported non-violence. For instance, a wing for long-term prisoners or featuring an enhanced regime might foster a settled and peaceful lifestyle in which residents would actively intervene to prevent two inmates arguing. Prison authorities also exercised a general influence on prisoners as they conducted their disputes. Prisoners sometimes considered the option of violence, but then decided against it because they felt they had too much to lose, for example if they were approaching a parole review or were concerned about having days added to their sentence as a punishment. In each case the benefits they expected from continued compliance outweighed the momentary gains they could get from assaulting another inmate.

Other social factors that reduced the chances an inmate would deal with a conflict by using violence included:

- jail experience – skills acquired after having served a long time in custody;

- location – inmates choosing the right time and place to work through a conflict; and

- courses that provided the prisoner with skills specifically suited to resolving conflicts.

Norms and attitudes

The second area that influenced disputes between prisoners and made non-violent outcomes more likely was the values held by the inmates concerned. Linked to the social constraint of official consequences, some prisoners spoke of a moment when they put things into perspective and realized that the cause of the dispute was not worth fighting about.

Other attitudinal influences that reduced the likelihood of a violent outcome included:

- independent thinking – not being coerced into using violence;

- empathy;

- an established practice of thinking before reacting;

- an explicitly stated commitment to finding non-violent solutions; and

- a desire to work on maintaining smooth relations with other inmates.

Peacemaking

We asked prisoners what they thought they could have done to prevent violence. A young offender said: 'I could have responded differently, but I don't know how.' This response implied that prevention was possible, if only the person concerned knew how to go about it. Despite our earlier emphasis on catalysts, which exacerbated disputes, we also analysed examples of what we term harmonizing techniques, tactics by which prisoners successfully resolved disputes.

The methods prisoners used to respond to conflict can be viewed in the context of a general theory of conflict management. For example, Black (1998: 74–94) identified five distinct types of response to conflict: self-help, avoidance, negotiation, settlement and toleration. His theory proposed that each style of response could be matched to a social structure in which it would thrive. Our studies enable us to cast a critical eye on Black's theories, and apply them to a particular social setting, the prison, and its specific expressions of conflict and conflict management.

By *self-help*, Black refers to the unilateral use of aggression to win a dispute. Such a response clearly tends to escalate rather than harmonize problem situations. He suggests that this method is most likely to arise when parties are of equal standing, there is relational and cultural distance, low spatial mobility, little economic interdependence and the presence of organized groups. These social-structural factors are common to prisons everywhere, including limited possibilities for movement, different cultures in close proximity, a high level of interactions with strangers and anonymous others, and prohibitions against trade (hence no officially approved economic interdependence). In the USA – though not in England – gangs are also common. The following story shows how the technique of self-help settled a dispute without physical harm:

> Spilsby borrowed a piece of foil from Norton and failed to return it. When Norton confronted him, he found Spilsby's response

sarcastic and dismissive. Norton took the foil back, crumpled it up and threw it to the floor. He described the sequence of events that followed:

'I'm walking away and he's right next to me – that's very aggressive in prison. He's very close, right in my personal space. At this point I knew there was possibly some violence here. I showed him a weakness. I can't remember what he said but he said something to provoke a response and I didn't say anything. It's like a dance and I missed a step. He had the upper hand then and he knew it. He leaned right over my shoulder. His lips were almost touching my ear. He thought I had lost my bottle. I immediately stopped and he bumped into me, and I turned round and we're nose to nose. He knew then I hadn't backed down. I said something like, "You're a fucking arsehole, you are". I had to say something, I had to assert my authority because now I'm in danger. He was shocked. I could see it on his face. He thought he had me and he didn't. That was the most crucial moment of all. It could have gone either way. He didn't move and neither did I. I thought that was it. I had the adrenaline rush but I felt quite scared. I did wonder if he had a tool and was going to stab me. After the moment passed, I took the chance. So I just said, "Arsehole", quietly, and turned away. I didn't know if he'd attack me. I walked to my cell and turned round and he was stood there – arms down and hands open – palms forward, like,"Come on, then" – but stood still and he said nothing.'

Both prisoners reacted to the problem with aggression. Both used hostile body language. Norton's early awareness that the dispute had the potential for serious consequences led him to use verbal abuse to confront Spilsby.

The social characteristics of prisons lead to the expectation that aggressive reactions to conflict would be widespread (as Norton's story illustrates). Our concept of catalysts expands the notion of aggressive reactions to include terms of abuse, threats and gestures. They functioned in prison conflicts like Blalock's concept of negative sanctions; that is, as mutually applied techniques of reacting to conflict that harmed the other party or denied them their interests. The tactics prisoners used to respond to conflict were typically:

- coercive (in that they closed off the other person's options);
- hostile (in their implied threats to personal safety); and

- power-based (in that they drove disputes towards an end determined by brute force rather than reasoning).

The frequency with which prisoners turned to catalysts when conflicts
arose seems to confirm that a setting with the characteristics Black
outlined would foster aggressive styles. Indeed, even in the 41 disputes
that were resolved without the use of injurious force, catalysts such as
threats and accusations were common. In a different setting Compstall
described a dispute that arose when Wilmslow accidentally slapped
him:

> I was in the dinner queue on the enhanced wing. The guys front
> and back of me were messing about. Wilmslow brushed my face
> with his hand. I said, 'What the fuck are you doing?' He goes,
> 'What are you on about?' I go, 'You just fucking slapped me in the
> face'. My mate comes over. 'What's wrong, Compstall?' I ex-
> plained, 'If I had slapped you, I would apologise; right?' He
> agrees. 'So why the fuck doesn't this punk?' Wilmslow apologised,
> 'I'm sorry. I'm sorry'. I walk off thinking, 'What a dickhead'.

No physical violence occurred – Compstall knew that even the slap
that initiated the dispute was accidental. But the tactics used in the
conflict included threats and accusations. The descriptions of the ways
prisoners conducted conflicts in Chapters 6 and 7 spell out in detail the
use of aggressive tactics in prison disputes, and therefore we will say
no more about this approach here.

Black's second type of response, *avoidance*, involves cutting oneself
off from the other party. Black believed that this response was most
likely to appear where there is social fragmentation, fluidity of
movement, no hierarchy, little interdependence and individual autonomy. Because of the lack of spatial mobility, avoidance might be
considered unlikely to appear in prison. However, the episodes drawn
from the conflicts study occasionally showed attempts at avoidance.
Indeed, Black's image of the suitable social setting, featuring fragmentation, low hierarchy or interdependence, fits the prisoners' situation in
some ways. None the less, although prisoners resorted to avoidance,
we found little evidence that it was an effective method of dealing with
conflict. Brief synopses of two disputes illustrate the uses of avoidance
in prison:

> One way to avoid conflict was to request protection. Malham
> witnessed an incident outside prison in which Retford, whom he

did not know, was humiliated. Years later, Malham arrived in the same prison as Retford. Almost immediately, Malham started receiving threats. Although he had done nothing to Retford, his knowledge of what had happened outside may have led Retford to fear that Malham would expose him and ruin his reputation. A woman visiting Malham was threatened. Then Malham heard that Retford had offered a payment to anyone who would assault him. Malham went to an officer and requested a transfer. Instead, he was placed on the VPU.

More commonly, avoidance was part of the problem. A typical example arose in the context of trade, when the debtor tried to avoid the creditor. In the next episode, avoidance could almost be considered a catalyst. Hixon's friend, Rochdale, asked him for drugs, and promised to repay him promptly at the end of the week. On Friday, Rochdale told a tale of woe and did not pay Hixon back. The following week Hixon went back to him, with the same result. This went on for three more weeks. Then Hixon saw that Rochdale had obtained drugs from someone else, and confirmed that he had paid for it. He went to Rochdale's cell, confronted him, and then assaulted him. Rochdale paid him for the drugs. Hixon commented: 'I could have just writ off the debt. Maybe I should have; not sold to him again. But him avoiding me was taking a liberty.'

Avoidance strategies were unlikely to be effective in prison. Not dealing with the conflict often exacerbated the tension between prisoners. McCorkle (1992) found that withdrawal was not a viable strategy for ensuring personal safety against the risks of predation from other prisoners. Even removal to a VPU or transfer to another prison does not genuinely resolve the conflict, as the vulnerable prisoner must remain vigilant against the possibility of a retaliatory strike.

Black's third type of response, *negotiation*, deals with conflicts by joint decision-making. The social structure that supports this type exhibits equality, social bridges between the parties, cultural closeness, mutual accessibility and suits corporate beings more than individuals.

The use of negotiation skills did not guarantee a non-violent outcome. Indeed, in the majority of situations, the harmonizing tactics that were used failed to prevent the fight or assault. Even so, the skills that prisoners demonstrated suggest that if the conditions were right, and their abilities to respond positively to conflict were supported, the potential for prisoners to resolve conflicts through negotiation was present. Techniques that showed the most promise were:

- distancing – gaining space or time from the urgency of a dispute;

- restraint – choosing not to react on instinct;

- explanation – carefully communicating one's interests;

- apologies;

- respectful attitude; and

- seeking further information.

Other conflict resolution strategies included appealing to the other person's reason, early recognition of trouble and intentionally non-aggressive body language.

Two stories illustrate prisoners' skills in peacefully resolving disputes when peer pressure was absent. In the victimization study, we were told a story that showed the capacity of prisoners to deal with conflicts in a constructive way. Firbank had a trusted job, and this was put at risk by the actions of Wisbech:

> I was in the chapel installing a sound system. When I turned my back someone took a microphone. I saw only one other person in the chapel. So I went straight to him and confronted him. I said, 'A microphone's gone missing. Did you nick it?' He shook his head. I said, 'Well, I need to get it back or it is on me'. I went back to work and he came to me ten minutes later and said, 'What did you say?' I repeated what I'd said, and explained I wasn't accusing him but he was the only one I'd seen so I had to ask him. He said, 'But now you're putting it on me'. And I told him, 'I wasn't accusing you, but you were the only one I'd seen'. He went away and returned with the microphone.

Although Wisbech seems to have inferred an accusation, he did not respond with a threat or other verbal abuse. Firbank handled the problem by asserting calmly how he saw matters and how he would be affected. Wisbech's objections were moderate; there were no threats or hostile gestures. Firbank's decision to leave Wisbech to think about it showed respect for his reasoning ability. And, fortunately, the issue was a private one, so that both parties could feel confident that they would not lose face.

In a second incident, Tainton and Stow resolved a problem that had been building up for some time:

> Stow and Tainton were in adjacent cells. Stow had a reputation for being immature, anti-authority, a bit rebellious. Tainton began to feel that Stow had some grievance against him:
>
> 'I really don't know why but I was getting these vibes off him that I'd done something, I don't know what.'
>
> About two weeks later, Stow appeared at Tainton's door. Tainton said that Stow was acting very aggressively. Tainton said he could see that Stow had come for a row. Tainton stepped out of his cell and spoke to Stow. Tainton recalled:
>
> 'Without thinking, I stepped outside and said to him, "Come in and sit down", in a really non-aggressive way. He changed suddenly and was okay. He came in and I said, "What's up; what's the problem?" and he said, "Well, you've been banging on the wall". I hadn't, actually, but I said "Well, I don't think I have, but if I've done it inadvertently well, I apologise". It seems he thought I'd said something. He'd maybe picked up certain things and sometimes you do tune in and it winds you up. I think he'd wound himself up.'

Tainton prevented violence by accurately interpreting Stow's expressions to mean that he felt anger towards Tainton. Tainton took the initiative in dealing with the problem. By taking the first step he could exercise some control over the way the conflict developed. His invitation to come into his cell and sit down showed trust in Stow, an expectation that he would be reasonable. And though Stow clearly was angry at Tainton, Tainton's concern disarmed Stow and got him talking. Tainton believed that Stow's first complaint was invented. But his willingness to resolve the differences between them was manifest when he apologized anyway. This led to a deeper trust between them.

Despite these demonstrations that negotiated resolutions are possible in prison, there are clear structural constraints that impede such an approach. To foster joint decision-making as a response to conflict, prisons would need to do far more to establish the necessary conditions of equality between prisoners, social bridges (such as, perhaps, wing consultation groups) and opportunities to work with conflicts in neutral, confidential and safe settings.

Black refers to conflict management in which the grievance is handled by a non-partisan third party as *settlement*. The most familiar examples are mediation, arbitration and adjudication. Black argues that this requires a social setting that features the presence of third parties equidistant from the adversaries. A third party does not need to be neutral in order to exercise a harmonizing effect on a clash. 'Friendly pacification' is sometimes possible. Here, for example, is a volatile situation that arose over personal property. This situation combines a number of Black's conflict management styles:

- *Self-help*, in that both participants used unilateral aggression (catalysts such as accusations and challenges).

- *Negotiation* as both openly communicated their feelings and supported their claims with evidence.

- *Avoidance*, as Bridport saw the potential for violence early and used spatial distancing.

- *Settlement*, through the roles of a cell-mate and prison officer. Other inmates showed a desire to settle the problem, and a third party relayed an apology.

Bridport describes the dispute:

> I had an argument with Chesterfield when she took my radio out of my room. She just left it out on association. I shouted down the wing, 'Who's nicked my radio?' She came up and said, 'I did. It's down there'. I pointed my finger at her and said, 'You're out of order. Don't you ever take my radio out of my room without asking!' She obviously thought I was quiet. She thought I would just leave it and say nothing. I went mad. Chesterfield shouted, 'Don't talk to me like that, making me look in the wrong'. Then I walked away, because I knew it was going to get into a fight. She came down, shouting and screaming, to my door. She was shouting in my face, right up close to me. I knew it was going to end in a fight and I am not losing days for anybody. I said, 'Let's forget about it. Let's drop the situation'. Poulton, my cell mate, got up and told her to go away from the door. Then an officer came down and told her to go back to her room. Loads of inmates came to our door to know what it was all about. They agreed that Chesterfield was out of order. They went to Chesterfield's door. A couple came over and said, 'Chesterfield is sorry. Can we drop it?'

Prisoners' conflicts often involved third parties. Although their influence sometimes functioned to end a dispute, many third parties aggravated matters. Settlement behaviour among inmates was uncommon because the necessary distance between a third party and each adversary rarely existed. There were obvious restrictions on staff intervening as third parties when disputes were so frequently related to illicit activities such as trade or drug use. Also, Burton (1990) cautions against settlements of conflict imposed by a more powerful third party, as the cessation of overt violence in such circumstances can disguise lingering tensions. None the less, there may be some potential for third-party prisoners to develop a role here, provided that training in mediation and conflict resolution could be made available to them and checks maintained to prevent abuses.

Finally, Black uses the term *toleration* to apply to inaction when a grievance might otherwise be handled. He believed that this style was most likely to be used when people are intimate, culturally close and socially inferior. We found evidence of toleration in prison conflicts, as in the following story, told by Bolton:

> Eldroth is on the phone and it's my time. I say to Eldroth, 'It's my time, can you come off the phone please?' He says, 'Yeah, in a minute'. Three minutes later I say the same thing again. He says, 'Yeah, in a minute'. Thirty seconds pass. 'Get off the fucking phone!' He starts saying goodbye straight away. He is coming off the phone. I calm down and go back to normal.

This situation was unusual in the extent to which toleration, in Black's sense, was mutual. According to Bolton, Eldroth was exploiting him by using time on the phone that was meant for him. In his account, he handled the clash of interests by politely asking Eldroth to get off the phone and then patiently waiting. The point of Bolton's story is that civility gets one nowhere in prison. Only when he threatened Eldroth did he give way. At that point, Eldroth exhibited toleration by backing down from a threat.

In just over a quarter of the 41 disputes that were resolved without physical violence, one person gave way. The immediate dispute was settled, but at a cost: one party submitted to the other, giving up their claim to their entitlements. In most of these situations, the person describing the events was not the one who gave way. Sometimes not becoming involved can be a sign of strength. It has ever been thus. According to Thucydides, historian of the Peloponnesian War, 'Of all manifestations of power, restraint impresses men most'. But backing down might arguably be seen as behaviour that contributes to violence by signalling weakness and vulnerability to exploitation. Both the victimization study and the conflicts study found that prisoners did not believe that backing down was workable in the long term.

Factors impeding prevention

Lack of trust

Before we describe what staff and management can do to minimize prison violence, we must first set this in the context of the situational factors in prisons that block efforts at prevention. There was strong evidence that prisoners did not trust staff. This led to a reluctance to report victimization, a problem that seems universal among prison populations. Dennis Cooley (1993: 490) found that Canadian prisoners told officials about their difficulties in only 9 per cent of incidents of victimization.

The extent to which problems went unreported in the victimization study is shown in Table 9.1. In more than 90 per cent of incidents a written report was not made. Verbal reports of cell theft were relatively common, probably because alerting the authorities to loss of goods might result in compensation and does not involve naming another prisoner, so the code against informing is not violated.

Table 9.1: Reports to staff

	Young offenders (Feltham and Huntercombe)			Adults (Bullingdon and Wellingborough)		
	No. victims	*% verbal*	*% written*	*No. victims*	*% verbal*	*% written*
Assault	172	14	8	113	14	6
Threats of violence	254	12	4	153	15	3
Robbery	59	17	8	25	8	8
Cell theft	157	38	10	197	28	10
Hurtful verbal abuse	321	10	5	153	14	7
Exclusion	103	10	7	40	22	10

Few inmates confided in staff when they were victimized. Some who did found that no action was taken. A few inmates reported victimization regularly, naming the perpetrators and sometimes submitting written complaints but, they said, to no avail. These people felt let down by the system. Staff will not be able to respond to victimization effectively where the culture of not confiding in them thrives. Thus, it

Table 9.2: Reasons given for not reporting victimization (per cent)

	Young offenders (Feltham and Huntercombe)	Adults (Bullingdon and Wellingborough)
Staff do not care	18	33
Staff could not do anything	16	29
Staff would not do anything	16	29
Could not prove it	14	20
Not serious enough	15	17
Fear of 'grassing'	49	40
Other	15	15

Column totals do not equal 100% as multiple responses were possible.

is useful to reflect on findings from the victimization study about the reasons prisoners gave to explain why they had not complained to an officer, as shown in Table 9.2.

Interesting differences emerged between the explanations provided by young offenders and adults. While both groups cited not wanting to be known as an informer as the most important factor, adults were markedly more cynical about the extent to which staff were interested or would do anything about a report. Unlike community crime surveys, the fact that the offence was not serious was seldom given as a reason for not reporting. Stating this finding the other way round, prisoners were reluctant to report to staff even when seriously harmed.

Given the problem of hidden victimization, officers could make better use of subtle indications that a given inmate is being picked on. Two types of victimization are likely to come to their attention: exclusion, which is observable, because by definition it takes place in public; and cell theft, which was the form of victimization most likely to be reported. When a prisoner was being excluded from games or isolated at meal times, it was also highly likely that he was being threatened, robbed, verbally abused or assaulted in ways that could not be directly observed by officers. Staff rarely become aware of threats of violence or robbery, but they do see exclusion and should note it carefully. Similarly, officers should be alert to the probability that someone reporting cell theft is being multiply victimized.

Misconceptions about the nature of victimization hamper attempts to formulate an effective response. As so little of what goes on is reported to them, members of staff may be misled into thinking that what they do hear about is typical and may make generalizations on this basis. There is a real risk that any intervention could be misinformed and even counter-productive if it is based on such partial information.

The danger of inappropriate interventions, based on inaccurate or partial information, was highlighted by the conflicts study. Fifty-eight prison staff were interviewed about their involvement in an incident; as witness, reporting officer or both. Although half of them had a good grasp of the background circumstances, the other half did not really know what the dispute was about. Only two said they could have done something to prevent the violence. Prison officers interviewed felt that they had little power to influence the course of inter-prisoner disputes or to prevent violent outcomes. When officers did not know the background circumstances, determining who was to blame was based on guesswork. Administrative action to protect an inmate labelled a victim or to punish a suspected perpetrator risked exacerbating the original conflict and was sometimes unjust.

Communication among staff was also lacking at times. The victimization study found that the methods designed to ensure continuity of approach, such as wing observation logs, security reports and personal history sheets, were used infrequently and inconsistently. In some cases observation notes, carefully entered by one shift, were not referred to, with the result that preventable assaults or robberies occurred.

Underlying the lack of mutual trust were pernicious values and attitudes. There was a resigned acceptance – shared by prisoners and staff – that violence is unavoidable. In the victimization study we found that the great majority of staff believed bullying to be a serious problem in prisons and young offender institutions. Yet, most felt it was an inevitable part of growing up and that it could not be prevented. In the conflicts study nine out of ten staff agreed with the statement 'violence is inevitable in prison': 'I agree, because of the types of people here – they are mainly violent and unpredictable people who act before they think.'

One impact of the belief that violence is inevitable was that many prisoners fought – not because they wanted to – but because they reached a point at which they could see no alternative. Hence, prisoners sometimes felt that their only option was to meet conflict with violence. Similarly, we observed that officers sometimes chose not to intervene, even when they held the potential to stop an argument, perhaps because they believed that violence could never be prevented, a case of corrupting pessimism.

In addition to being seen as inevitable, violence was quite often believed to be legitimate (see Table 7.2). Just over half the prisoners in the victimization survey felt that informers deserved to be bullied.

There was a greater consensus, especially among young offenders, that sex offenders deserved to be bullied, although one in four adults did not subscribe to this view.

Staff, on the other hand, were virtually unanimous in their view that no prisoner deserved to be beaten up. Only one of 58 interviewed for the conflicts study adopted a contrary position: 'I couldn't condone a beating but I wouldn't help them. I'd turn a blind eye. I wouldn't do it myself or expect another officer to do it.'

The staff role in preventing violence is only one aspect of the background to prison violence. The patterns that emerge from this book point to a broader link between the prison setting and violence: namely, the ways prison settings nurture the seeds of violence by denying basic human needs.

Basic needs and cycles of violence

In an early work, Burton (1979) listed nine basic human needs: consistency in response, stimulation, security, recognition, distributive justice, appearing rational, meaningful responses, a sense of control and defending one's role. Later, Burton (1990) claimed that conflict emerges from unfulfilled needs and cannot be repressed or prevented through coercive means, but only by identifying the needs that are neglected and working to meet them. He stressed that these needs are not material interests, and his proposed solutions are not a matter of throwing money at the problem. From this vantage point, the creation of safer prisons need not require major financial investment.

Burton's theories neatly correspond to Toch's list of prisoners' primary areas of concern, which were (1992: 21–2): privacy, safety, structure, support, emotional feedback, activity and freedom. Toch recognized that different groups of prisoners place different orders of priority upon each of these areas. His theory of congruent settings is particularly helpful in this context. He pointed out, for example, that young offenders will place a higher value on activity, while older inmates will value security and married prisoners will place a greater emphasis on emotional feedback. Environments that meet the psychological requirements of prisoners foster contentment. One size fits all approaches are inappropriate. Toch writes instead of a policy of 'orchestrated diversity' (ibid.: 6) to realign environments with individual needs.

Some of the needs cited by Burton and Toch are virtually identical: security and safety; consistent responses and structure; stimulation and activity. In previous chapters we presented evidence that established the failure of the prison environment to provide personal security,

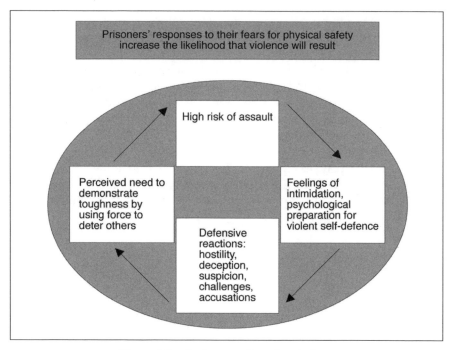

Figure 9.1   Cycle one – force begets force.

consistent responses and privacy. It seems clear to us that, as Burton and Toch suggest, the failure to fulfil these basic human needs foments interpersonal conflict between prisoners. When invasions of privacy (e.g. rub-downs and cell searches by staff) are combined with the damaging impact of imprisonment on family relationships, it is not surprising that conflicts result. When two prisoners get into a fight after having difficult visits, the background circumstances to the violence reflect the deprivation of intimacy, imposed by the prison.

The work of Toch and Burton provides insights into ways that a prison community can slide into cycles in which conflict is constant and violence becomes routine. A prison with high rates of assault and threats of violence fails to meet the human need for safety, rationality and a sense of control. Prisoners in such a setting might grasp violence as a means of reasserting some control over their circumstances, given the assumption that potential predators are likely to respect shows of force. This cycle of violence is shown in Figure 9.1.

High rates of theft and robbery signal a failure to uphold prisoners' needs for distributive justice, consistent responses and personal security. Norm-enforcing motivations would lead some prisoners to manage

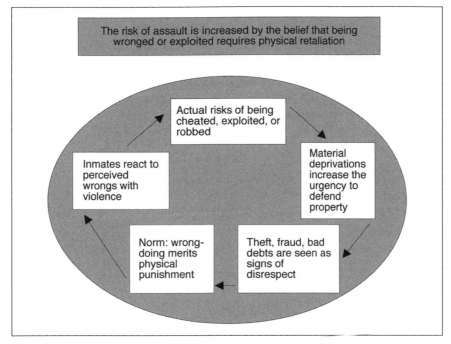

The risk of assault is increased by the belief that being wronged or exploited requires physical retaliation

Actual risks of being cheated, exploited, or robbed

Material deprivations increase the urgency to defend property

Inmates react to perceived wrongs with violence

Norm: wrong-doing merits physical punishment

Theft, fraud, bad debts are seen as signs of disrespect

Figure 9.2   Cycle two – dynamics of retribution.

these risks by inflicting punishment on suspected thieves. This cycle is shown in Figure 9.2.

These cycles are exacerbated by regime factors such as a lack of useful activity. When prisoners are deprived of adequate stimulation, they may lose a sense of role and feel that they have little control over their future. The lack of incentives that jobs otherwise provide – improved standards of living, time out of cell, opportunities to prove one's reliability – means that prisoners may feel that they have little to lose if they resort to violence.

To some extent, prisoners' behaviour reflects the way they are treated. When their safety is neglected, they will decide what they need to do to defend themselves. When conflicts of interest arise between management and inmates, and the outcome is determined without consultation, the prisoners' tendency to shape their own conflicts into win–lose confrontations is given tacit official validation. When problems between staff and prisoners are decided by the superior physical force of officers, the power values that many prisoners bring to prison are reinforced. When prisons leave no room for individuality, inmates become ever more jealous of the little autonomy they possess, realized in interactions with other prisoners, and prepare to defend their personal integrity with whatever it takes.

The prominence of any of these cycles in a particular prison may vary, as Toch's work implies, and indeed we found that the extent and nature of violent victimization were affected by the type of prison and the nature of its population.

Women used weapons far less frequently than men, and their weapons of choice were to hand rather than fabricated in advance. Women prisoners almost never used violence as a means of settling differences. Rather, they viewed violence as legitimate when it was used to punish those who had wronged them or offended their community. Females were more likely than males to intervene to stop a fight or assault. The female prison community disapproved of violence in most circumstances.

Young offenders were more likely than the rest of the sample to have experienced a recent fight or assault. They fought back when they were threatened or attacked; readily turned to violence to settle their differences; and believed that using violence would protect them from future victimization. They served their time in a hair trigger society. They did not foresee the damage their violence might do to their future relationships with other prisoners and staff.

Adult men in the local prison were a more heterogeneous group. They were more likely than others to use force in retaliation or revenge. A greater proportion of their conflicts concerned bullying and intimidation. These prisoners often justified their use of force as a means of standing up for themselves or self-defence.

Prisoners in the *high-security prison* identified conflicts earlier than those in other prisons and showed an ability to anticipate the consequences of a fight or assault. In general they were older, serving longer sentences and jail wise. The culture of a settled community meant that they had incentives to prevent the escalation of conflict into violence. They also showed that they were able to use their deeper knowledge of their peers to resolve conflicts without violence.

Toch's concept of finding 'congruent solutions' provides the basis on which safer prisons can be planned. In this book, we have highlighted the ways that assaults emerge from the routine victimization and conflict that characterize prison life. A focus on the processes, rather than the outcomes, of violence may enable staff to identify potential disputes earlier. The model of the conflict pyramid set out in Chapter 6 provides a framework for understanding volatile interactions. Finally, a recognition that the functions of violence may be defined in different ways in different prisons (convention, regulator, disruption or rebellion) can guide authorities in devising solutions that are tailored to local situations.

Creating safer prisons

From an institutional perspective, interpersonal violence is defined in terms of the fights and assaults that come to the notice of staff and are brought to an adjudication. The typical prison response to a violent incident is to determine, from the facts brought before the adjudicating governor, whether there is proof that the prisoner did indeed use injurious force as charged. If so, the usual solution is twofold: the prisoner is punished (often by taking away privileges) and separated, if need be, from the person he assaulted (or the fighters are separated one from the other). In short, the principles of responding to fights and assaults are fair finding of guilt, punishment and segregation.

Prevention targets intelligence and administrative measures, primarily founded on identifying which prisoners are violent types and restricting their opportunities to deploy force. Thus the risk of violence is managed through the identification of violence-prone prisoners, and the determination of guilt and punishment for those who cause harm and are apprehended and prosecuted.

Two fundamental problems with this approach undermine the capacity of prison staff and management to reduce the levels of assault. First, our research has shown that most of the violence that takes places between prisoners goes unreported. Hence, information available to management about the sources of violence is partial and potentially distorting. As Bottoms (1999: 231) observed:

> In a context where the vast majority of violent acts are apparently undetected, it should be clear that those who are formally identified as repeat offenders may well be atypical of the larger universe of those who are prepared, when occasion demands, to resort to violence to achieve their own ends.

Secondly, the segregation and punishment of an assailant are often counter-productive. Recalling Goffman's insights about adjustments to total institutions, Paul Keve, a former warden in the USA, wrote about the reciprocal effect of repressive regimes (1983: 48):

> With such curtailment of freedom, certain prisoners react with those forms of rebellion that are needed for support of their own

satisfying self-images. It is, after all, an altogether normal human need, however inept or even self-destructive the prisoner's means of gratifying it. Necessarily, official response from the custodians is to impose still more repression (time in punitive isolation, perhaps) which further promotes the prisoner's hostility. And so we sustain the correctional quicksand – and the prison's crimi-nogenic character.

The credibility of measures such as anti-bullying programmes depends in large part upon accurate identification of persistent victimizers. As we saw in Chapter 4, bullying is a slippery concept and even at an abstract level it can be difficult to work with. Staff interviewed in the victimization study believed that 'bullies' could be distinguished by certain common characteristics. For example, many officers mentioned demeanour and stated that inmates who were arrogant to staff were likely to victimize other inmates. This is a dangerous bias, because it can easily lead to the wrongful identification of 'loud' inmates as potential 'bullies'. It was not necessarily the case that inmates who were hostile to staff were hostile to other inmates.

Further, as conflicts and victimization are pervasive, and as many victimizers are also victims, dedicated units can have little impact on overall levels. A focus on 'violent people' diverts attention from the interactions that lead up to fights or assaults. Inaccurate identification of candidates for these units compromises their legitimacy. Active victimizers can go undetected while others, identified as vulnerable, can begin to prey on fellow inmates if relocated to a VPU. Furthermore, the inmates who are grouped together – even on anti-bullying units – can continue to victimize each other. The fact that an inmate, already on a specialist unit, can continue to victimize others is a powerful demonstration of the limited value of segregation. It is also a reminder of the importance of overlap.

One of the key findings we present in this book is the extent of the overlap for certain types of victimization and the limited value of thinking in strict terms of victims and perpetrators as separate groups. Lifestyle factors partly explain the overlap as certain routine activities increase the opportunities for a prisoner to find a suitable victim or to be seen as vulnerable himself. There might also be a direct link between an inmate's experience of victimization and offences they commit. The threats of violence that a prisoner uses one week might result in their being assaulted the following week; an attempted robbery may result in a retaliatory attack; prisoners in fights assault those who assault them. The boomerang effect of violence must not be underestimated.

Sparks, Bottoms and Hay (1996) focused on the options open to prison managers in their efforts to maintain social order in prison. Although the analysis they offered necessarily encompassed the decisions prisoners made as rational agents, their book approached the problem of order primarily from an institutional perspective. Alison Liebling and David Price (2001), in their book, *The Prison Officer*, were also concerned about the smooth running of prison communities, but they took as their reference point the experience and insights of prison officers.

The victimization and conflict studies, in contrast, were intended to reflect the prisoners' lived world. Although both these studies gathered information from staff, we have not worked the staff dimension into the structure of this book, preferring to concentrate on the experience of prisoners. Although it would be unfair to summarize the staff aspect of our research in a few paragraphs at this late stage, we can build on our understanding of conflict and violence in the prisoners' world to respond to a number of the key themes in the work of Liebling and Price, and Sparks, Bottoms and Hay.

Sparks *et al.* described social order in prison as an aim of prison management. They drew a contrast between *situational* and *social* methods of maintaining order. By situational controls, they referred to efforts to reduce or eliminate opportunities for prisoners to disrupt the regime. These included, for example, improved surveillance, the control of movements using lockable gates and timetables, and strict enforcement of rules.

Richard Wortley (2002) has teased out the situational perspective in some detail. He proposed a two-stage model, in which, 'behaviour is first initiated by situational conditions, and only then does the consideration of opportunity come into play' (ibid.: 217). He gave the example of self-harm, where prison conditions may contribute to feelings of hopelessness that are followed by a search for a suitable method, such as a ligature or a piece of sharpened glass. Similarly the opportunity to escape from an open prison is not acted upon unless other situational factors, such as mounting debts or a family problem, make escape a desirable option. The challenge for prisons lies in striking a balance between precipitation control and opportunity reduction. It is too early to be sure about how this balance will be found, due in large part to the 'particular paucity of microanalyses of disorder and the prison environment' (ibid.: 224). Hopefully the research findings we have presented will ease the passage of future attempts to test the boundaries of Wortley's model.

Opportunity-reduction policies can easily shade into a punitive, over-controlling approach which may lead to restrictive and oppressive regimes. Therefore, situational crime prevention must be seen as one component of a broader strategy which confronts the underlying causes of victimization and conflict.

Social controls are based on changing the culture, strengthening relationships, ensuring that the exercise of power is seen as legitimate by most prisoners most of the time, and developing mutual trust. Crucially, neither social nor situational methods advocate the maintenance of order through the enforcement of rules alone.

More generally, Sparks *et al.* characterized responses to prison violence on a continuum of control, from ultra-tight regimes of prisons like Marion, Illinois, to the lax approach pursued in HMP Wymott at the time *Prisons and the Problem of Order* was written. They suggested that coercive policies tend to minimize opportunities for fighting, while liberal regimes honour prisoners' need for autonomy. They acknowledged the risk that liberal regimes can also increase the levels of violence (1996: 327): 'The niggling doubt remains as to whether [a] lesser prioritisation of situational control exposes some prisoners, and perhaps staff, to unacceptable levels of risk.'

The distinction between liberal and repressive regimes is at heart a question of how strictly rules are enforced. Our research points out an alternative to the dichotomy between liberal and repressive methods of addressing prison violence. A conflict-centred approach implies a profoundly different set of policy considerations. From the perspective of the prison manager, the first step is to recognize that the origins of violence lie in conflicts. Building on the work of Burton and Toch, and our own victimization survey, a policy of violence prevention would entail a systematic audit of each prison, to determine levels of victimization and fear and to identify which basic human needs are unfulfilled. As Toch advised, the priorities among these needs must be set in collaboration with prisoners, because each community of prisoners will have its unique set of key concerns. The links between needs, fears, conflicts and violence strongly suggest that the prison that most successfully fulfils the basic human needs of the people it holds will be seen as a place of legitimacy and safety.

The conflict-centred method also has implications for the policies management set for prisoners. The reasons for disputes and competition between prisoners are varied. However, four factors stand out as underlying much of the interpersonal violence that occurs in prisons:

1. (relative) material deprivation;

2. danger (the ever-present risk of being victimized);

3. power struggles (made more intense by a general loss of personal autonomy); and

4. lack of skills in dealing constructively with conflict.

As the analysis in previous chapters has demonstrated, violence in prison arises from clashes that prisoners are unable to resolve peaceably. We found that many prisoners did not want to fight, but faced with a conflict, they felt that they had no option. In general terms, the prison must be proactive in providing the means by which these inevitable conflicts can be mediated and resolved. For example, exploring conflicts in an open way might require outside, independent and impartial mediators. Restorative justice conferencing might provide more effective responses to fights and assaults; and a number of prisons, including Bullingdon, have been trying out just such an approach. In addition, as prisoners' methods of handling conflict very often increased the risk of a violent outcome, many fights could be prevented if prisons provided prisoners with training specifically in conflict-resolution skills.

Halting the cycles of conflict calls for local problem-solving, informed by careful empirical study of the specific roots of conflict and victimization, and by consultation with prisoners to determine the primary areas of concern in each establishment. One manager might find that the prisoners' sense of personal security is under such threat that intimacy or privacy are less important to them. In another prison, the key concerns might be a need for stimulation (activity) and opportunities to find a meaningful role. Still other prisons might find that the key areas in which needs are neglected are distributive justice and consistency in responses (for example, where there are strong indications of discrimination on ethnic grounds). There may also be particular parts of the physical environment that promote fear (e.g. showers or segregation units) and the possibility of designing out some elements of the problem should not be dismissed. The ways that particular prisons fail to meet basic needs differ widely, and so the means of reducing potentially violent conflicts that we propose cannot be elucidated in a single, detailed prescription.

Liebling and Price (2001) produced a wide-ranging understanding of the officer's role. They gave particular attention to the definition of right relations between staff and inmates. They argued that staff must balance controls to enforce social order on one hand with rewards and fairness to maintain their legitimacy on the other. Rules were used as resources, drawn upon selectively to negotiate order rather than rigidly to enforce the law. While they recognized the limitations (and the costs) of coercive power, they also saw that policies of appeasement could reduce personal safety. Summing up the developments in the officers' role in the late 1990s, they wrote (ibid.: 128): 'prisoners traded in relative freedom, fear and chaos for restraint, order and security, and the knowledge that staff (and not other prisoners) were in control.'

Recalling Sykes's insight that officers must surrender some of their power to ensure the maintenance of order, they found that a key to the prison officer's role was discretion. Liebling and Price (2001: 124) labelled the decision not to enforce a given rule, 'peacekeeping': 'The "un-exercise" of power in prison is hugely significant . . . deployed in an appropriate manner, the under-use of power constitutes "the best" form of prison officer work: what we (and others) have called peacekeeping.'

Three points arise from this interpretation of peacekeeping. First, it is unfortunate that the officers whose views supplied the raw material for *The Prison Officer* saw peacekeeping in such a narrow and limited way. While Liebling and Price stressed that right relations require a broader understanding of the officer's powers than rule enforcement, the officers themselves described peacekeeping entirely within a rule-bound function.

Secondly, the officers' emphasis on discretion indicates a role that mediates between the interests of inmates and management. Failing to enforce a rule in a given situation might ease tensions that arise when the demands of management are unrealistic, but a partial application of the rules is likely to foment problems between the prisoner whose transgression was overlooked and others who were punished. As a technique of conflict management, this is bound to lead to mixed results. Toch (1992: 124) has written of the importance of conventions about how rules are to be applied. The reliable and equitable application of the rules is a prerequisite for stability. The formal level of discipline in an institution may be less relevant than the consistency with which it is employed.

Thirdly, Liebling and Price's sketch of the peacekeeping role did not provide guidance on what, in the context of conflicts between prisoners, is arguably the most important part of the officers' role: namely, how officers can intervene appropriately to facilitate the resolution of conflicts between prisoners.

The conflict-centred approach that we advocate would envisage peacekeeping by staff in the following broad terms:

- Developing methods of preventing or minimizing violence through the sensitive handling of inmates' disputes by focusing on the interests, values and needs at stake.

- Identifying the tactics each party has used and intervening to stop prisoners using catalysts such as insults, threats, accusations, hostile gestures and challenges.

- Improving communication between the parties.

- Searching for options for win–win outcomes.

- Striving to create a culture that favours negotiation and the fulfilment of basic human needs over coercive controls.

This rendering of the peacekeeping role requires far more than the occasional under-enforcement of rules. It is clear from Liebling and Price's valuable work that prison officers have a very limited sense of a peacekeeping role if, as we believe, this refers to a duty to reduce the sources of conflict between inmates (not just between inmates and staff or inmates and management) and to prevent conflicts from escalating into violence. To some extent, the detailed descriptions in Chapters 6–8 of this book begin the task of enabling officers to identify conflicts and understand their dynamics. However, concrete guidance to staff about how they can intervene and help to resolve conflicts awaits research focused on that specific function. A general analysis of the prison officer role cannot provide the required detail.

None the less, the point is not that the enforcement of rules is irrelevant to the officer's job. Effective policing is essential in response to victimization. Prisoners assign a deep significance to being exploited by other prisoners. Thus, one way to reduce assaults is to pay greater attention to preventing exploitation of prisoners by prisoners. They are often willing to resort to violence if they think another person has gained some material advantage over them. The fact that theft, threats of violence, robbery and assault are routine experiences in prisoners' lives – and are unlikely to be brought to official notice – highlights the serious problem faced by the Prison Service in meeting its obligation to maintain people in safe custody. In this area of prison life, the non-enforcement of rules by officers is as far as possible from keeping the peace, especially if it is inconsistent.

More generally, if prison officers are to have any hope of reducing levels of violence, the way the Prison Service defines their role must shift from the reactive (using force when fights break out) to the preventive, and from enforcing (or not) the rules to a broader more engaged sense of peacekeeping as conflict resolution.

It is unacceptable for officers to shy away from a genuine peacekeeping role through a belief that violence is inevitable. True peacekeeping means that officers must be trained to recognize potentially volatile situations as they arise between prisoners, to know the circumstances in which it would be beneficial to intervene and to deal with conflict so that their interventions are not counter-productive.

It is clearly difficult to provide prison environments which are safe all the time. Prisons will continue to be places that generate conflict. But that is all the more reason to promote a non-violent ethos, to explore new ways of giving prisoners access to mediation, in order to promote settlement activities, and to provide programmes which develop prisoners' skills in handling disputes. If the problems of prison violence can be ameliorated there may be a diffusion of benefits, in that safer prisons contribute to safer societies. Rather than thinking of a subculture of violence in prisons it might be more productive to think in terms of a subculture of uneasy peace. Supporting this imperfect peace is the key to creating safer prisons.

Appendix

Escalator

I walked off. We both got banged up.

I pushed him back. An officer rang the alarm.

He pushed me a second time.

Exeter offered me double or nothing. He lost. I laughed. He stood up and pushed me.

I was playing computer football with Exeter. He was losing and I was taking the piss – moving the ball around out of reach.

Supplementary questions

> **Intentions and consequences**
> *Step 1.* Q. What were you hoping to achieve by taking the piss?
> A. When you play someone who isn't good, you might as well make it more interesting.
> Q. What was the effect on him?
> A. It got him pissed off and more frustrated.
>
> *Step 2.* Q. Why do you think Exeter pushed you?
> A. Make himself feel better.
> Q. How did that affect you?
> A. I thought he was going to hit me. I wanted to hit him cos I thought he was going to hit me, but I thought it weren't worth it. If he had punched me I would have gone. I wouldn't have let him. When it happened I was pissed off but I was more concerned with just getting away.

> **Prevention**
> Q. Was there anything you could have done to prevent the incident? [Indicates step 1 – when Exeter was losing.]
> A. I wouldn't have played, or I would have let him win.
>
> Q. Was there anything he could have done? [Indicates step 2 – when Exeter offered double or nothing.]
> A. Stop betting, or if it was pissing him off, stop playing.

Bampton versus Stroud

Bampton	Stroud
My cell mate told someone else she had got some gear in on a visit. Lots of women kept coming to the door to hassle her for it.	
My mate and I went to the video room to get away from the hassle.	I was in the TV room watching telly. The incident did not start in the TV room, but that is the first I knew of it.
A girl was sitting in front of us. Totton [Stroud's cell mate] came in putting pressure on my mate. Not threats, just, 'Give it to me'.	She was already in there, sitting just behind me.
I said, 'Why didn't you just tell her to fuck off?'	I found what she was saying offensive. She was talking to her friend about my pad-mate. She obviously hadn't seen me.
The girl in front talked over her shoulder, telling me to shut the fuck up.	Words were exchanged.
I replied, 'I won't shut up'.	She denied she had said what I heard her say. I said, 'Leave it. Just shut the fuck up'. She said, 'No, you shut up'.
She stood up and started walking towards me.	
I stood up. We were face to face.	I stood. We squared up to each other. We were two inches apart. My hands were down. I cannot remember what was said. I was fuming, livid.
She head-butted me. My head was down and I was bleeding badly.	Her hands were like she was going to grab me. My reaction was it was either her or me, so I head-butted her.
I grabbed her hair and pulled her down.	We grabbed each other.
Other inmates stepped in and pulled us apart.	Other inmates intervened.
Officers came in.	

Leyland versus Hapton

Leyland	Hapton
	Some time ago some inmates started being rude after I had a short shower.
	It got worse and Leyland was dissing me every time he saw me – and everyone else.
	In the showers one day he said to me, 'If I piss on you, what will you do?' and I carried on washing. I told him I'd kill him but he just carried on dissing me. I made my mind up then that I would fight him.
I'm doing kit change. Hapton comes in and I said, 'What's going on, smelly arse?'	Two days later when I came down to kit change he started again.
He said, 'Who are you calling smelly?' I said the same again – he moves the table out the way and comes into the kit room.	I wasn't having it any more.
I was laughing and said, 'Come on then', but I was laughing and I didn't mean it in an aggressive way.	
He comes right up to me and hits me in the face.	I pushed the table aside and punched him.
I started punching him back.	We had a fight – punching each other.
We were separated by other inmates.	Another inmate came between us.
Staff came in and bent him up and took him down the Block.	The officer comes in and pulls me out. The alarm bell was pressed and other officers arrived, bent me up and took me to the Block – overnight.
	In the adjudication I was charged with assault.
Don't know what's going to happen – I'll have to wait and see when I see him.	I've seen him since and we don't talk. I think it's over.

Glastonbury versus Atworth

Glastonbury	Atworth
Atworth came on the wing. He was acting strange – giving me funny looks.	I came on the wing.
I asked him 'What are you playing at?'	
He waved a razor at me. I left it.	
Then later, I was playing pool. Atworth got two cups of hot water and came to the pool table.	Three or four days later, Glastonbury insulted me.
	He called me a nonce.
He made comments about my girlfriend being really young.	He swung down off the bars, like he was about to kick me. I backed away.
He jumped up and grabbed the suicide netting. The water spilled.	He flicked cold water at me and was still insulting me.
I said 'Piss off. You're a nonce'. He said 'I'll wipe the floor with you'.	
One day passes.	Next day.
I had a visit. He came back at dinner time.	I flicked cold water on him.
He hit me with cold water.	He said, 'Did you flick water at me?' I said 'No. I didn't'.
I said, 'What are you playing at?' He laughed and walked away.	
I took my dinner back to my cell and then went out to get some hot water.	Glastonbury went to his cell.
On my way back, I passed Atworth's cell. He said something.	Glastonbury came back to my door with his cup of water.
I stood at his cell door. He stepped back.	I was near the door.
	Glastonbury called me a name and punched me twice on the jaw.
I stepped into the cell and slapped him on his cheek once (backhanded).	My reaction was to throw water on him – in self-defence, retaliation. I thought my water would be colder than Glastonbury's. Glastonbury got angry and chucked his water on me.
He hit me with the scalding water.	
I tried to get my jumper off.	
Atworth reached for a second cup, but his cell-mate knocked it out of his hand.	Officers arrived and sent Glastonbury back to his cell. They shut me in my cell.
Officers arrived.	

Sutton versus Whaley

Sutton	Whaley
I argued with an Officer about lunch. Whaley interrupted and tells me to stop talking to the officer. He said, 'Be quiet'.	An argument between the Officer and Sutton. I intervened and said, 'Leave it'.
I said, 'Shut up. This has nothing to do with you. No one's talking to you'.	Sutton gets upset and a big argument starts between the two of us.
Whaley starts shouting and using threatening language. Whaley comes towards me and a screw stepped in.	I moved towards Sutton and an officer restrained him and then banged him up.
The screw drags me out of the servery and locks me up till later. I came out on association while Whaley was on a visit. I had a weapon with me.	After lunch I'm still pissed off with him but go for a visit and I had forgotten about it till I saw him again.
Whaley comes back on the wing and starts arguing and threatening me. He says, 'In the shower!'	On the wing an argument develops – others get involved. I invited him in the showers.
We go in but staff came and no blows were exchanged. Whaley saw the weapon.	We go in to have a fight. He had a weapon. It made me shocked and angry. No blows were exchanged as staff came in.
Back on association, it carried on, arguing and cussing each other. We agreed to fight in the cell later.	Still on association we were exchanging words and stares. We agree to fight in cell.
At the end of association I followed him to his cell and we had a fight. The door got pushed to. He hit me with a battery and I scratched him with the weapon. We were exchanging blows.	I go into my cell, he follows, with a weapon. We have quite a serious fight. We both get injured.
Whaley pressed the alarm bell and a screw came. I walked out.	Staff open the door. I was still pissed off after the fight even though I won. I was furious. I wanted to kill him.
The adjudication next day did nothing. I was still angry.	After the adjudication we were let out for a few days and didn't speak to each other. By Wednesday I decided to see if we could forget it. We shook hands, and said, 'It's squashed'.
Two days later, Whaley came along and asked me to look after his laundry. We talked about it and shook hands. It's over.	

Milford versus Shap

Milford	Shap
I've been under pressure on the servery with a bit of bullying and intimidation from a few of the other servery inmates. Shap was always more personal than the others.	A loudmouth on the wing had been insulting my mother, saying, 'When I get out I will make your mother pregnant'. It made me lose it. In the morning I was in tears of rage. I never got a chance to finish it. I was still bubbling.
He took too much food at the end of dinner and I'm on portion control. He's always doing it, so I said, 'Look, you're taking the piss'.	I wanted an extra yoghurt. Milford challenges me for it. An argument develops.
He reacts badly and an argument follows. He said, 'Get lost or you'll get a slap'. I said, 'Don't be so bloody stupid. We're only talking about food here'.	
He raised his hand, not to hit, but in an aggressive gesture. I said, 'Don't raise your hand to me'. He says, 'What are you going to do about it?' And we squared up.	I tell him to shut up and I raised my arm in a dismissive gesture, like, 'Oh, go away. I ain't interested'. He takes it as an aggressive gesture, opens his arms and says, 'Come on, then'.
I said, 'Okay, let's do it', and we started to fight.	I had a bowl of curry in my hand and I hit him with the bowl. We were grappling. He threw a few more blows and we were skidding all over the place.
We fell over amongst the food and we were exchanging blows but not hurting each other.	
One of us leant against the bell. We didn't know, because it doesn't sound in the kitchens, and suddenly officers arrived.	He fell against the bell I gave him a couple more digs. I heard their boots coming.
We stopped immediately. They questioned us but didn't put us on report. We were warned and made to clean the servery alone. We didn't lose our jobs.	Screws arrived. We'd stopped fighting before they got there. They asked about it. We said nothing and they made us clean the servery.
Shap and me shook hands and had a laugh and a joke whilst we were cleaning up. It's over, but he still tries to get at me like before.	We shook hands and had a laugh. It's over.

References

Adams, K. (1992) Adjusting to prison life. In M. Tonry (ed.) *Crime and Justice: A Review of Research. Vol. 16*. Chicago, IL: University of Chicago Press.

Aijmer, G. and Abbink, J. (eds) (2000) *The Meanings of Violence: A Cross Cultural Perspective*. Oxford: Berg.

Alternatives to Violence Project (1996) *Supplement to the Basic and Second Level Manuals*. New York: Alternatives to Violence Education Committee.

Anderson, E. (1999) *Code of the Street: Decency, Violence and the Moral Life of the Inner City*. New York: Norton.

Arendt, H. (1970) *On Violence*. London: Allen Lane, The Penguin Press.

Atlas, R. (1983) Crime site selection for assaults in four Florida prisons. *Prison Journal*. LXIII: 59–72.

Augsburger, D.W. (1992) *Conflict Mediation across Cultures: Pathways and Patterns*. Louisville, KT: John Knox Press.

Beck, G. (1995) Bullying among young offenders in custody. In N.K. Clark and G.M. Stephenson (eds) *Criminal Behaviour: Perceptions, Attributions and Rationality. Issues in Criminological and Legal Psychology* 22. Leicester: British Psychological Society.

Berger, P. and Luckmann, T. (1967) *The Social Construction of Reality: A Treatise in the Sociology of Knowledge*. New York: Anchor Books.

Black, D. (1998) *The Social Structure of Right and Wrong* (revised edn). San Diego, CA: Academic Press.

Blalock, H.M. (1989) *Power and Conflict: Toward a General Theory*. London: Sage.

Blumer, H. (1969) *Symbolic Interactionism: Perspective and Method*. Englewood Cliffs, NJ: Prentice-Hall.

Bosworth, M. (1999) *Engendering Resistance: Agency and Power in Women's Prisons*. Aldershot: Ashgate.

Bosworth, M. and Carrabine, E. (2001) Reassessing resistance: race, gender and sexuality in prison. *Punishment and Society* 3: 501–15.

Bottoms, A.E. (1999) Interpersonal violence and social order in prisons. In M. Tonry and J. Petersilia (eds) *Crime and Justice: A Review of Research. Vol. 26*. Chicago, IL: University of Chicago Press.

Bowker, L. (1980) *Prison Victimization*. New York: Elsevier.

Burton, J. (1979) *Deviance, Terrorism, and War: The Process of Solving Unsolved Social and Political Problems*. New York: St Martin's Press.

Burton, J. (1990) *Conflict: Resolution and Prevention*. London: Macmillan.

Clemmer, D. (1940) *The Prison Community*. New York: Holt, Rinehart & Winston.
Coady, C.A.J. (1986) The idea of violence. *Journal of Applied Philosophy*, 3: 3–19.
Cooley, D. (1993) Criminal victimization in male federal prisons. *Canadian Journal of Criminology* 35: 479–95.
Cooney, M. (1998) *Warriors and Peacemakers: How Third Parties Shape Violence*. New York: New York University Press.

Davies, W. (1982) Violence in prisons. In P. Feldman (ed.) *Developments in the Study of Criminal Behaviour. Vol. 2*. Chichester: Wiley.
Davis, A.J. (1977) Sexual assaults in the Philadelphia prison system and sheriff's vans. In C.D. Bryant (ed.) *Sexual Deviancy in Social Context*. New York: Franklin Watts.
Denzin, N.K. (1989) *Interpretive Interactionism. Applied Social Research Methods Series. Vol. 16*. London: Sage.
Dodge, K.A., Price, J.M., Coie, J.D. and Christopoulos, C. (1990) On the development of aggressive dyadic relationships in boys' peer groups. *Human Development* 33: 260–70.

Edgar, K. and Martin, C. (2000) *Conflicts and Violence in Prison* (final report to Economic and Social Research Council, Violence Research Programme). Oxford: University of Oxford, Centre for Criminological Research.
Edgar, K., Martin, C. and O'Donnell, I. (2003) Institutional violence. In E. Stanko (ed.) *The Meaning of Violence*. London: Routledge.
Edgar, K. and O'Donnell, I. (1998) Assault in prison: the 'victim's' contribution. *British Journal of Criminology* 38: 635–50.
Edgar, K., O'Donnell, I. and Martin, C. (2002) Tracking the pathways to violence in prison. In R.M. Lee and E. Stanko (eds) *Researching Violence: Methodology and Measurement*. London: Routledge.

Farrall, S., Bannister, J., Ditton, J. and Gilchrist, E. (2000) Social psychology and the fear of crime. *British Journal of Criminology* 40: 399–413.
Farrington, D. (1993) Understanding and preventing bullying. In M. Tonry (ed.) *Crime and Justice: A Review of Research. Vol. 17*. Chicago, IL: University of Chicago Press.
Felson, R.B., Baumer, E.P. and Messner, S.F. (2000) Acquaintance robbery. *Journal of Research in Crime and Delinquency* 37: 284–305.
Foster, J. (1995) Informal social control and community crime prevention. *British Journal of Criminology* 35: 563–83.

Gagnon, W. and Simon, J. (eds) (1973) *The Social Sources of Human Sexuality*. Chicago, IL: Aldine Publishing.

Galtung, J. (1975) *Essays in Peace Research. Vol. 1.* Copenhagen: Eilers.

Gambetta, D. (2002) *Crimes and Signs: Essays on Underworld Communication.* Oxford, typescript.

Garland, D. (1990) *Punishment and Modern Society.* Oxford: Clarendon Press.

Giddens, A. (1984) *The Constitution of Society: Outline of the Theory of Structuration.* Cambridge: Polity Press.

Gilligan, J. (2001) *Preventing Violence.* London: Thames & Hudson.

Girard, R. (1977) *Violence and the Sacred.* Baltimore, MD: Johns Hopkins University Press.

Goffman, E. (1961) *Asylums: Essays on the Social Situation of Mental Patients and Other Inmates.* New York: Anchor Books.

Grapendaal, M. (1990) The inmate subcultures in Dutch prisons. *British Journal of Criminology* 30: 341–57.

Hale, C. (1996) Fear of crime: a review of the literature. *International Review of Victimology* 4: 79–150.

Hemmens, C. and Marquart, J.W. (1999) Straight time: inmates' perceptions of violence and victimization in the prison environment. *Journal of Offender Rehabilitation* 28(3–4): 1–21.

Hindelang, M., Gottfredson, M. and Garofalo, J. (1978) *Victims of Personal Crime.* Cambridge, MA: Ballinger.

Hood, R. and Joyce, K. (1999) Three generations: oral testimonies on crime and social change in London's East End. *British Journal of Criminology* 39: 136–57.

Hough, M. (1995) *Anxiety about Crime: Findings from the 1994 British Crime Survey.* Home Office Research Study 147. London: Home Office Research and Statistics Directorate.

Human Rights Watch (2001) *No Escape: Male Rape in US Prisons.* Available at www.hrw.org/reports/2001/prison/report.html

Ireland, J (2000) 'Bullying' among prisoners: a review of research. *Aggression and Violent Behaviour* 5: 201–15.

Irwin, J. and Cressey, D.R. (1962) Thieves, convicts and the inmate culture. *Social Problems* 10: 142–55.

Katz, J. (1988) *Seductions of Crime.* New York: Basic Books.

Kemper, T.D. and Collins, R. (1990) Dimensions of microinteraction. *American Journal of Sociology* 96: 32–68.

Keve, P. (1983) The quicksand prison. *The Prison Journal* LXIII: 47–58.

Killias, M. (1990) Vulnerability: towards a better understanding of a key variable in the genesis of fear of crime. *Violence and Victims* 5: 97–108.

Liebling, A. and Price, D. (2001) *The Prison Officer.* Leyhill: Prison Service Journal.

Luckenbill, D.F. (1977) Criminal homicide as a situated transaction. *Social Problems* 25: 176–86.

Lyng, S. (1990) Edgework: a social psychological analysis of voluntary risk taking. *American Journal of Sociology* 95: 851–86.

McCorkle, R.C. (1992) Personal precautions to violence in prison. *Criminal Justice and Behavior* 19: 160–73.

McCorkle, R.C. (1993) Living on the edge: fear in a maximum-security prison. *Journal of Offender Rehabilitation* 20: 73–91.

McEvoy, K. (2001) *Paramilitary Imprisonment in Northern Ireland.* Oxford: Clarendon Press.

McEvoy, K. and Mika, H. (2002) Restorative justice and the critique of informalism in Northern Ireland. *British Journal of Criminology* 42(3): 534–62.

McGurk, B., Forde, R. and Barnes, A. (2000) *Sexual Victimisation among 15–17 Year-Old Offenders in Prison. Occasional Paper* 65. London: Home Office Research, Development and Statistics Directorate.

McVicar, J. (1972) Postscript. In S. Cohen and L. Taylor, *Psychological Survival: The Experience of Long-Term Imprisonment.* Harmondsworth: Penguin Books.

Meier, R.F. and Miethe, T.D. (1993) Understanding theories of criminal victimization. In M. Tonry (ed.) *Crime and Justice: A Review of Research. Vol. 17.* Chicago, IL: University of Chicago Press.

Morris, T. and Morris, P. (1963) *Pentonville: A Study of an English Prison.* London: Routledge & Kegan Paul.

Nagel, W. (1976) Prison architecture and prison violence. In A.K. Cohen, G.F. Cole and R.G. Bailey (eds) *Prison Violence.* Lexington, Mass: D.C. Heath & Co.

O'Donnell, I. and Edgar, K. (1996) *The Extent and Dynamics of Victimization in Prisons* (final report to the Home Office Research and Statistics Directorate). Oxford: University of Oxford, Centre for Criminological Research.

O'Donnell, I. and Edgar, K. (1998a) *Bullying in Prisons. Occasional Paper* 18. Oxford: University of Oxford, Centre for Criminological Research.

O'Donnell, I. and Edgar, K. (1998b) Routine victimisation in prisons. *The Howard Journal of Criminal Justice* 37: 266–79.

O'Donnell, I. and Edgar, K. (1999) Fear in prison. *The Prison Journal* 79: 90–9.

Olweus, D. (1993) *Bullying at School: What We Know and What We Can Do.* Oxford: Blackwell.

Pinar, W.F. (2001) *The Gender of Racial Politics and Violence in America: Lynching, Prison Rape and the Crisis of Masculinity.* New York: Peter Lang.

Riches, D. (ed.) (1986) *The Anthropology of Violence.* Oxford: Blackwell.

Robben, A.C.G.M. and Nordstrom, C. (1995) The anthropology and ethnography of violence and sociopolitical conflict. In C. Nordstrom and A.C.G.M. Robben (eds) *Fieldwork under Fire: Contemporary Studies of Violence and Survival.* Berkeley, CA: University of California Press.

Sabo, D., Kupers, T.A. and London, W. (eds) (2001) *Prison Masculinities*. Philadelphia, PA: Temple University Press.

Sattar, G. (2001) *Rates and Causes of Death among Prisoners and Offenders under Community Supervision. Research Study* 231. London: Home Office.

Sim, J. (1994) Tougher than the rest? Men in prison. In T. Newburn and E. Stanko (eds) *Just Boys Doing Business? Men, Masculinities and Crime*. London: Routledge.

Smith, P.K. (1991) The silent nightmare: bullying and victimisation in school peer groups. *The Psychologist: Bulletin of the British Psychological Society* 4: 243–8.

Sparks, R.F. (1982) *Research on Victims of Crime: Accomplishments, Issues and New Directions*. Rockville, MD: US Department of Health and Human Services.

Sparks, R., Bottoms, A.E. and Hay, W. (1996) *Prisons and the Problem of Order*. Oxford: Clarendon Press.

Sykes, G.M. (1958) *The Society of Captives: The Study of a Maximum Security Prison*. Princeton, NJ: Princeton University Press.

Sykes, G. and Matza, D. (1957) Techniques of neutralization: a theory of delinquency. *American Sociological Review* 22: 664–70.

Toch, H. (1992) *Living in Prison: The Ecology of Survival* (revised edn). Washington, DC: American Psychological Association.

Toch, H. (1997) *Corrections: A Humanistic Approach*. New York: Harrow & Heston.

Van der Wurff, A., Stringer, P. and Timmer, F. (1986) Feelings of unsafety in residential surroundings. In D. Canter, C. Jesuino, L. Soczka and G. Stephenson (eds) *Environmental Social Psychology*. Dordrecht: Kluwer.

Walmsley, R., Howard, L. and White, S. (1992) *The National Prison Survey 1991: Main Findings. Home Office Research Study* 128. London: HMSO.

Wolfgang, M.E. (1957) Victim-precipitated criminal homicide. *Journal of Criminal Law, Criminology and Police Science* 48: 1–11.

Wortley, R. (2002) *Situational Prison Control: Crime Prevention in Correctional Institutions*. Cambridge: Cambridge University Press.

Index

acceptance, of violence, 198
accusations, 114–15
acquaintance robberies, 68
Adams, K., 4–5
adaptations, to prison environment, 4–5,
    8, 48
adult institutions
    cell theft, 35
    rates of victimization, 29–30
    violence in, 185
adult offenders
    overlap between victim and
        victimizer, 66f
    reporting victimization, 196–7
    self-reported victimizing, 31
aggression
    conflict resolution, 189–90
    influence on interactions, 166–7
    protection from robbery, 149
    to secure personal safety, 95
Aijmer, G. and Abbink, J., 23
Alderley versus Thorpe, 120, 147–8, 168
Anderson, E., 138, 154
anti-bullying programmes, 204
arguments, use of threats to win, 41–2
Arkle versus Wilton, 112
Ashby versus Cerne, 182
assault, 42–7
    influence of relationships on, 107–10
    rates of victimization, 30t
    risk of victimization, 62–3
    robbery accompanied by, 53–4
    victim's contribution to, 60–4
    see also sexual assault
assessment, of fellow prisoners, 70
associates, disputes between, 108
Aston versus Cautley, 152
Atlas, R., 91
attitudes, conflict resolution, 187–8
attractivity, fear of crime, 81

Atworth versus Glastonbury, 124–5, 215
Auckland versus Sowerby, 170–1
authority, showing disrespect for, 120
avengers, 75–6
avoidance, 190–1

Baldersby versus Nantwich, 125–6, 153
Bampton versus Stroud, 109, 213
Barnton versus Dudley, 156
barons, 74–5
basic human needs, cycles of violence,
    199–201
Beck, G., 55
behaviour, reflection of treatment, 201
Belsay versus Orton, 119
Berger, P. and Luckmann, T., 166
Binegar versus Nailsea, 170
Bion of Smyrna, 32–3
Black, D., 26–7, 168–9, 188
black prisoners, victimization of, 98
Blalock, H., 26, 140, 161, 189
Blumer, H., 12, 126–7, 132
Blythe versus Consett, 169–70
Blyton versus Romney, 110–11
body language, 121–2
Bolton versus Eldroth, 195
Boston versus trader, 118
Bosworth, M., 7–8
Bosworth, M. and Carrabine, E., 160
Bottoms, A., 5, 6, 10, 84–5, 87, 203
Bowker, Lee, 69
Bridport versus Chesterfield, 194
Broadway versus Fleet, 134
Brough versus Darwin, 139–40, 151–2
Buckden, versus Irlam, 106
building tender system, 93
bullies, staff perception of, 204
bullying, 55–6
    as an expression of power, 169–70
    defining, 23

223